The American Assembly, *Columbia University*

THE FUTURE OF
FOUNDATIONS

Prentice-Hall, Inc., *Englewood Cliffs, N.J.* A SPECTRUM BOOK

Library of Congress Cataloging in Publication Data

Main entry under title:

The Future of foundations.

(A Spectrum book)
Background papers for the 41st American Assembly at
Arden House, Harriman, N.Y., Nov. 2–5, 1972.
1. Endowments—United States—Addresses, essays,
lectures. I. Heimann, Fritz F., ed. II. American
Assembly.
HV97.A3F87   361.7'6'0973   72–13906
ISBN 0–13–345983–7
ISBN 0–13–345975–6 (pbk)

Printed in the United States of America.

10 9 8 7 6 5 4 3 2 1

PRENTICE-HALL INTERNATIONAL, INC. (*London*)
PRENTICE-HALL OF AUSTRALIA, PTY. LTD. (*Sydney*)
PRENTICE-HALL OF CANADA, LTD. (*Toronto*)
PRENTICE-HALL OF INDIA PRIVATE LIMITED (*New Delhi*)
PRENTICE-HALL OF JAPAN, INC. (*Tokyo*)

Table of Contents

iii

Preface

The participants in the Forty-first American Assembly at Arden House, Harriman, New York, November 2–5, 1972, addressed themselves to the problems of American foundations, which for the purposes of their deliberations they defined as "privately managed sources of funds dedicated to public purposes." Their final report of findings and recommendations—which may be had as a pamphlet from The American Assembly—focused primarily on private grant-making foundations. So does this volume, which was organized and edited by Fritz F. Heimann, Associate Corporate Counsel of the General Electric Company, as background reading for the Arden House Assembly.

But the volume is also intended for the general reader; for, as the Assembly report pointed out, there are more than 25,000 grant-making foundations in the United States, and the existence of such diversified and decentralized sources of money is of great importance to our entire society, even in the face of the enormous expansion of governmental activities during the past generation.

The chapters which follow contain the opinions of the authors themselves and not of The American Assembly, a nonpartisan educational forum which takes no official position on matters it presents for public consideration at Arden House and in other meetings across the nation. Furthermore, the following persons and organizations who partially funded this Assembly program (and whose support is gratefully acknowledged) must not be thought of necessarily as sharing the opinions herein: DeWitt Wallace, Douglas Dillon, Robert O. Anderson, Robert W. Woodruff, The Rockefeller Foundation, The Henry Luce Foundation, and the William Benton Foundation.

Clifford C. Nelson
President
The American Assembly

Fritz F. Heimann

Introduction: The Issues and Their Setting

Foundations have played an active role in American life since shortly after the beginning of the twentieth century. However, their presence has rarely risen to a level of broad public visibility. This has usually been occasioned by political attacks on particular foundation activities. The public interest has generally been narrowly focused and of short duration. In the 1910s, it was on foundation involvement in anti-union activities. In the early 1950s the target was foundation support for left-wing organizations. In the mid-sixties Congressman Patman highlighted self-dealing and other forms of tax abuse. Usually after a splash of headlines, the politicians, the media, and the public have gone on to other matters and the foundation field has returned to its placid ways, of continuing interest chiefly to "philanthropoids," tax lawyers, university presidents, and other fund raisers. Because the attacks on foundations have been narrowly focused and episodic, while the continuing interest has been mostly parochial or self-serving, the basic issues regarding the role and rationale of foundations have hardly ever been examined.

FRITZ F. HEIMANN *is associate corporate counsel of the General Electric Company. During 1969–70 he served first as associate director and then as executive director of the Peterson Commission on Foundations and Private Philanthropy.*

1

The year 1969 appeared to be different. As part of a broad tax reform drive, a prolonged debate ensued over the foundation provisions to be incorporated into the Tax Reform Act. Among the issues debated were foundation involvement in voter registration campaigns; political favoritism and other abuses in grants to individuals; foundation participation in social controversies, such as the New York City school decentralization battle; self-dealing transactions between foundations and their donors; foundation control over business corporations; and even limitations on the life of foundations and curtailment of their tax-exempt status. While the debates of 1969 were far-ranging, an objective reappraisal suggests that the examination of the issues was relatively superficial. The question whether foundations had a continuing rationale was hardly touched upon.

The one effort launched in 1969 to deal with more basic questions, the Peterson Commission on Foundations and Private Philanthropy, landed between two stools. The commission got under way in the late spring of 1969. Its original objective of examining the more basic questions regarding the role of foundations was quickly overshadowed by the rapidly developing events before Congress to which the commission devoted much of its attention. After the political storm in Washington had abated, the subject of foundations had become passé. When the commission's report was finally issued in the middle of 1970 it aroused all the interest of a review of last year's fashions.

The present volume, and the American Assembly program for which it is prepared, represent an attempt to grapple with the basic issue of the rationale for foundations and their proper role for the future. Enough time has passed since the storm of 1969 to make possible an objective examination of the changes in the law which were then enacted. Even more importantly, no new crisis has yet surfaced, and it is therefore possible to examine fundamental questions without the distraction of some immediate and specific crisis.

Our first chapter provides necessary background. It answers the threshold question: what is a foundation and what is not? It supplies facts and figures regarding the number of foundations, their assets, and their grant-making activities. It analyzes the reasons why foundations are established, describes their principal accomplishments, and provides an historical account of the various controversies over foundations. This chapter is written by Thomas Parrish, a writer associated with Berea College in Kentucky, who has long been active in programs (foundation-financed and otherwise) dealing with the problems of Appalachia. In 1969–70 he worked on the staff of the Peterson Commission on Foundations and Private Philanthropy.

FOUNDATIONS AND PUBLIC CONTROVERSY

The second and third chapters debate the issue of foundation involvement in public controversies. This debate places into focus one of the major questions regarding the nature and role foundations should play in American life. The movement of some foundations in the 1960s toward direct involvement in such matters as registration of black voters, the decentralization of New York City's public schools, and the organization of protest movements by various minority groups, was undoubtedly one of the factors which led to the congressional onslaught on foundations in 1969. Thus one of the major issues for the future is whether foundations should restrict themselves to educational and cultural activities which are some distance away from the battlelines of political controversy. If foundations should endeavor to have a more direct impact on contemporary problems, how deeply should they become involved? In particular, how far into our governmental and political processes should foundations be permitted to venture? Congressional lobbying? Financing analytical studies for executive departments? Bringing lawsuits to challenge government regulations? Supporting election campaigns? These questions raise complex issues concerning not merely the nature of foundations but also the nature of our governmental processes. They must be considered not only on a conceptual level but also from the standpoint of practical ground rules.

The case against "social activism" is presented by Jeffrey Hart, professor of English at Dartmouth College. He is an articulate spokesman for the conservative point of view and is an editor of the *National Review*. The case for foundation involvement in public controversy is developed by John Simon, professor of law at the Yale Law School. He is president of the Taconic Foundation, which has supported voter registration activities in the South and other programs of an activist nature.

THE 1969 TAX REFORM ACT

The fourth and fifth chapters analyze the basic legal structure governing the organization and conduct of foundations. During the debates over the 1969 Tax Reform Act, the level of rhetoric escalated to a point where it became almost impossible to determine how serious the consequences of the new law would turn out to be. Some spokesmen for foundations predicted the end of their world, while some of the critics argued that the new restrictions did not go nearly far enough. In "The 1969 Tax Reforms Reconsidered" John Labovitz analyzes each of the changes in the law in the light of the actual experience since they were enacted in 1969. He describes the interpretative regulations adopted by the Treasury Department and draws on extensive interviews with foundation administrators throughout the country to provide an assessment of the actual impact of the law on the conduct of foundations. Mr. Labovitz is currently directing a study of the foundation provisions of the Tax Reform Act for the American Bar Foundation and was assistant director of the Peterson Commission.

Boris I. Bittker, of the Yale Law School, one of the nation's leading tax authorities, examines the 1969 Tax Reform Act from a different perspective: the relative position of foundations compared to other tax-favored organizations. In "Should Foundations Be Third-Class Charities?" he analyzes the premises underlying one of the most important consequences of the 1969 tax reform: placing foundations in a significantly less favorable position than operating philanthropies, such as universities and hospitals, or charities which draw on broad public support, such as community chests.

FOUNDATIONS AND GOVERNMENT

Perhaps the single most pervasive change affecting foundations during the past generation has been the steady expansion of the role of the federal government in all of the traditional areas of foundation activity. The *annual budget* of the Department of Health, Education and Welfare alone is now around three times as large as the *total assets* of all foundations. Many other government agencies are, of course, active on a very large scale in the same fields in which foundations work. This represents a radical shift from the first half of this century, when foundation grants in such fields as higher education and medical research were very substantial compared to government funding.

Any effort to think about the future must deal realistically with the impact of the federal government on foundations. This area is largely unexplored. Clichés about the virtues of pluralism are no substitute for real thinking.

The relationship between foundations and government is a multi-faceted one. At least five separate levels can be identified:

First, as already noted, the government is a powerful competitor in practically every field of foundation activity.

Second, foundations and government agencies can act as collaborators in areas of mutual interest.

Third, the government acts as a regulator of foundation activities, conferring benefits and enforcing the restrictions and penalties imposed by the tax law.

Fourth, on a level beyond regulation, both Congress and the executive branch act to encourage or discourage foundations: the 1969 legislation represents the most recent encounter on this level.

Fifth, the government can become a subject of foundation programs. With the ever-growing scope of the role of government programs, the need for external criticism and evaluation of government programs is of increasing importance and foundations can help to fill this need.

Richard Friedman, who has written our chapter on "Private Foundation-Government Relationships," is uniquely qualified to discuss this subject on a practical and meaningful level. He is the regional director for the Midwest of the Department of Health, Education and Welfare. In that role he has taken pioneering steps in developing working relationships between foundations and government programs in the human services field. Earlier in his career, Mr. Friedman was assistant attorney general of the state of Illinois with responsibility for state regulation of charitable organizations, including foundations.

THE OPERATION OF FOUNDATIONS

Our seventh and eighth chapters deal with the actual working of foundations. H. Thomas James, president of the Spencer Foundation of Chicago, deals with the internal functioning of foundations. He writes from the perspective of a newcomer to the foundation field, who, during the past two years, has been responsible for the organization of a new foundation. In the course of this work, he has had to think through and deal with the principal questions of foundation management: how should trustees be selected, from what backgrounds, and how long should they serve? How necessary is a professional staff and what is meant by "professionalism"? How deeply should foundations become involved in the activities of recipient organizations? To whom should foundations be accountable, and what is the proper scope of foundation disclosure and reporting?

In "Do We Know What We Are Doing?" Dr. Orville G. Brim, Jr., deals with the evaluation of foundation programs. Dr. Brim retired in 1972 after ten years as president of Russell Sage Foundation, the preeminent foundation in the field of social science research. He deals knowledgeably and with style and humor with a matter of great importance to the effectiveness of foundation programs.

The book concludes with some of my own views on a rationale for foundations, on amendments to the tax law, and on foundation-government relations.

Thomas Parrish

1

The Foundation: "A Special American Institution"

The Givers

Philanthropy, as it is generally thought of, is the love of mankind as manifested in good works, these good works usually involving at some stage the transfer of money from a donor to a recipient. About 50 years ago a pioneer social worker named Lillian Brandt wrote a little book in which she looked into this love of mankind and the works it produces. She called her inquiry *How Much Shall I Give?* The answer to this fundamental philanthropic question depends, she thought, not only on one's resources but on one's individual reasons for giving. Deciding what the reasons really are, however, is no easy matter, since—like minerals—human motives (including altruism) are not found free in nature but occur in varied compounds.

On analyzing the motivations that underlie private giving, Miss Brandt concluded that they are made up of seven elements. The

THOMAS PARRISH *has written books and articles on public affairs and other subjects and has had extensive experience in editing and publishing (Maco Magazine Corporation, Rutledge Books, and other houses). At present, he divides his time between writing and serving the Appalachian Center of Berea College (Kentucky).*

first one, which is "fundamental, primitive, probably instinctive," is *sympathy for suffering.* The second element is *desire for divine approval*—the feeling that the practice of philanthropy is "a means of escaping hell or winning heaven." Even 50 years ago, it appears, this was a fading motive and one to which public opinion and the courts set narrow limits. A will in which a lady left her entire fortune to charity for this explicit reason was, at the request of her less spiritually inclined survivors, set aside by the court, on the ground that she had been "suffering from a delusion." The third element in philanthropy is giving *to meet the expectations of associates*—philanthropic chic, we might call it today.

The fourth element is *familiarity,* one's firsthand knowledge of the needs of the local children's home or the work of familiar agencies like the Red Cross. *Loyalty,* giving out of association and affection, is the fifth motivational element; alumni fund drives and similar campaigns depend on it.

The sixth motive is giving *for the pleasure of doing good*—philanthropy for the "glow" and "exhilaration" such acts can bring. The seventh is giving because of *intellectual and esthetic forces,* factors such as one's sense of justice or sense of decency. This is the kind of explicit motivation that finds expression in phrases like "for the benefit of mankind," "to improve living conditions," and so on.

But, particularly when one is speaking of the very rich, are not some of these motives much less important than others? Is not guilt, whether motivated by fear of the eternal or of public wrath, behind much of the giving? Even in the case of the most ruthless tycoon, Miss Brandt says, it is not so simple: "No man is a chemically pure captain of industry." It is perfectly possible for a man to exploit the workers in his mines or factories and yet endow a hospital out of a variety of the higher motives on the list. The most rapacious profiteer can be moved, like Shylock, "by the impulses common to the human heart."

It will be noted that among Miss Brandt's motives and impulses appears nothing on the order of *benefiting from a tax deduction* or *retaining control of a corporation* or *preserving an estate from the ravages of the inheritance tax.* Her omission of such fiscal considerations is, of course, simply a reflection of the fact that in 1921 the income tax (1913) and the estate tax (1917) were still too new and their bites too gentle for them to have become factors of significance in charitable giving. If Miss Brandt were constructing her motivational list today, she would no doubt include such points under a suitable heading, one recognizing the fact that the government's tax policies have tended to create a whole new dimension of philanthropy, which might be termed giving that is of direct financial benefit to the donor.

It will also be noted that Miss Brandt's list refers to the motives that she believed to lie behind charitable giving in general. She is speaking of the entire field of private philanthropy, not of any subdivision of it. But the most spectacular private giving in the two decades preceding 1921 had in fact been the establishment of a remarkable series of philanthropic foundations by two of the most famous private givers in all of history, Andrew Carnegie and John D. Rockefeller. Since Miss Brandt herself was associated with a foundation, it is surely safe to assume that such benefactions were among those she considered as she composed her list. We cannot know how clearly she foresaw the special place that foundations would come to occupy in American life, and the continuing special attention that would therefore be given to the motives of those who create and direct them.

What Is a Foundation?

We speak of foundations as though everybody automatically knew what they are, and certainly most people who think about these institutions at all do have a definite idea of them: foundations are institutions—nongovernmental institutions—that make grants. Just as a college is a teaching institution, in this view, a foundation is a grant-making institution. It is the fact of grant-making that causes the Ford Foundation, for notable example, to be famous among people who have no idea of any particular grants it has ever made.

So far as it goes, this commonsense definition is quite useful. But there are, of course, refinements. Although there is no single, universally agreed-upon definition that will enable one to determine infallibly whether a given entity is or is not a foundation, several authoritative ones have been offered. In the Tax Reform Act of

1969, Congress describes a "private foundation" as, in effect, a charitable organization that receives its contributions from relatively few sources and spends its funds through grants or through operating programs. In its report, published in 1970, the Commission on Foundations and Private Philanthropy (usually known as the Peterson Commission) emphasizes the distinction between foundations and philanthropic organizations that are broadly supported by the general public. The commission observes that "two basic characteristics distinguish foundations from other charitable organizations: first, they receive their contributions from a single person or a relatively small group, and second, their major function is *giving (grant-making) rather than doing*" (italics in original).

In his book *Philanthropic Foundations*, F. Emerson Andrews, president emeritus of the Foundation Center, presents a detailed definition that has been widely accepted. A foundation, he says, is "a nongovernmental, nonprofit organization having a principal fund of its own, managed by its own trustees or directors, and established to maintain or aid social, educational, charitable, religious, or other activities serving the common welfare." Unlike Congress or the Peterson Commission, Andrews regards the possession of an endowment as essential to a true foundation. There are, he says, good reasons for this refinement: "the prestigeful name *foundation* has been adopted by many organizations which . . . have no proper right to its use. These include agencies which solicit contributions instead of disbursing from an established fund, and some which are trade associations, pressure groups, or outright rackets." The Peterson Commission was clearly aware of considerations of this kind, but its report simply says that "as long as the sources of contributions are relatively narrow, we did not think the presence or absence of an endowment made a major functional difference."

If we can introduce one further point, and talk about *large* and *famous* foundations—Ford, Rockefeller, Carnegie and so on, the foundations that to laymen embody the concept of foundation—it will readily be seen that, formally at least, Andrews' definition fits them precisely and that the possession of a large endowment is perhaps their chief identifying characteristic. The congressional and Peterson Commission definitions, being less detailed, also apply.

Even though some foundations that meet every other test have as part of their activities directly operated programs (medical research, for instance), certainly their "major function" has been giving through grants.

The great, characteristic American foundation is, accordingly, a philanthropic agency having a large endowment and accomplishing its purposes primarily through the making of grants. Foundations of other types and dimensions will by no means be excluded from our discussion but, as will become evident, there are advantages of scope and clarity to be gained from focusing for a moment on the famous foundations. Foundations of this kind are not only symbolic of the breed, they were first in the field—whether called foundations, endowments, corporations or something else—and they gave the word *foundation* a meaning that one would have found in no dictionary at the beginning of the twentieth century.

These are the foundations that made the grants to the persons who discovered insulin and developed polio vaccine and discerned the double-helical structure of DNA. They made the grants that led to control of yellow fever and hookworm. They financed the birth-control pill, hybrid corn, Dr. Kinsey's discoveries, the two-hundred-inch Mt. Palomar telescope. Dr. Norman Borlaug, who is identified with the Green Revolution, is funded by one of these foundations. So have been the 2,811 Carnegie-endowed libraries in the United States and Britain.

These great foundations are the products of a particular time and place, and they owe much of their distinctive character to the circumstances of their origin. It will be instructive to take a look at these circumstances.

The Millionaires' Problem—and the Answer

"Foundations are a special American phenomenon," Robert M. Hutchins once observed, and "the public ought to know about them." The remark was made in the wake of a 1954 congressional proceeding that, Hutchins felt, had in fact told the public nothing worth knowing about foundations. We shall return to that particular proceeding later. The immediate point here is that an indispensable way to "know" about foundations and why they are, indeed, special American phenomena is to know something about their origins.

Scholars who study the history of human philanthropy can point to endowments and charitable trusts of one kind or another in the ancient civilizations of the Near East. As might be expected, these generally appear to have had an other-worldly orientation—to assure the best possible reception of the donor in the next life. A remarkable example from later antiquity is Plato's Academy, which was endowed by the founder with valuable farmlands and cattle and lasted until closed by the Emperor Justinian some nine hundred years later (truly remarkable longevity when we consider that there was no legal mechanism whereby the Academy could be perpetuated; Plato willed it to a nephew, who in turn passed it on to an heir, and so on through all those centuries).

Early in the Christian era the Church acquired the right to receive legacies and to use the income, and other resources, for charitable purposes. Throughout the Middle Ages, philanthropic giving was dominated by what have been termed "ecclesiastical foundations." Donors were enabled to make gifts in perpetuity, though some of the bequests have a less-than-philanthropic ring today; for example, a fund to make sure that the Church always had on hand plenty of "faggots for the burning of heretics."

Still, these "foundations" were not a great deal like the characteristic American foundations of today. The private, secular side of philanthropy began to take on importance with the breaking up of the monasteries and the confiscation of Church lands in Tudor England. Oxford's Bodleian Library, for instance, dates from Sir Thomas Bodley's benefaction of 1602. In the American Colonies, remote from the attentions and restrictions of the central government—and from its welfare activities as well—private initiative showed signs of flourishing from the outset, in philanthropy as in other fields of activity. John Harvard made a gift that has attracted some subsequent attention, although the first educational bequest may have been that of Benjamin Sims, also of Massachusetts, who left "200 acres of land and the milk and increase of 8 cows for the maintenance of an earnest and honest man to keep a school."

A pioneer in American philanthropy as in most things was Benjamin Franklin, who in 1743 founded the American Philosophical Society, which has many of the characteristics of a foundation; Franklin also left to Boston and Philadelphia famous bequests of a thousand pounds each, which are still compounding today. According to some authorities, the first United States foundation was the Magdalen Society of Philadelphia, a perpetual trust which exists today as the White-Williams Foundation. Its aims have been somewhat modified from those it was given in 1800, which were "to ameliorate the distressed condition of those unhappy females who have been seduced from the paths of virtue and are desirous of returning to a life of rectitude." After more than a century of patient attempts to keep going in the face of the chronic insufficiency of unhappy females desirous of rectitude and of the frequent intractability of those who did present themselves, the trustees voted in 1918 to broaden the work of the foundation.

On the whole, despite these philanthropic beginnings, the seventeenth and eighteenth centuries, and the first part of the nineteenth as well, were from our vantage point more important for the fostering of attitudes than for actual foundation-building achievements. There is a simple reason for this: before the Civil War, nobody had enough money to be a great benefactor of mankind. One can imagine what Franklin might have done—either as donor or as adviser of donors—had he lived a century or so later.

PROBLEM OF PROFITS

Only after the Civil War, as a rather unsympathetic critic of foundations wrote in the 1930s, "did the problem which faces the modern millionaires begin to appear." The men who created the monopolies and trusts that characterized the era began to reap huge profits—profits that far exceeded the opportunities of reinvestment or the spending powers of even the most dedicated sybarite. And, of course, there was no income tax. It was observed by Professor Eduard C. Lindeman, also writing in the 1930s—a decade in which the rampant capitalism of the post-Civil War era found few sympathizers—that under the American system "accumulations of unexpended and unneeded wealth would inevitably arise." And "if surplus money cannot be spent entirely on luxuries, and if increased speculations result in cyclical depressions, there is still the remaining outlet of philanthropy. At this point foundations arise." This, in Lindeman's view, is simply a logical evolution from ordinary individual benevolence: "The distinction between ordinary private charity and large-scaled philanthropy is the difference between a small and a large surplus."

This tidy explanation leaves small room for the complex of motives which Miss Brandt ascribed to donors. It ignores, in fact, "bad" motivations as well as "good" ones, in favor of an economic-determinist or historical-force principle. But, nevertheless, it is unassailably true that the historical force *was* there. Private wealth in unprecedented amounts was piling up in the 1870s, the 1880s, and the 1890s. What was to be done with all the money (even historical necessity requires conscious, articulate spokesmen and agents)?

CARNEGIE AND ROCKEFELLER

An enthusiastic and creative standard for donors was raised in 1889, when Andrew Carnegie proclaimed what has become famous as his "gospel of wealth" (the term, applied by detractors of Carnegie, was intended ironically; he blandly accepted it). Already, in 1887, Carnegie had told W. E. Gladstone that "it is disgraceful to die a rich man." Now he described the millionaire as a "trustee for the poor, intrusted for a season with a great part of the increased wealth of the community, but administering it for the community far better than it could or would have done for itself."

A man of positive ideas, as the latter point suggests, Carnegie knew what the community needed: universities, libraries, hospitals, medical schools, parks, swimming "baths." At first he tried to "administer" his wealth through detailed, personal giving, but this proved too limited and too slow. He turned to larger gifts, which funded endowments with aims that were more or less specific (for example, the Carnegie Foundation for the Advancement of Teaching and the Carnegie Endowment for International Peace). Finally, in 1911, he created the broad-purpose Carnegie Corporation of New York—Andrew Carnegie, Inc., one writer has termed it. "The Pittsburgh steelmaker turned philanthropist was a dramatic figure on the world stage," says F. Emerson Andrews, "and he had the ear of the wealthy men of his time"—notably, John D. Rockefeller, who invited Carnegie to serve as a trustee of his own first foundation, the General Education Board, incorporated in 1903.

Rockefeller had not been philanthropically idle before setting up the General Education Board. His most prominent personal benefaction had been the new University of Chicago (ultimately, the gifts amounted to $35 million). And in 1901 he had established a special-purpose foundation, the Rockefeller Institute for Medical Research. In 1913, amid sound and fury we shall presently discuss, came the Rockefeller analogue of Carnegie's broad-purpose foundation, the Rockefeller Foundation.

The dominant idea behind Carnegie's benefactions appears to have been the undesirability (even the pointlessness) of dealing with poverty and ignorance by palliative measures and the importance of "the placing of ladders upon which the aspiring can rise." As it might be put nowadays, in his own way he sought to help people realize their potential. This notion of amelioration, making the world better, was shared by Rockefeller in his statements of aims, and it became a cornerstone concept in foundation thinking generally. As will be obvious, there has always been debate about the extent to which foundations have lived up to the concept, or have tried to do so, but since the early days they have distinguished themselves from conventional charities by this kind of emphasis.

Because of the bold and sweeping benefactions of Carnegie and Rockefeller, the first dozen or so years of the twentieth century were the years when organized large-scale philanthropy acquired its distinctly American cast. The day of the foundation had come—the foundation that was, in Lindeman's phrase, "the unique American answer" to the millionaires' problem. It proved to be a popular answer. Russell Sage, Phelps-Stokes, Rosenwald, Duke, Guggenheim, Kellogg, Mellon—within two decades all these foundations, each bearing the name of a great fortune, came into being. Despite advancing income taxes, fortunes—and foundations—have continued to flourish and multiply: ten of the thirteen largest foundations have been funded mainly since World War II. The most prominent mem-

ber of this group is The Ford Foundation, which is by far the largest
of all (and the gigantic funding of which was in fact stimulated by
the tax structure).

The Foundation Landscape

NATURE OF THE TERRAIN

The word "gigantic," it should be pointed out, has one meaning in a foundation context, another meaning when applied to the
field of private philanthropy as a whole, and still another—and
greatly different one—when one is speaking of governmental activities. Certainly private philanthropy is big business in the United
States. As the report of the Peterson Commission says, "it stands on
a distinctive plane of its own, not remotely approached in any
other nation." And yet, as a slice of the gross national product,
private giving is not as big as the attention it gets might lead one
to believe. For some years now, according to the best available estimates, it has averaged somewhat less than 2 percent of the GNP. In
1970, private giving amounted to about $18.3 billion, not including
the value of millions of hours of donated time. The philanthropic
gross is thus rather less than the General Motors gross, which suggests that 2 percent of a large economy is still a lot of money.

It is of particular interest to note that foundation giving—that is,
grants made by foundations—accounts for only a relatively modest
part of the philanthropic total. The great bulk of this total, from
three-fourths to four-fifths, comes as contributions from individual
living persons. For 1970, for instance, the estimate was 78 percent,
amounting to $14.3 billion. The other figures break down this way:
individual after-death bequests—$1.4 billion, or 8 percent; founda-
tion—$1.7 billion, or 9 percent; corporate giving—$0.9 billion, or
5 percent. As a percentage of the gross national product, foundation
expenditures are thus very small indeed. Compared with the federal
budget, they amount to a little less than 1 percent. The point is put
this way not to minimize the importance of foundation spending,
which can and sometimes does have significance far beyond its
actual size. But it often appears that people in general have a more
or less clearly defined idea that foundations and government play
in the same league. To switch the metaphor, the foundations simply

do not have the horses. Once they did. Fifty years ago, foundations spent more money in education, for instance, than the federal government did. But that was a long 50 years ago. Now federal spending for education amounts to several times the total of foundation spending for all purposes.

The figures above are adapted from a set compiled by F. Emerson Andrews, and may be presumed to be in accordance with his definition of a foundation. But this definition and the others that were offered were all general, covering the whole field. One thing that becomes clear on looking at this field today is the variety of types and sizes it contains. Our notion of a foundation as being built on a large fortune turned over to it by a rich donor was useful as a way of understanding the development of the foundation idea, but we must modify it in looking at the total picture today. It is still true of the famous foundations, of course, but for every Rockefeller Foundation there are a thousand or more that are purely local or receive modest annual contributions or give for only a specialized purpose or differ in other ways. Most of the great foundations have as their primary aim the furtherance of education and research. Lesser foundations have a variety of more limited aims.

One indication of the diversity of the field is suggested by the fact that Andrews divides foundations into five types. The Fords, Rockefellers and the like are *general* or *general research* foundations. These have the broad aims, such as Rockefeller's "to promote the well-being of mankind throughout the world." As was suggested earlier, their purpose is not alms-giving or palliative treatment of problems, but "prevention, research, discovery."

Special-purpose foundations are, as one might imagine, more modest in scope and very often are the expression of a specialized interest or even obsession of a donor. Most are conventional and quite laudable in aim, but many have offered rich material to the humorist and the student of anachronisms and to the legal profession as well. Out of a number of comic possibilities one thinks of the fund (set up by an American) to enable French peasants to dress as matadors or hula maidens because the donor felt that there was no degradation that the French would not stoop to for money, or the fund to provide one baked potato at each meal for every girl at Bryn Mawr. Even trusts that were perfectly sensible when they were established have become flagrantly outmoded by changing times. Resistance to amending the original terms appears to have been much greater in the United States than in Great Britain. American courts apparently tend to sympathize with the cry of Plato: "Oh ye gods, how monstrous if I am not allowed to give or not to give my own to whom I will!"

Company foundations, largely post-World War II phenomena, are devices for facilitating corporate giving, and in doing so they confer definite financial advantages on the company. The point will be taken up presently.

Family or *personal* foundations are established by living donors and commonly serve as channels for the personal giving of the founders (such foundations have been nicknamed "incorporated checkbooks"). As Andrews points out, "The same high tax rates in the upper brackets which now tend to prevent large accumulations of wealth have encouraged, through the provisions for charitable deductions, annual contributions to family foundations." These tend to be small (interestingly, the Ford Foundation was launched in 1936 as a family foundation with an endowment of $25,000), and they have as legitimate a place as other types. But it is some of the foundations of this kind that, through self-dealing and other kinds of manipulation, have stimulated much of the criticism of foundations as tax dodges, rackets, and so on. This point, too, will recur.

Community foundations are funds, usually city-wide, in which gifts and bequests from numerous sources are combined into a single whole. They have conferred undoubted benefits on their municipalities and also, it has been observed, on the trust companies that manage their portfolios.

The system of classification just enumerated gives a good view of the kinds of elements that make up the foundation landscape. But, for purposes of study and reflection, two other approaches may add something to the picture. First, it is possible to think of all foundations as falling into two categories: (a) those that are essentially independent—"pure," perhaps—philanthropic entities, with a staff and purpose of their own, existing quite apart from any donor, company or other external entity, and (b) all the others—channels for company giving, incorporated checkbooks, tax shelters dreamed up by lawyers and accountants, and so on. This is in no sense a criticism of all the foundations in category (b); the point is the solid, independent existence of the foundations in (a). They are basically independent, professional, philanthropic personalities. (As a practical matter, of course, most of the foundations in category (a) began their lives in category (b).)

The second approach divides up the field in a somewhat different way—a way that is more subjective, because it calls for judgments about intentions. This approach would classify foundations as (a) sincere (or reasonably so) attempts to benefit society and (b) sincere attempts to benefit a donor or a company or other founding organization. There is more to this distinction than the identification of some "foundations" as blatant tax dodges. A number of others might wander from one category to the other if they felt little need to improve their investment performance, for instance, or to spend as much of their income as possible for philanthropic purposes. (The Tax Reform Act of 1969 specifically addressed itself to such points, but tendencies to do no more than grudgingly comply with the law may remain.)

If these two approaches are combined, they yield as the stars of the foundation scene a group of genuine philanthropies, most of them having considerable independence and all of them together —as the following discussion will show—having most of the money.

RESOURCES

In 1969, which was the year that foundations came under intense congressional scrutiny and, not entirely by coincidence, under the scrutiny of the Peterson Commission on Foundations and Private Philanthropy, an interesting question emerged: just how many foundations are there? Since there was no agreed-upon definition, it is hardly surprising that numbers varied—and varied widely. A zealous critic, Representative Wright Patman of Texas, apparently lumping foundations with various other kinds of tax-exempt organizations, had put the number at about forty-five thousand. Those who do not view foundations as quite so appalling a specter on the American scene tended to put the number somewhat lower. The Foundation Center, which is the most useful source of worked-up data, gives a figure of about twenty-six thousand foundations in the current edition of its *Foundation Directory*. This number represents, essentially, the center's calculation of all the organizations in Andrews' five categories.

Although it is considerably less than 45,000, this is still a very large number. The *Directory* observes, however, that about 20,000 of these foundations are really quite small and, although they meet the formal criteria, financially are "relatively negligible." This means that none of them gives as much as $25,000 a year in grants or has as much as $500,000 in assets. The residue of this winnowing-out process amounts to 5,454 foundations. These foundations have estimated assets of about $25.2 billion and make grants of about $1.5 billion a year (based on the year of record, which is not the same for all the foundations). If the other 20,000 foundations were added, the totals would be increased only slightly.

Whether this $25 billion or so is a huge or merely a large pool of capital depends on what one compares it with. If, for instance, all twenty-six thousand foundations combined their assets and turned them over to a broker, he would not, in a typical year, have enough to buy the outstanding shares of IBM stock. The largest aggregation of United States capital is that held by life-insurance companies, which have about eight times the resources that foundations have. Savings-and-loan associations are a good second, with perhaps seven times the holdings of foundations. Corporate pension funds are likewise large—about four times the amount of foundation assets. Mutual funds total about twice as much as foundation holdings.

Another interesting comparison is relative holdings in corporate stocks. Here foundations take precedence over other nonprofit organizations. Their portfolios hold not quite twice as much as those of all universities combined and one-third more than those of all the other nonprofit organizations. This says nothing, of course, about holdings in bonds or real estate and other physical assets. Most foundations operate without elaborate physical facilities.

Although the 5,454 foundations control all but a fraction of total foundation assets, they are far from homogeneous in size. There are a great many more at the bottom of the scale than at the top. Foundations with assets of less than $1 million each number 3,275. Another 1,830 are in the $1 million–$10 million range. Only 331— out of the more than 5,000 included in the listing—have assets of more than $10 million. "An understanding of the concentration of assets is crucial to an understanding of the foundation structure in America," says the report of the Peterson Commission. "Thus, the twenty-six largest foundations hold over $10 billion in assets—at least one-third of total foundation assets—and account for over $475 million in grants per year or slightly less than one-third of the annual grants." From the point of view of assets, we might therefore describe the foundation landscape as made up of three topographical levels—a wide plain, a ring of foothills, and a cluster of massive peaks.

An additional refinement must be added to the picture. One foundation—the Ford Foundation, of course—is larger by far than any other, its assets (as nearly as can be judged) amounting to perhaps one-ninth of all foundation assets. Table I, compiled by the Foundation Center, shows the value of the assets of the sixteen largest foundations (those having assets of more than $200 million).

Table I

(Dollar Figures in Millions)

Foundation	*Rank*	*Assets*
Ford Foundation	1	$3,371
Johnson (Robert Wood) Foundation	2	1,180
Lilly Endowment	3	928
Rockefeller Foundation	4	832
Kresge Foundation	5	717
Mellon (The Andrew W.) Foundation	6	671
Kellogg (W. K.) Foundation	7	488
Pew Memorial Trust	8	481
Duke Endowment	9	425
Mott (Charles Stewart) Foundation	10	392
Sloan (Alfred P.) Foundation	11	329
Carnegie Corporation of New York	12	320
Rockefeller Brothers Fund	13	238
Hartford (John A.) Foundation	14	233
Mellon (Richard King) Foundation	15	215
Houston Endowment	16	208
Totals	16	$11,028

EXPENDITURES

The question naturally arises, what do foundations do with the income earned by their assets? How do they spend the $1.5, 1.6 or 1.7 billion they distribute in grants each year? A fondness for precise statistical answers must not lead us to suppose that this question is easily dealt with. Reporting is incomplete and of varying quality (in fact, the foundation world has traditionally varied between simple shyness and obsessive secrecy), although the Tax Reform Act of 1969 is bringing about changes. Besides, foundation activities do not fall neatly into categories that make it possible to compile easy and accurate totals.

Two analyses of foundation spending are available. One comes from the report of the Peterson Commission, which in its survey of foundations asked them to classify their expenditures by type of recipient and purpose of grant. Many observers (including, doubtless, those who believed that foundations spend large amounts on political or quasi-political activities) were surprised to see figures indicating that 94 percent of all grant dollars went from foundations to *other* charitable organizations—the kinds of organizations to which an individual taxpayer may make deductible contributions. The remaining 6 percent were divided between individuals and a variety of foreign and noncharitable organizations, from nonexempt social welfare groups to ghetto business enterprises. The grants to individuals were almost all for scholarships, fellowships, research, and support for artistic and other creative endeavors.

Analyzed by purpose, total foundation grants broke down pretty much as might be expected from the preceding answers: education, 31 percent; health and medicine, 21 percent; general welfare (United Fund, etc.), 14 percent; cultural institutions, 11 percent; religion, 4 percent; community services, 4 percent. The remaining 15 percent went to various kinds of research, conservation activities, services to individuals (food, clothing and the like), and so on. Less than half of 1 percent went for purposes explicitly related to the political process (voter registration and similar projects), although some of the community services involved work with community groups that, whether or not it was political, drew political fire. The figures, it might be remarked, were received with some sadness by many who had imagined that in a troubled time foundations have been serving as society's daring developers of desirable change.

The Foundation Center, too, encourages foundations to report on their grant-making activity. Table II summarizes this over a ten-year period. It does not include all grants—only those over ten thousand that were reported to the center. In any case, it essentially confirms the emphases discerned by the Peterson Commission.

These emphases are, of course, drawn from the whole foundation field, and one may well wonder whether the patterns are the same among foundations of different types and of different orders of magnitude; for instance, a large general-purpose foundation like the Rockefeller obviously has different priorities and purposes from those of a smaller foundation whose main function is supporting social agencies in St. Louis or nourishing the Toledo Art Museum. And so the fact proves. Smaller foundations, those that are closely tied to donors (either individuals or companies), present a pattern of giving that corresponds closely to that of individual donors. Thus they indeed tend to be incorporated checkbooks or perhaps slightly more detached extensions of individual desires and impulses. Compared with the expenditures of the large foundations, a higher proportion goes for health, religion and civic enterprises like the Community Chest. A really signal difference between large foundations and the others is in the size of individual grants. Those reported by the 331 top foundations average a little more than $20,000 each, whereas foundations in the middle group ($1 million– $10 million in assets) make grants averaging only about $3,600, and the bottom foundations have an even lower average—about $1,700.

Two questions asked by the Peterson Commission throw a different sort of light on the variations among types of foundations. Foundations were asked about grants they considered controversial and those they considered innovative. The responding foundations in the bottom (under $1 million) group had made *no* grants they regarded as controversial, but 38 percent of the very top (over $100 million) foundations had done so—although such grants amounted to only 3 percent of their total. Innovation, a claim foundations often make, in fact proved to be relatively rare, but the bigger foundations were very much in the lead. The very top foundations reported that 37 percent of their grants were innovative, and the next

Table II

(Dollar Figures in Millions)

Fields	1962 Amount	%	1963 Amount	%	1964 Amount	%	1965 Amount	%	1966 Amount	%	1967 Amount	%	1968 Amount	%	1969 Amount	%	1970 Amount	%	1971 Amount	%
Education	$145	46	$83	26	$186	33	$164	25	$157	24	$191	33	$308	41	$202	30	$281	36	$343	36
International Activities	52	17	82	25	74	13	128	20	141	21	84	15	93	12	75	11	59	7	106	7
Health	32	10	35	11	129	23	103	16	62	9	81	14	77	10	106	16	121	15	156	15
Welfare	20	6	24	7	44	8	104	16	81	12	82	14	74	10	102	15	136	17	174	17
Science	45	14	47	14	58	11	60	9	69	11	79	13	106	14	114	17	93	12	111	12
Humanities	16	5	48	15	39	7	39	6	117	18	39	7	73	10	37	5	52	7	103	7
Religion	5	2	5	2	26	5	51	8	34	5	24	4	23	3	41	6	51	6	73	6
Totals	$316	100	$324	100	$556	100	$649	100	$661	100	$579	100	$753	100	$677	100	$793	100	$1066	100

highest percentage was only 8. Overall, one must conclude that the foundation world has traditionally been judged by the performance of its most prominent members and that the judgment of that performance has very often (usually, in fact) been wrong. Except in science, the foundation world would not appear to have had a great deal to do with radical change. This is not to say, by any means, that it cannot or should not. Thus far, however, it has not.

What Foundations Have Wrought

Having taken a look at the foundation landscape and its financial substratum, we can turn to a discussion that is somewhat more concerned with causes and criticisms. Foundations confer two types of benefits—those that accrue to society and those that accrue to the people who create them. In the same way, they incur two types of criticism, which might be categorized as the philosophical and the fiscal. Accordingly, there are reasons for society to encourage the creation of foundations and other reasons for donors to create them. Likewise, there are reasons for observers to object to foundations in principle and to the conduct of donors in practice.

FROM SOCIETY'S VIEWPOINT

The fact that foundations have brought some great benefits to society is not really questioned by anybody. Earlier, we touched on a few of the famous achievements, in the control of diseases, in agriculture and nutrition, and in other fields. At times in the past, medical research and public health have actually appeared to owe their very existence to foundations (notably, Rockefeller), and the work continues in the present, although the field now receives great infusions of federal funds. Dr. Philip R. Lee, assistant secretary of health, education and welfare in the Johnson administration, and a member of the Peterson Commission, observes of foundations that "their present pioneering efforts in the area of medical care may in the future prove to be as important as have their past activities in other areas." Foundations are humming in the other areas, too. If you like *Masterpiece Theater,* for instance, you will thank the Ford Foundation for having kept noncommercial television alive—to the tune of more than $180 million since the mid-

1950s—and the Carnegie Corporation for showing how a public network could be established. Carnegie also gets the credit for *Sesame Street*. And to continue in the media, at this very moment writers are writing, dancers dancing, and painters painting because foundation grants give them the opportunity to do so.

Again, in whatever field—medicine, communications, the arts, welfare, whatever—foundations have made contributions in the past and are making contributions today. Nobody doubts it. They are able to do so partly because, as mechanisms of discovery and change, they have two advantageous and actually unique traits. In the first place, they have funds that are not committed to built-in, ongoing activities. They have money—substantial amounts of it—that (unlike, say, a university) they can spend next year for purposes quite different from those now being pursued, and they can plant seed money without having to force it into premature bloom within the same fiscal year (unlike many an office dispensing government funds).

The second point is that a foundation with an endowment does not have to go out and raise new money every year. Corporations, universities and government agencies all must, in one way or another, win the approval of external forces in order to continue operating. In the case of government agencies, of course, this factor is behind the pressure that they sometimes put on grantees to produce quick results with even the most unyielding problems. But if a foundation can stand a little heat, it can be almost wholly inner-directed. (It is true that in 1969, when the Tax Reform Act was being framed, foundations received more than just a little heat, but the restrictions written into the Act do not appear to have had any great inhibiting effect. We shall return to this point.)

Obviously, this freedom from outside financial controls and vetoes combines with the freedom from internal fixed obligations to give foundations a great deal of flexibility. They are in the happy position, it has been observed, of having all assets and no liabilities. Since our society, through tax policy and in other ways, has made it possible for foundations to have this degree of freedom, we have presumably believed that the benefits they offer, or can offer, justify it. The point has been made that this unique status was never really conferred, in a purposeful way, by society; foundations, as latecomers to the philanthropic scene, simply rode on the coattails of schools, churches, and hospitals. It has often been asserted, too, that foundations actually have less to show in the way of achievements than they ought to have, in view of the freedom they have enjoyed, and that the government or some other mechanism could have used the money better. This is a point that students of the foundation world will want to consider in looking to the future, but whether or not one agrees with it, the fact is that foundations have occupied and continue to occupy a uniquely advantageous position.

FROM THE DONOR'S VIEWPOINT

One of the things that everybody, friend or foe, knows about foundations is that they are tax-exempt institutions and that the money donated to them is tax-deductible. Under the Tax Reform Act, foundations are required to pay the Treasury 4 percent of their investment income as a kind of auditing fee, but notwithstanding this "excise" tax, they remain technically exempt from the federal income tax. The principle behind tax exemption is quite clear. As Robert M. Hutchins puts it, "Tax-exemption is conferred for the purpose of facilitating the performance of a public task by a private agency."

In her list of the motivations underlying acts of philanthropy, Miss Brandt was not concerned with tax-exemption. As we saw, she regarded motives as mixed, but the philanthropic deed itself was pure: a donation was a donation. In those days, and later, philanthropic action for public purposes was not only an accepted part of the American tradition, it was viewed as a highly desirable alternative to governmental expenditures for the same purposes (on this point, for instance, a reading of some of President Hoover's speeches during the first two years of the Great Depression, with their fervent appeals for private relief efforts, is not only instructive but incredibly so). Tax-exemption was, accordingly, not a motive question of much prominence until tax rates began to rise in the 1930s and, more significantly, during and after World War II.

After the end of the war, the enduring high taxes on incomes, inheritances, and corporation profits confronted the "modern millionaires" with their second great problem. If finding ways to dispose of surplus wealth was the prime source of *angst* in Andrew Carnegie's time, keeping the federal government from legalized confiscation appeared to be the principal postwar task. Fortunately, the tax laws continued to recognize the desirability of private philanthropic giving; the tax rates guaranteed that numbers of persons who had money to give would in fact do so. Extremely wealthy givers were able to make contributions for only a few after-tax cents. And, from many a donor's point of view, the most advantageous contribution was not a gift to an operating charity but the turning-over of assets to a foundation.

Contributions to foundations were deductible just as were contributions to any other charitable enterprise, and bequests were not subject to estate taxes. But giving to a foundation had one advantage that the ordinary charitable deed lacked. A donor could obtain the tax deduction and yet continue to exercise a significant measure of control over the donated assets. By establishing his own foundation, the donor was in essence saying that the income from the contributed assets would—in due course—be devoted to philanthropy. The assets themselves would remain intact, and the donor could determine when and to whom the income would be paid out. If the donor's contribution consisted of stock in a closely held corporation (Ford was a famous instance), the donor could maintain control of the corporation either by voting the stock given to the foundation or by classifying the foundation's stock as nonvoting. Before the adoption of the 1969 law, and emphatically before the imposition of some restrictions in 1950, a donor could use a foundation as a sort of private bank. Subject—after 1950—only to a vague arm's length or "reasonableness" standard, a donor could lend himself money or make other personal use of the assets. With all these advantages, and in view of the alternatives, it is hardly a wonder that, as Robert Bremner observes, "the foundation was irresistible." In fact, foundations began to seem, as another observer says, the "museums of the money world," devoted to keeping fortunes intact.

Ever mindful of Miss Brandt, we must not forget that the foundation had other types of attractive qualities, too. It enables a donor to even out his charitable giving by contributing more in a profitable year than in a lean one. It makes it possible for a donor to make an ongoing contribution that will continue to exist after his own death and even be able to change to fit new circumstances. It enables a donor to make some types of contributions that would not be tax-deductible if he made them as an individual. There are still other advantages, including the notable feature that one can name a foundation after oneself or a loved one and thus acquire or confer status, and a measure of immortality.

But there is no, or not much, gainsaying the fact that of the 5,436 foundations for which the Foundation Center has the necessary data, 4,911 have been established since 1939, and about half of these—2,546—were founded in the 1950s. (That decade, because of the Korean War excess-profits tax, was a boom time for company foundations.) About one-fourth—1,231—were established in the 1960s. And it must be remembered that these figures say nothing about the 20,000 foundations that were too small to be included in the *Foundation Directory* listing. Some estimates are that the percentage of foundations established in the last three decades or so is not 90 (as the figures above would suggest) but closer to 99. The point is especially instructive when one learns that in the early 1940s it was feared that the age of foundations was coming to a premature end, because the income-tax rates would prevent the accumulation of private wealth. Instead, as tax expert J. K. Lasser pointed out, the tax structure was destined to have a benign effect on "the natural impulses to give to charity."

Foundations on the Defensive

EARLY SKIRMISHES

It was remarked earlier that foundations have been strongly criticized on both theoretical and practical grounds. The principal targets of both kinds of criticism have been the donors themselves. Sometimes they have been accused of using their noble and sweeping aims—"the welfare of mankind," and so forth—as disguises for selfish and sinister operations that really were contrary to the welfare of society. Sometimes (increasingly during the recent past) the criticisms were more down to earth: donors were setting up dummy, or almost lifeless, foundations for the sole purpose of controlling money that would otherwise go in taxes. Sometimes, of course, the theoretical and the practical kinds of criticism have been intertwined.

At the very outset, the great foundations were in a rather odd historical position. They grew out of the industrial and financial empires of the late nineteenth century, but the first real foundation decade (1900–1910) was also a decade of reaction against the "robber barons." It was the Progressive era, the age of muckraking and trust-busting. Among the trusts up for busting in 1910 was Rockefeller's Standard Oil, while at the same time the Rockefeller Foundation was seeking a charter from Congress. The donation creating the foundation consisted of $50 million of Standard Oil stock. Reformers raised an old anti-Rockefeller cry: "Tainted money!" and even President Taft frowned on "the proposed act to incorporate John D. Rockefeller." After three years of unsuccessful effort, the Rockefellers dropped the idea of federal incorporation (which had not actually been necessary in the first place) and instead sought action from the New York legislature. It was promptly forthcoming.

A congressional investigation was not far behind, although it was not launched with this explicit purpose. As a result of labor wars in the Colorado coal fields, including those of the Rockefeller-controlled Colorado Fuel & Iron Company, Congress had established a Commission on Industrial Relations, headed by Senator Walsh of Massachusetts. It was supposed to look into the "general conditions of labor in the United States." This mandate took in the Colorado labor wars, and it became extended to take in other Rockefeller interests and influence, particularly the new foundation—and, before long, all foundations. Were they dangerous concentrations of wealth and influence, free of all control and able to extend the donor's malign power from business to fields that ought to be unrelated?

It is interesting to look at two or three opinions that were offered to the commission. A J. P. Morgan partner felt "no concern whatever" about the influence of foundations, but he did make the point that this view was predicated on full and frequent disclosure by foundations of their investment activities and disbursements. Henry Ford said that he had not thought enough about foundations to have an opinion worth expressing. John D. Rockefeller, Jr., stated quite candidly that the Rockefellers had not "drawn sharp lines between our business and philanthropic interest." The point seems to have been that the same advisers served in both areas.

A United Mine Workers official uttered a bitter footnote to testimony that the Rockefeller Foundation had numbered among its benefactions the funding of refuges for birds and relief for Belgium (World War I had come): "There are thousands of Mr. Rockefeller's ex-employees in Colorado today who wish to God that they were in Belgium to be fed or birds to be cared for tenderly." Opponents of foundations seemed to have an underlying view that the "vast fortunes" that made them possible had been squeezed from working people, who could make better use of the money if only they were allowed to keep it.

One witness advanced several specific proposals for the regulation of foundations. In view of more recent legislative discussion, this 1915 list is striking: 1) foundations should operate under federal, not state, charter; 2) foundations should not be perpetual; 3) there should be a limit on size; 4) foundations should not be permitted to accumulate income; 5) the federal government should be represented on boards of trustees.

The Walsh Commission, as it was known, issued a majority report which stated that foundations were in fact large and dangerous influences over corporations (an arresting idea) and over such fields as education as well. But no one, in Congress or out of it, seems to have paid any attention to the Walsh Report. By the time the report was published, the Progressive era was dead.

Foundations were not to be troubled by congressional attentions for a good many years. But in the 1930s, for what appears to have been the first time, some serious private studies of the phenomenon were made. This being the era of general disillusionment with big business, much of the criticism had a Marxian flavor. Philanthropy was viewed primarily as a device whereby capitalism eased dangerous social pressures or bemused the masses who would otherwise see how near the entire edifice was to disintegration. Less severe critics felt that even with the best intentions foundations could not be of much fundamental importance, because they depended for their own survival on survival of an unsatisfactory status quo.

Critics then and later were greatly concerned with one particular aspect of the foundation world, the nature and lineage of the persons who sat on the boards of trustees. Eduard C. Lindeman, in particular, studied four hundred of them. The point behind concern of this kind was the belief that the interests and limitations of the trustees were bound to govern the actions (and the limits of

action) of even the best foundations; i.e., that foundations were and
logically had to be little more than reflections of the interests of the
trustees. Here is the kind of point that critics made. "Editorial writers and popular apologists," wrote Horace Coon, "are inclined to
point out how wonderful it is that these important men . . . have
found the time and the social consciousness to devote a part of their
thought and energy to humanitarian, philanthropic work. . . .
What an admirable economic system it is that can develop such
beneficent institutions as philanthropic foundations!" Coon commented: "The popular apologists do not seem to realize that these
philanthropic interests are all part and parcel of the job these
gentlemen have undertaken of running the economic system. . . .
Philanthropic and business interests are not merely complementary,
they are identical."

In the days of the Walsh investigation, some concern had been expressed about "interlocking directorates" among foundations. Now
Lindeman's study provided deeper statistics and interpretations.
They may be summarized by saying that he found the typical trustee
to be about what might have been expected—a rich or near-rich
Ivy League graduate living in the New York area; "in short, he is a
member of that successful and conservative class . . . whose status is
based primarily on pecuniary success." Just as New York was the
headquarters of corporations, it was the headquarters of foundations. In all these respects, Lindeman's findings still apply today.

Many of "these gentlemen," Coon observed, "probably believe
that their philanthropic and business interests are separate. . . .
But it would be very stupid to imagine that the money, the power,
the influence of the foundations could be used for anything except
the safeguarding, promotion, and enhancement of the group in society which the trustees serve and to which they belong."

"Interlocking directorate," "group in society": one can see these
critics groping for a phrase that had not yet come into being,
C. Wright Mills's "power elite." The trustees and therefore the
foundations were instruments of—elements of—the American power
elite. But as Mills himself cautions, "We cannot infer the direction
of policy merely from the social origins and careers of the policy-
makers." The actual deeds are important, too. To ignore such con-

siderations is to be "guilty of a rather simple-minded biographical theory of society."

This notion concerning the power elite is important in itself and is a question to be considered today. But it should also be kept in mind because of what at least appear to be the very different charges hurled at foundations two decades after Lindeman's study. In passing, however, we should note that in 1950, as a result of an investigation conducted by Senator Charles W. Tobey of New Hampshire, the internal-revenue code was revised with the aim of cleaning up the foundation field by eliminating some of the worst tax dodges. It was then that transactions between a donor and his foundation were restricted to "arm's length" or "reasonable" dealings. Although some of the more brazen nonphilanthropic foundations were thereby put out of business, the "arm's length" proved to be a highly elastic unit of measure. Congress returned to this "self-dealing" point in 1969.

FRIGHT IN THE FIFTIES

In talking about the various attacks that have been made on foundations since the early days, persons in the field will often point out that the accusations have varied from one extreme to the other. In the Progressive era, foundations were charged with being agents of "creeping capitalism." By the early 1950s, when the McCarthy era was upon us, the accusations had become just the opposite: foundations were being attacked as creeping, perhaps even galloping, agents of communism. The inference drawn is that foundations exist in the eye of the beholder and therefore can expect to be attacked, without rhyme or reason, by anyone so disposed. A closer look, however, suggests that this may not quite be the case. There is, perhaps, a consistency to the attacks.

In the 1950s, there were two Congressional scrutinies (one, at least, hardly qualifies as an investigation). These were carried out by the Cox Committee of the House in 1952 and the Reece Committee in 1954. Officially and explicitly, the Cox Committee was trying to determine which foundations "are using their resources for un-American and subversive activities or for purposes not in the interest or tradition of the United States." About 40 witnesses, pro and con, were called, and nothing of much note was discovered except that foundations are "important and vital." In the climate of the time, however, it was significant that the committee unanimously cleared the foundations of the procommunist charges.

This feeble result apparently dismayed Representative B. Carroll Reece of Tennessee, who renewed the campaign in 1954. His scrutiny was more haphazard, more biased, and funnier than that of the Cox Committee. The goal seemed to be to prove that foundations were engaged in an anti-American conspiracy—"diabolical," it was said to be—but only one foundation representative was allowed to appear before the hearings were abruptly adjourned. Particularly evil, in the view of some members of the committee, was foundation support of empirical research. But foundation people fought back. If they could be censured for supporting empiricism, they said, they might soon be charged with using syntax and practicing Presbyterianism. The Reece proceeding was so farcical and patently unfair that its inhibitory effect on foundations was less than was feared likely at the time.

It must be obvious to anyone that no member of the Cox or the Reece Committee can seriously have believed that the Rockefellers or Paul Hoffman (president of the Ford Foundation in 1952) or such men as John Foster Dulles (a foundation trustee) were actually promoters of communism. Some critics may have thought that these men were stupid enough to hire communist sympathizers who would invisibly work to dismantle the institutions of the country. With the Alger Hiss case in mind, one might maintain that without having to offer any actual evidence of misconduct. But these investigations were really about something else at least as much as they were about communistic activities. This something else was political, and more than political. The antifoundation people were also partisans of Robert A. Taft and opponents of Dwight Eisenhower for the 1952 Republican presidential nomination. What better way to discredit Eisenhower than by discrediting Dulles, Hoffman, and other "liberal Republicans" as communist well-wishers or dupes? These Eisenhower supporters were characterized as "the Eastern crowd"—in other words, sophisticated foes of the folks in the hinterlands; in other words, the power elite. One is reminded of the way the Chicago *Tribune* used to employ the word "Eastern," all by itself, as a term of condemnation. So the right-wing attacks of the 1950s turn out to have had, in good measure, the same targets as the Marxian criticisms of the 1930s and the Walsh Commission of the Progressive era—not so much the actual deeds of foundations as the rich and powerful men who created and controlled them.

THE 1960s

In the 1960s (one is tempted to say, at last) a more openly populist attack was launched—the continuing investigation by Representative Wright Patman of Texas. Unlike almost all the previous congressional probings, this one has yielded practical results, not through any specific legislation offered by Patman but through his highly individual performance as a gadfly and a goad. He began in 1961 with the charge that "foundations have become a force in our society second only to that of Government itself" and that the public lacked any effective control over these powerful agencies. As was noted earlier, the congressman's definition of "foundation" was the broadest one possible, perhaps because he was suspicious of all tax-exempt institutions and regarded the word "foundation" as an effective bit of rhetoric. Certainly his anticorporation, anti-Wall Street views have been well known during his many years in Washington.

In any case, Patman succeeded to an unprecedented extent in prying open the reluctant foundations and extracting facts and figures about their operations; he passed his findings on to the public, the Congress, and the Internal Revenue Service in a series of reports. These reports described the sophisticated ways in which the foundation mechanism was being used not for philanthropic ends but for the shoddiest and most selfish purposes, all such being designed to enrich the "donors." And many of the more genuinely philanthropic foundations were compelled, for the first time, to reveal their holdings.

Although it is generally agreed that the reports contain a great many unsupported assertions and errors of fact and interpretation, it is also true, as a prominent member of the foundation world reluctantly concedes in *Foundation News,* that Patman "has contributed toward the improvement of reporting rules and practices, and he has called attention to the abuses of several foundations which deserve to be corrected." In general, he prodded IRS and the Treasury Department as a whole to pay more attention to foundations and, notably, to produce (February 1965) a highly valuable report with recommendations. This Treasury report carefully distinguished between genuine philanthropic foundations and those that seemed to exist for the sake of tax evasion. Strangely, even the noblest foundations do not appear to have made much effort to put up this kind of defense on their own; they seem to have been content for years to be lumped in the public mind with the speculators, the accomplished self-dealers, and the incorporated doctors and lawyers who transformed their professional activities into fake philanthropies.

Finally, in 1969, the foundation world came under detailed scrutiny that was part philosophical, part practical, and certainly a good bit political. Whatever the varied motivations behind it, it was an examination whose time was overdue. Foundations were indeed big business, they were influential, they flourished with only the skimpiest of social or fiscal controls, they still offered a tempting mechanism to the tax evader as well as to the genuine philanthropist. Also, they had been in the headlines in some spectacular ways.

Early in his investigations, Representative Patman had drawn attention to relationships between various little-known foundations and the Central Intelligence Agency. The relationships turned out not to be mysterious at all: the foundations were pipelines through which CIA money flowed to a number of diverse organizations that were not publicly known to have anything whatever to do with the CIA. It was most embarrassing, and it brought updated echoes of the old cry, "Tainted money!"

But this was small stuff compared with the excitement, even rage, stirred up by activities of the Ford Foundation. In 1967 the foundation made a grant of $175,000 to the Congress of Racial Equality (CORE), of which $38,750 was used for a voter-registration program in Cleveland. The grant was announced during a mayoral campaign which resulted in the victory of Carl Stokes, who clearly benefited from it. Critics charged that such activity was political, not really educational, and therefore not philanthropic. The same accusation was made about Ford's involvement in the furious and complex New York City school-decentralization struggle, and the foundation's grants to Chicano youth groups and other minority-oriented programs angered officeholders. Where foundations had built up a tradition of "arm's length" dealing with social problems, if they had any such dealings at all, Ford now appeared to be rushing to embrace problems, and in fact the foundation did manifest a new kind of activism in a number of areas as the crises of the 1960s exploded.

What may have angered congressmen as much as anything were the actions of an obscure fund called the Richmond Foundation. This foundation began to channel money to various ethnically oriented clubs and organizations in the Brooklyn district represented in Congress by John J. Rooney—which might have been all right with Rooney except that Frederick W. Richmond, the foundation's donor, was running hard for Rooney's seat in the House of Representatives. Rooney told his colleagues of the threat to his tenure posed by the "awesome financial resources of a tax-exempt foundation," and warned that this "can—and probably will—happen in your districts." The point seemed to sink in.

For these and similar reasons, Congress began its 1969 examination of foundations in what appeared to many observers as a punitive spirit. Much of this was the traditionally latent, sometimes active, animosity that dated back to the Walsh Commission. But, though foundations were slow to recognize the common threat and therefore to build up a common front, for once they were not passive. One historian calls their efforts "the most intensive publicity campaign in their history." But throughout the congressional debate, foundations found themselves in something of the position of foreign countries hoping for aid—they had no voting constituency to support their cause, not even a resident ethnic minority. Here and there, recipients of grants made representations to members of Congress, but for all the money they had spent in the twentieth century, foundations seemed essentially to be without allies. The power elite did not appear to be as powerful as it was supposed to be.

Some of the leaders of the foundation field had recognized before the 1969 congressional hearings began that the foundations were having trouble defending themselves. As a result of meetings of concerned persons brought together by John D. Rockefeller 3rd,

Peter G. Peterson of Chicago, then chairman of the Bell & Howell Company, was asked to head a Commission on Foundations and Private Philanthropy. The announced objective of the commission was to make a far-ranging study and to issue a report containing long-range policy recommendations with respect to foundations and private philanthropy. All accounts agree that Peterson ran the commission free from foundation control. When the commission began its work in the spring of 1969, few observers expected Congress to move fast enough to produce a new law in 1969. The feeling was that there would be plenty of time for the commission to explore the issues and to present its own conclusions before Congress would take action.

Because of the speed with which Congress moved in the summer and fall of 1969, the commission (not without some doubts and disagreements) became more involved with the legislative process than had originally been anticipated. The commission had developed data that existed nowhere else and had attempted to consider objectively some of the same issues which were being debated before Congress. Thus it was not surprising that congressional leaders invited Peterson to appear and present the commission's preliminary findings. One of the commission's major recommendations—that foundations should be required to make annual distributions to charity in the range of 6–8 percent of the market value of their assets—was strongly opposed by some foundation spokesmen. The adoption of the payout requirement in the 1969 Act is almost certainly due to the Peterson Commission's advocacy of the idea. This provision gave Congress a viable alternative to the proposal to limit the life of foundations to a fixed term which had gathered strong support.

THE 1969 ACT

In spite of all the fear and trembling and the apocalyptic forecasts, the bill that was signed into law in December 1969 was milder than was expected and contained a number of reforms designed to make foundations more responsible agencies. The principal objections that members of Congress had to foundation practices (or what were believed to be foundation practices) can be seen in the specific restrictions placed on foundations. In the financial area, the "arm's length" standard for self-dealing was completely abandoned; a foundation is absolutely prohibited from having dealings with persons related to it. It is also prohibited from making speculative investments. Foundation ownership of the controlling interest in a business is curbed by several complex restrictions. From the point of view of deductibility of contributions, foundations come under some inhibitions that do not apply to other charitable organizations. And, as mentioned earlier, a foundation must pay an "excise tax" of 4 percent of its investment income.

A key provision of the law, affecting both financial and program areas, is the requirement that a foundation must annually spend its net income (or an amount equal to a specified minimum percentage of the value of its assets) for charitable purposes. This provision, which keeps foundations on their investment toes and likewise keeps them from idly building up their wealth, was proposed by the Peterson Commission.

Several restrictions are placed on program activities. A foundation may not attempt to influence legislation "through an attempt to affect the opinion of the general public" or through direct contact with law-makers, except in the most general sense that it may publish the results of nonpartisan research and study. A foundation may not spend funds to try to influence the outcome of a particular election (thus voter-education projects are placed under some inhibition). Grants to individual persons (a fiery issue in 1969 because of Ford Foundation grants in 1968 to several persons who had been members of Robert Kennedy's staff) are likewise restricted. A foundation must monitor the activities of certain types of grantees, and it must make an annual report available for public inspection.

As is evident, the law is complex, and it is not exactly precise. How has it worked in practice? It caused a number of organizations to have to decide (with the help of the Internal Revenue Service) whether they were "private" foundations or "private operating" foundations or something else; its 4 percent excise tax created considerable resentment among foundation officials; its program restrictions fostered some fresh timidity toward social action and related fields—but the prevailing view in the foundation world was reported to be that of Merrimon Cunninggim, president of the Danforth Foundation. The law, he said, "has not hurt foundations as much as they expected it would, and it has not hurt them much. Both." One reason for this, apparently, is the restrained view the Treasury Department has taken of foundation activities that might be considered by some to relate to legislation or public policy.

Certainly foundations have not been forced to abandon social action. Folksinger Joan Baez, who supports a foundation, neatly sums up the continuing advantages of the foundation mechanism: "All the concerts I do are benefits because the money from them can be funneled through the foundation to things like the Georgia Draft Resistance, or whatever. You can't just plunge in and write out a big check, because then you get taxed for the whole thing, and you might owe the government $10,000 for what you just gave somebody as a gift." But another commentator talks sadly about the "bitter comedy of being 'researched' at great cost by foundations who won't give a penny to a project meant to correct the conditions being looked into." This is an old complaint, to be sure, heard before the 1969 Act as well as after it.

One thing the 1969 discussion showed was that foundations tend to resemble individual persons. When a particular trait or quality is generally popular, foundations like to claim it as a prime characteristic. When it is in disfavor, they passionately deny that they ever thought or did anything of the kind. When social action is popular, foundations cheerfully accept praise for being, as the semiofficial cliché has it, society's "cutting edge." When political or other powerful forces frown on anything that looks to be a serious social-action project, foundations hasten to assert their innate level-headedness and conservatism.

Today and Tomorrow

It has been remarked several times, in different ways, that foundations are a characteristic or special American institution. Those who have had dealings with foundations in other countries may have thought this a crude example of philanthropic chauvinism. But the point has simply been that philanthropic foundations have occupied a position of much greater prominence in the United States than they have elsewhere, they have been closer to the center of the life of the country, and they have provided the inspiration and the example for the development of foundations in other countries. As a student of the field says, "this type of philanthropy, based upon English laws of charity . . . thrives today, with modifications, in many countries of the world."

It is often advisable to look to other countries for guidance as well as to our own past, but foreign foundation practices do not appear to hold any startling lessons for us in the United States today. These foundations perform a variety of tasks and social roles, as ours do, although in general they are perhaps more traditional in focus than American foundations. It is of interest that other countries have not made much use of tax incentives as stimuli to philanthropic giving, so that foreign philanthropy in that respect may be "purer" than the domestic variety. But it is also true, compensatingly, that personal giving is often carried out in other countries through foundations in order to divert the attentions of tax collectors from the contemplation of donors' personal assets. As Miss Brandt implied, purity of purpose is no more common in philanthropy than in any other human activity.

As the discussion of the American foundation past has shown, tax policy has developed from its early unimportance (nonexistence, even) to become one of the most important questions having to do with foundations. It remains so even after the Tax Reform Act. That Act, and the hearings that led up to it, dealt with a number of the important policy questions concerning foundations, but it was hardly the last word. In some respects, actually, the debate seemed to be more an overdue first word, and many of the questions it took up were either turned aside or given only partial answers. Some of these questions cannot really receive satisfactory answers in legislation until society clarifies its ideas and expectations about foundations.

Besides, there is more to the foundation picture than issues of law and government policy. These ultimately turn on public attitudes, and the criticisms and attacks, from the Walsh Commission until today, have emphasized a wide variety of concerns. They have raised very durable questions about the place of foundations in American life. If, as we customarily say, we value pluralism and diversity, we shall believe in the value of private philanthropy and, in particular, in the value of foundations. But because these unique institutions have a great deal of independence and a great deal of money—money that is not committed to fulfilling explicit obligations and that forms a corpus of which only the income must be spent—we shall want to ask what we ought to expect from them. What should they try to do? What kinds of social and governmental control are called for? How should foundations relate to fields in which government is a prominent (or the chief) actor? Who should govern and manage foundations, and what kinds of persons should serve them as staff members? How should foundations conduct their operations? How should they deal with controversial subjects, inasmuch as it is often impossible to determine what is "political" and what is "nonpartisan," and the nonpolitical and the safely nonpartisan may also be the nonproductive and nonneeded?

Overall, we can decide whether or not foundations are to be useful forces in the troubled, seething world we inhabit today. Everyone knows the magnitude and the intensity of the needs facing established agencies and institutions. In dealing with these needs, government often appears inadequate or poorly structured. Can private groups, including foundations, help develop and carry out answers? Or, if foundations are to be little more than Community Chests and other gentle philanthropies of the kind, is some other mechanism desirable?

It may be time for society to determine just how special the "special American institutions" are to be.

Jeffrey Hart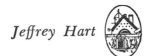

2

Foundations and Social Activism: A Critical View

Popular Wariness

In both practical and theoretical terms, the tax-free foundations face serious difficulties, and, for those who have eyes to see, neither category of difficulty seems at all likely to fade silently away. May I say that this situation is by no means a source of joy to me, since I do think the foundations have a valuable role to play in our society—though, as will be seen, my conception of that role differs from the one widely if not generally held in the foundation world. But, on the other hand, I cannot grieve overmuch for the foundations in their predicament, for they themselves have done much to create it, and they continue to exacerbate it. As in Greek tragedy, here too character may be destiny. In any case, as I see it, the prospect before the foundations today is one of deepening public malaise and festering rebellion, with, off at the end, only bleak prospects.

During the campaign leading up to the 1972 elections, we heard a great deal about a resurgence of "populism," and politicians as diverse as James Buckley, Harold Hughes, Fred Harris, George Mc-

JEFFREY HART, *professor of English at Dartmouth College, is a syndicated newspaper columnist for King Features and a senior editor of* National Review. *He is also a member of the National Council of the National Endowment for the Humanities.*

Govern and George Wallace, sensing the national mood, made one form or another of populist appeal. The common denominator in all of this was the feeling on the part of the ordinary American that he was being put upon by one or another feature of the system— that vested interests, government agencies, the Supreme Court, the rich, or the tax structure were impinging upon his life in a malign way and that he, himself, could do little about it. George McGovern, on the left, campaigned against "tax loopholes," among other things; on the right, George Wallace has attacked busing orders, pointy-heads in the bureaucracy, and tax-free foundations. But beneath these differences in formulation the appeal was essentially the same; it is a recurrent one historically and as old as the republic; it is essentially the appeal to the principle of equality and against privi-lege, recognizable in Jacksonian democracy or in the movement that followed William Jennings Bryan, and it becomes a powerful po-litical current when it speaks to the condition of important segments of the population, as it apparently did in 1972.

But this populism is not merely an election-year phenomenon, especially as it bears upon the tax-free foundation. Beginning in February 1969, the House Ways and Means Committee, under the chairmanship of the formidable Wilbur Mills, began a long-awaited and widely feared inquiry into the behavior of the foundations, and Mills' recommendations at length passed through the legislative process and were included in the Tax Reform Act of 1969, about two-thirds of which is devoted to the regulation of foundations. This law, incidentally, represents the most extensive regulation yet at-tempted by Congress of the more than twenty-six thousand widely varying American foundations.

The Act does not appear to have been found to be particularly onerous by the foundations. Accountability and auditing procedures were tightened up in response to the legislation; the 4 percent tax on foundations' investment income produced a modest return to the federal government. So on the surface all seems tranquil. In the Act, however, a kind of floating mine is present in the form of the pro-vision which prohibits foundations from using their tax-free funds to "influence any legislation through an attempt to affect the opin-ion of the general public or any segment thereof." So far this and other provisions of the Act bearing upon the political behavior of foundations have been broadly interpreted and have not—it is generally agreed—much inhibited the activities of the foundations. That floating mine in the Act is therefore, as it were, unarmed; but it is also clear that any unduly risqué political initiative on the part of the foundations would result in the prompt arming of that floating mine.

Foundation Vulnerabilities

The hearings in 1969 before Chairman Mills' committee were not, of course, the only prominent manifestation of public concern about the activities of the foundations. At about the same time, a private commission headed by Peter Peterson, Charles Percy's successor as chairman of the board at Bell and Howell, was raising its own questions about foundations. *Ramparts* magazine on the left, as well as *National Review* and the American Conservative Union on the right, were calling attention to what they perceived, from their different standpoints, as the abuses of foundations. And of course the legendary Wright Patman, congressman from the First District of Texas—and genuine populist long before the current vogue of populism—had been conducting throughout the decade of the 1960s an exhaustive investigation of the foundations and accumulating thousands of pages of testimony.

By 1969, the year of the Tax Reform Act, the tax-free foundations had entered into the general political consciousness as an issue, as, indeed, a problem. The provisions of the Tax Reform Act, moreover, ought to be regarded by the foundations with a loud sigh of relief, the best they could hope for under the circumstances. For by 1969 the position of the foundations was highly vulnerable. In 1972, in addition to the populist noises made by George Wallace and others, Representative Patman announced that his Banking and Currency Committee was getting ready to reopen the entire question of the foundations.

As the decade of the 1960s came to an end, the foundations found themselves suddenly vulnerable for three main reasons. The first two are straightforward enough: (1) many were operating wholly or in large part as tax dodges, and (2) many were frivolous to the point of kookery in the way they disposed of their tax-exempt funds.

Though these two kinds of abuse are serious, they are not especially complicated, and the Tax Reform Act of 1969 moved, at least tentatively, to correct them. The third reason for the foundations' vulnerability, however, is a deeper and more complicated thing. The huge foundations, such as Ford and Rockefeller, dispose of enormous amounts of money and exercise considerable power; yet they are run by men elected by no one, and accountable only to self-perpetuating boards of directors. During the 1960s, moreover, these large foundations to an increasing degree involved themselves in the political arena. Their power was brought to bear for various interests in the nation and against others. Yet this power was perceived, correctly, as arbitrary power, unaccountable and therefore, in the strictest sense of the word, irresponsible.

Before returning to this third, and difficult question about the foundations, a word or two about the first two problems may be in order. First of all, foundations have been proliferating at a fantastic rate. Two thousand new ones came into existence in 1968 alone. And the criteria for starting a foundation seemed almost infinitely elastic. Wright Patman turned up foundations supporting mistresses, widows, divorcées, foundations to recruit football players, and foundations to underwrite banquets. One man set up a foundation, donated his house to the foundation, then continued to live in the house, charging his expenses off to the foundation. The possibilities seemed endless. Your foundation could have your portrait painted or your biography written, thus making contributions to "art" and "history." Foundations such as Ford ($3 billion), Lilly ($900 million), Rockefeller ($830 million), Duke ($425 million), and Carnegie ($320 million) are the stratospheric peaks of the Foundation Range. Down in the foothills, however, there are some small but in their way gorgeous protuberances. Most foundations are in fact quite small, relatively speaking. Two-thirds have assets of less than $200,-000, and make grants totaling less than $10,000 annually. Some of the smaller foundations are marvels to behold. Stewart Mott, Jr., for example, set up his own foundation called Spectemur Agendo, Inc., which gives away some $80,000 per year. Mott proudly described the recipients of his largesse as "a variety of organizations in the fields of extra-sensory perception, human sexual response, aberration and hippie-oriented urban service." In 1972, Mott's fancy turned much more political.

But the gut issue concerning foundations is neither their use as tax dodges nor their use by kooks and eccentrics. The deep issue concerns the role of the larger foundations as a kind of shadow government, disposing of substantial political and social power, and using that power in ways that are in fact highly questionable. Though the foundations to an increasing degree are acting as a political force, and though they make no bones about their desire to act as a political force, they are not responsible to any electorate and so cannot be voted out of office if their political policies are perceived as undesirable. Because of their tax-exempt status, moreover, they are undertaking these activities with public money— money, that is, which otherwise would have found its way into the federal treasury and been used for public purposes.

Now in reply to these points it could well be urged that foundations are not the only politically potent entities enjoying tax exemption. It could be pointed out that the income of labor unions is tax-exempt and that labor union dues are tax deductible. The income of veterans' organizations is tax exempt. Businesses have a good deal of latitude as regards the activities they can deduct as business expenses. And these entities are often active politically in ways both direct and indirect. Why, then, single out foundations for special opprobrium?

Two answers may be given. First, the political activities of labor unions, for example, are the subject of extensive regulation. Tony Boyle, president of the United Mine Workers, faced a five-year jail term for violating such regulations. And, in general, the political use of tax-exempt money is the subject of continuing federal scrutiny.

But beyond that, however, is the fact that there is a difference in kind between, on the one hand, labor unions, veterans' organizations and businesses, and, on the other hand, the foundations. Each of the former represents a specific, concrete interest in the community. It is generally recognized that the members of labor unions have common interests; it is also recognized that some of those interests are political; and it is generally agreed that it is right—the agreement is embodied in legislation—that those political interests be pursued. The same is true of veterans' organizations and businesses. They are concrete, identifiable interests. But this is not true of the foundations. What interest do the foundations represent? What, indeed, *is* a foundation but a large amount of money presided over by a small number of executives, individuals largely unknown outside their own circle, whose opinions and goals are themselves largely unknown. It is by no means obvious that the foundations, politically considered, represent an interest in the community which ought to be fostered. The analogy between the tax-exempt foundation and the tax privileged entity like the labor union therefore breaks down immediately.

Political Action and Social Change

Until recently, the eleemosynary activities of the foundations, insofar as the general public apprehended them at all, were relatively noncontroversial. The foundations supported medical and scientific research, they provided some support for scholarship and the arts, they were much involved with education and conservation. By rough common consent, all this was "legitimate" activity for tax-exempt capital. In addition, such benign activity was self-evidently consistent with the intentions—on the surface, at least, altruistic—of the men who had started the foundations.

During the 1960s, however, all this underwent a sharp change, and once again, as in the days of the robber barons, *Ford* and *Rockefeller* were in a fair way of becoming hated names in the land, for the great foundations began to involve themselves aggressively in political activities, bringing their vast resources to bear in ways that pit one group against another. "In the U.S.," as *Fortune* noted approvingly, "the foundations have developed into a powerful force for social change and human betterment—a third force, as it were, independent of business and government."

A "third force" indeed! The country has made up its mind, as above, about the legitimate activities of labor unions, veterans' groups, and businesses—but it is only beginning to consider the role of the tax-exempt foundation.

And while I am quoting *Fortune*, I would like to ponder, indeed to savor, some of its rhetoric, because I have found that rhetoric echoing in many a place: "the foundations have developed into a powerful force for social change and human betterment." It seems here as if "social change" and "human betterment" are almost the same thing, or even exactly the same thing. And I would like to remember that adjective "powerful."

But the expression "social change," which has such a positive connotation in *Fortune*'s rhetoric, and in the rhetoric of foundation meetings, conferences, symposia and apologia, is, after all, a complicated and ambiguous thing.

The fall of Troy, after all, was a "social change." The Greeks no doubt considered it a change for the better. The Trojans might have entertained their doubts. If the Grecian assault upon Troy had been carried out with funds to which the Trojans themselves had contributed—if, for example, the wooden horse had been built with tax-exempt funds accumulated in Troy itself—then, on a reasonable view, the Trojans would have had grounds for complaint.

In the American context, one man's desirable social change may be another man's ruined neighborhood, or disrupted way of life, or lost election. There is in fact no reason why the phrase "social change" should have a hopeful ring at all. Change is, after all, merely change. And when you get down to specificities, here is what the major foundations really mean by that hopeful phrase, "social change":

1. In 1967, the Ford Foundation, working through the Congress of Racial Equality (CORE), put $175,000 behind a voter registration drive in the Negro areas of Cleveland, Ohio. McGeorge Bundy has defended this, with spectacular disingenuousness, as merely an effort to expand "democratic participation." But, as he knows, there was no way in which such a drive could fail to help Democratic nominee Carl Stokes, a Negro, who, in fact, was elected. Insofar as Seth Taft, Stokes' opponent, paid higher taxes because of Ford's tax-exempt status, Taft was actually contributing to his opponent's election. Insofar as the large number of voters who voted against Stokes were paying higher taxes for the same reason, they too were subsidizing with their own money the campaign of the man to whom they were in fact opposed.

The hypocrisy here on the part of the Ford Foundation goes very deep. Bundy invokes "democratic participation" as the neutral rationale for his voter registration drive. Apparently some groups are more "democratic" than others, or their "participation" is more desirable. It is commonplace that lower and working class voters turn out in lower percentages than those higher in the scale. This description would fit many Negro voters, such as those in Cleveland. Yet it is not recorded that Bundy's democratic evangelism has extended to working class Italian and Irish districts, for example. He was not observed to be active in support of the recent campaign of Rizzo in Philadelphia. "Democratic participation" evidently is not the only thing that is desired. As everyone knows, there is a card concealed in the shirt cuff.

2. In the fall of 1969, the Ford Foundation helped to finance various school decentralization experiments in New York City. On paper, at least, such decentralization seems to have much to recommend it. Yet in the Ocean Hill-Brownsville district, the teachers felt that Ford money was being used to destroy their union, destroy the laboriously built-up standards of the public schools, and corrupt key members of the Board of Education by giving them "grants." It may be that school decentralization is desirable. Or the opposite may be true. What is certain here is that Ford money was poured in on whim. "Decentralization" somehow automatically has an appeal; it has an appeal to me; but its concrete effects may be rather different from the idea in the upper middle class mind. Consider this summary by Daniel P. Moynihan:

> Seemingly it comes to this. Over and again the attempt by official and quasi-official agencies, such as the Ford Foundation, to organize poor communities led first to the radicalization of the middle class persons who began the effort; next, to a certain amount of stirring among the poor, but accompanied by heightened racial antagonism on the part of the poor if they happened to be black; next, to retaliation from the white community; whereupon it would emerge that the community action agency, which had talked so much, been so much in the headlines, promised so much in the way of change, was powerless. . . . to bitterness all around.

3. The Ford Foundation also put its resources behind "open housing" in the suburbs, evidently deciding on its own hook that

integrated living is what people ought to have, whether they want it or not.

4. The Ford Foundation put $5 million into a scheme which turns out, on closer inspection, to be a political operation benefiting what can loosely be called a group of Kennedyite political operatives. A product of the merging of three other organizations, the Center for Community Change was based in Washington. Its president was Jack Conway, Walter Reuther's assistant for fifteen years. On its board of directors were: Burke Marshall, a former assistant United States attorney general and a Kennedy functionary; Frank Mankiewicz, Bobby Kennedy's press secretary and one of the principals in the McGovern presidential organization; Fred Dutton, executive director of the Robert F. Kennedy Memorial Foundation, and another McGovern functionary; and the Rev. Channing Phillips, a supporter of RFK, and, titillatingly, the signer of a statement suggesting that the murder of a white policeman by black citizens was "justifiable homicide."

5. Making its way even further out and into the fever swamps, the Ford Foundation supported a variety of extremist groups, regardless of their impact on a local community. Representative Henry Gonzalez, for example, a liberal Texas Democrat, revealed that the Ford Foundation contributed $630,000 to an umbrella organization which then channeled the money to such groups as MAYO (Mexican American Youth Organization). Gonzalez said that members of MAYO traveled regularly to Cuba and distributed pro-Castro propaganda among Mexican-Americans in Texas. The president of MAYO, Jose Angel Gutierrez, spent his time making speeches denouncing "gringos" and calling for their elimination "by killing them if all else fails." Gutierrez was also on the payroll of the Mexican American Legal Defence Fund (MALDF), which, as you might expect, received $2.5 million from Ford. According to Representative Gonzalez, MALDF offices in San Antonio were festooned with pictures of Ché Guevara.

It is worth pausing here to wonder why Ford finds an individual like Gutierrez so eligible a recipient for its largesse. The answer must be the one discovered by Tom Wolfe in his laughing-through-tears essay "Mau-Mauing the Flak-Catchers." Wolfe found that of-

ficials of the War on Poverty in California tended to regard as most
"authentic" those blacks and Chicanos who "Mau-Maued" them—
that is, who spouted the most extreme rhetoric, who presented the
most exotic appearance, who were, in fact, fountains of anti-white
racism. All this validated them as minority spokesmen, in the eyes
of white liberals. But, Wolfe also noted, by rewarding extremism—
often handsomely—the liberal officials were also helping to create
it. When there is a ready market, someone will produce the product.

Ford money in San Antonio also underwrote a vague entity called
the Universidad de los Barrios, which was not in fact a university
at all, and had no curriculum. In actuality, it was a local gang operation, and the young thugs who were part of it, according to Representative Gonzalez, "have become what some neighbors believe to
be a threat to safety and even life itself." Gonzalez made it clear that
all of these Ford-supported extremist groups were loathed by the
vast majority of Mexican-Americans.

I have chosen to dwell on this Mexican-American example because
it will probably not be quite so familiar to most readers. Large
chunks of tax-free foundation money have also gone to a variety of
black extremist groups; but this is so well known as not to require
lengthy discussion.

6. The Ford Foundation granted $315,000 to the so-called Na-
tional Student Association, the title of which is misleading. The
NSA was in fact a tightly controlled and self-perpetuating left
pressure group about which few students were aware. The Ford
grant was supposed to be used for "training schools" where "promising students" [sic] could sharpen their skills in pressing for "curriculum reform" and in "dealing effectively with faculty and
administrators." In other words, and to speak bluntly, the Ford
Foundation was putting its money—i.e., tax-free and therefore partially public money—behind the campus revolution.

7. For sheer open arrogance, nothing, not even the above, perhaps, can match the Ford Foundation's grant of $131,000 to eight
former aides of Senator Robert F. Kennedy in 1969. Frank Mankiewicz, who got Ford money through the Center for Community
Change, got more Ford money through this one: $15,692 for a study
of Peace Corps operations in Latin America. Mankiewicz, as previously noted, slid easily off this vacation and into the George Mc-

Govern operation. Testifying before Wilbur Mills' committee, McGeorge Bundy had the effrontery to defend these grants as "educational." As anyone could see, however, they were really severance pay for benignly regarded political functionaries. Ford money was not bestowed, to my knowledge, on former Reagan or even Humphrey aides.

Let us sum up the argument to this point: At the present time the tax-free foundations represent a conspicuous form of irresponsible power. By this I mean that they can intervene in a variety of ways in political and social matters, and they can do so without any restraining influence by those whom their actions damage. To the above list of instances, many others could be added. And to make matters worse, the activities of the foundations, because of their tax-exempt status, are in a sense partially financed by those whose interests are being damaged.

There emerges from this a political equation of virtually Euclidean clarity. To the degree that the foundations involve themselves in controversial political and social activity, the demand will be raised, and justifiably so, for legislative regulation. Furthermore, the *more* controversial the activity, the tougher and stricter will be the regulation demanded: and again, in my opinion, justifiably so.

Social Conditions and Foundation Motivation

We have been considering here the manifest desire, yes, the manifestly growing desire, on the part of some of the larger foundations to play an activist role politically and socially, to promote what they euphemistically call "social change." It is worth asking why this desire has come to the fore in relatively recent years, and whether the assumptions upon which it is based are in fact valid. The riot in Watts and, perhaps especially, the riots following the assassination of Martin Luther King, Jr., in 1968 probably had much to do with it. The rhetoric of ethnic suffering, as orchestrated by James Baldwin, Malcolm X and others, which has filtered into the mass media, probably also fuels the desire. Many have drawn the conclusion that the social fabric is in jeopardy, that a national crisis is at hand, and that—something has to be done.

Oddly enough, none of these conclusions seems to be true; at

least, none of them is supported by the available evidence. Edward
C. Banfield writes:

> The plain fact is that the overwhelming majority of city dwellers live
> more comfortably and conveniently than ever before. They have more
> and better housing, more and better schools, more and better transporta-
> tion, and so on. By any conceivable measure of material welfare the
> present generation of urban Americans is, on the whole, better off than
> any large group of people has ever been anywhere. What is more, there
> is every reason to expect that the general level of comfort and conven-
> ience will continue to rise at an even more rapid rate through the fore-
> seeable future.

Banfield goes on to say that "there is still much poverty and *much*
racial discrimination, but there is less of both than ever before."
Conclusions like these, solidly based upon empirical evidence, do
not support the assumption that the society is in crisis. Banfield further shows that the riots mentioned above had little to do with
poverty or absence of opportunity and were not importantly motivated by "racial" feeling. And he shows that the problems that do
exist are for the most part highly resistant to infusions of money
by government or by the foundations.

And yet, he notices, "Doing good is becoming—has already become—a growth industry, like the other forms of mass entertain-
ment, while righteous indignation and uncompromising allegiance
to principle are becoming *the* motives of political commitment." It
is clearly in the interest of the "growth industry" he designates to
define problems as "critical" and to demand the authority to "do
something" about them. It is clearly in the interest of that growth
industry to claim that unless something is done, disaster will occur.

Here we have, I think, a clue to the syndrome that afflicts those
who evangelize for social activism in the world of the foundations.
Against all the objective evidence, they exaggerate the seriousness of
our various social difficulties. They falsely suggest, and may even
believe, that the activities they propose and sponsor will ameliorate
those difficulties—though the reverse is more often the case. And it
certainly pleases the ego of the foundation functionary to feel that
he is coping with vast crises and apocalyptic dangers, as well as dealing with exotic types from the ghettoes and barrios. But it seems to

me the more prosaic truth is the one articulated by Edward C. Banfield in the conclusion of *The Unheavenly City*:

> The import of what has been said in this book is that although there are many difficulties to be coped with, dilemmas to be faced, and afflictions to be endured, there are very few problems that can be solved; it is also that although much is seriously wrong with the city, no disaster impends unless it be one that results from public misconceptions that are in the nature of self-fulfilling prophecies.

The conventional rhetoric of crisis, from that perspective, is not at all part of the solution, but a principal source of the problem, for it perpetuates a veritable reign of error.

Knowledge and Beauty

The pity is that the foundations, for all their social activist fancies, do have an important role to play in our society. And there follows from the above discussion a clear recommendation, i.e., that the foundations concern themselves with activities that will be perceived as beneficent by all segments of the national community. Indeed, so far as I can see, the tax-exempt status of the foundations enjoins them to pursue such a policy.

To be sure, the foundations have long supported scientific endeavor. No segment of the community is likely to object to the use of tax-exempt funds for cancer research or research into heart disease, nor is anyone likely to find it anything but praiseworthy for the foundations to support attempts to discover through experimentation better methods of giving instruction in reading or arithmetic. The social sciences also afford a wide range of possibilities for the use of tax-exempt funds in ways which will benefit the entire community. This first recommendation, for support of the sciences and social sciences, might be termed the case for disinterested—but not, therefore, frivolous or useless—knowledge.

Knowledge, disinterested knowledge, is surely one entirely noncontroversial good. Even a little knowledge is not a dangerous thing; though, as Pope said, a little learning may well be. But there is another disinterested good, complementing Knowledge, and it is the basis for my second recommendation. If the scientific pursuit of

Knowledge has broad claims, so too does the creation of Beauty. One thing that has struck me forcibly about the foundation world is its obsessive and oppressive moralism. Foundation people, as I meet them—and it must by now be obvious that I meet them as a kind of anthropologist amidst a strange tribe—tend to be interested in what is immediately useful, as they conceive of it, and what is morally good, as they conceive of it. There is an immense irony here, from the standpoint of the cultural anthropologist. Many in the foundation world, especially among the activists and reformers, think of themselves as critics of society and agents of change. Yet in nothing are they so continuous with previous American culture as in their moralism and utilitarianism. Their spiritual ancestors were freeing the Negro: they are still freeing the Negro. Their spiritual ancestors were packaging breakfast cereals or making Model T's: they are still, though less usefully, fiddling with the nuts and bolts of society. Like the nineteenth-century millionaires whose money they are now spending, these twentieth-century reformers are moralists and utilitarians, civilizationally speaking brothers under the skin to Ford, Kellogg, Carnegie and all those other flinty, moralistic, but not especially civilized types.

I would now like to present my second proposal. It is serious intellectually, and serious in the sense that I would like to see it come to pass; but not serious in the sense that I expect it to come to pass.

I would like to see some powerful corrective to our pervasive moralism and utilitarianism come into existence in America. Will the puritans and the mechanics, in their latter manifestations, never stand down—even when they are doing no demonstrable good? I think it might be generally perceived as a benevolent and disinterested good if the foundations summoned the courage to behave like Florentine Medici or the Renaissance Popes. The creation of beauty, after all, is a function of status and luxury; the Sistine Chapel was not conceived of in a spirit of utilitarianism or moralism. And, after all, things like the Ford Foundation, and the others, are creatures of status and luxury.

It is also true that to bring about the creation of beauty a great deal of money may have to be wasted. Not every Renaissance artist was a Michelangelo. But the foundations would seem to be in an ideal position to do this. In fact, they are wasting a great deal now.

And I would urge that they shift a good deal of their expenditure to the arts, cast their bread (no pun intended) upon the waters, in support of painting, architecture, music, and so on. Not just a piffling amount, either: at least a couple of hundred million—as befitting the modern equivalent of a tax-free Renaissance prince. Beauty, like Knowledge, is not divisive. It is a disinterested value. It shines on all alike. And if the foundations supported not only science, which is universal, but also aesthetic endeavor, which is universal too, perhaps with a little luck this civilization will make some permanent contribution to the human spirit and be interesting to people five hundred years from now.

Addendum

I have been given an opportunity to read Professor Simon's essay, which comments on a number of points in my own essay, and also the opportunity to reply to Professor Simon if I so desire.

In general, I prefer to let the two essays speak for themselves. It is clear that Professor Simon desires the foundations to involve themselves in liberal social and political initiatives, and, furthermore, feels that it is relatively safe for them to do so. I disagree. A careful reading of the "cautionary guidelines" set forth at the end of his essay, however, suggests that we may in fact be more in agreement than would be gathered from the rest of his essay.

One or two brief comments on his opening points may be valuable. In arguing that museums, hospitals, and research agencies can be controversial, Professor Simon seems to me to disregard the all-important question of degree. There is a sense, to be sure, in which even buying a stick of gum is a political act, since the Wrigley company is part of "the system." But I would not expect to hear it argued that it is just as political as the activity of the Ford Foundation in its highly selective voter registration project. Similarly, I would regard Professor Simon's contention that "all kinds of change produce social change" as bordering on sophistry—and, indeed, as involving a kind of pun on the word "change."

John G. Simon

3

Foundations and Public Controversy: An Affirmative View

Introduction

THE AVOIDANCE OF CONTROVERSY

For all foundations, controversy is the way of life. Every foundation grant is ultimately controversial—i.e., involves the taking of sides—in one of two ways. First, the recipient of even the blandest "general support" foundation grant is likely to be an institution whose structures or policies are the subject of contention. For example, museums seem good and gray and safe enough—and yet more than one museum has been accused of paving over its parkland, representing too few black artists on its walls or too few young people on its board. Then there is the good and gray hospital which maintains a nonunion custodial work force, refuses to admit chiropractors to residency, or permits vivisection; the good and gray university which declines to fire Communists, offers football scholarships, or maintains a quota for women. Not to speak of the good and gray church, which dissents from a war in Vietnam, opposes contraception, or runs blockades in Biafra and Bangladesh.

JOHN G. SIMON, _professor of law at Yale, is also president of The Taconic Foundation. A coauthor of_ The Ethical Investor, _Professor Simon is chairman of the Cooperative Assistance Fund and a member of the steering committee of the National Urban Coalition._

58

Does a general support grant help to sustain the policies that prevail in these institutions? Plainly so. A foundation can protest that its grant implies no approval of the museum's intrusions on parkland or the church's position on South America; on that question the donor insists that it remains "neutral." And yet the resources the foundation makes available to the institution's managers help them to keep the organization solvent, thereby assisting them to retain their positions and also to resist the demands of other donors who wish, as a condition of gift, to change the institution's controversial policies. Moreover, the no-strings grant is usually viewed as carrying with it an unspoken intimation of general approval: "Would they, after all, have given us the money if they did not think we were doing a good job?"

To avoid this variety of involvement in institutional controversy, the foundation might seek to replace all grants to institutions with grants to individuals for research, artistic pursuits, scholarships, or temporary relief of poverty. But here we encounter a second aspect of controversy. The very act of allocating charitable resources to one activity instead of another is inherently controversial. For example: research grants for studies of minority group problems? The late Whitney Young urged scholars to stop studying blacks and start studying whites for a change. Scholarships for private secondary schools—thus diverting both resources and able students from the undernourished public school systems? Relief grants to the needy— at a time when legislative efforts are being made to put the needy to work? Support of "aesthetic endeavor" in the tradition of "Florentine Medici or the Renaissance Popes," as urged by Professor Jeffrey Hart—when there are too few artificial kidneys to go around?

Nor are these controversial allocation decisions likely to escape public notice. Representative Patman scolded the Bollingen Foundation for using "tax-free dollars to finance . . . exotic" research into the "origin and significance of the decorative types of medieval tombstones in Bosnia and Herzegovina," rather than "Pittsburgh poverty." And Professor Jeffrey Hart's suggestion that "support of . . . the social sciences" is an activity that will "be perceived as beneficent by all segments of the national community," overlooks the fierce criticism Congressman Reece's committee directed at the foundations in 1954 for their support of the "so-called 'social sciences' "; the committee alleged that these programs emphasized excessively "empirical" research methods that impaired "our basic moral, religious and governmental principles," in addition to promoting "collectivism," "moral relativity," a "one world" philosophy, and other vices.

The Spirit of Controversy seeks us everywhere, and even when we retreat to Samarra, he will greet us with a smile. It is a smile, we may note, not of triumph but of companionship. For controversy is not only inevitable but, as Albert M. Sacks has observed, wholly compatible with philanthropy:

> This notion that philanthropy, to retain its character, must remain noncontroversial represents a fundamental misunderstanding of the institution which not only perverts its historical development, but also destroys its essential values. The most traditional of charitable purposes ordinarily require the acquisition, development, and dissemination of information and ideas, and they are not rendered the less charitable because such information or ideas are disputable and disputed.[1]

Perhaps it is for this reason that in 1959 the Treasury abandoned its earlier position that a group claiming educational status under Section 501(c)(3) of the Code must strive to be "noncontroversial."

THE AVOIDANCE OF "SOCIAL CHANGE"

A similar theme of inevitability haunts the recurrent discussion of a companion question: should foundations participate in the process of "social change"? If I am correct that social change means a change in the relationships of group to group and individual to individual—changes having to do with economic or political power, or with the way people live together, or the way institutions respond to people—then all kinds of change produce *social* change. Any modification in what people consume or what they learn, or in the conditions of their homes or their bodies, affects their capacity to cope with their surroundings and therefore their capacity to cope with other men and women and other groups. For this reason, even charitable activities that are merely ameliorative—which do not

[1] Sacks, "The Role of Philanthropy: An Institutional View," 46 *Va. L. Rev.* 516, 529 (1960).

profess to alter anything—do effect social change. And so, just as foundations cannot avoid controversy, they cannot avoid a social change function.

The question, therefore, is not controversy *vel non*, or social change *vel non;* the question becomes one of the *ways and means* of participating in controversy or social change—e.g., whether the participation should be direct or indirect, explicit or unstated, contentious or purportedly "neutral." Rather than discuss these questions in the abstract, I should like to focus on one issue that embraces these matters of ways and means: the issue of foundation involvement in "public affairs."

THE SCOPE OF "PUBLIC AFFAIRS"

For purposes of this paper I will define the "public affairs" activities of foundations as those activities which seek to study, criticize, inform people about, and modify the actions of the executive, legislative, and judicial branches of government at all levels. They include such diverse activities as "public interest" litigation; lobbying and other attempts to influence legislation; monitoring, and attempting to affect the practices of, presidents, governors, mayors and other executive officers—or administrative agencies. And they include grants to government bodies (like the Ford Foundation's grants to the state of North Carolina) to encourage experimentation with new and often politically controversial methods of providing public services. They therefore include activities now permitted to foundations and some that are not. In short, the term "public affairs" embraces that broad range of activities that the House Ways and Means Committee, in May 1969, tentatively proposed to place off limits to foundations: "any activities intended . . . to influence the decision of any government body. . . ." [2]

---

[2] House Committee on Ways and Means, Press Release No. 10, May 27, 1969, p. 4. For a discussion of the value and techniques of foundation-funded monitoring of executive branch action, see Harold C. Fleming, "Riding Herd on Government Programs," *Foundation News*, May/June 1972, p. 5. With respect to litigation, the provisions of the Civil Rights Act of 1964, the housing provisions of the Civil Rights Act of 1968, and the Air Quality Control Act of 1970, all express a congressional desire to rely in large part on private groups to enforce norms of national policy in the courts; many of these groups receive foundation support.

My definition does not, however, include participation in election campaigns on behalf of any candidate for public office (an activity forbidden to all charitable organizations under Section 501(c)(3) of the Code). I omit this category not only because a special case can be made for its inappropriateness as a charitable activity, but also for the *realpolitik* reason that it would be wholly jocular to propose a repeal of this particular prohibition.

To illustrate the kinds of activity under discussion, here is a list of activities which I ask us to imagine being undertaken (either as "in-house" projects or as grants to other organizations) by a foundation concerned about better government performance in the environmental field:

1. Conducting research which yields general conclusions about the necessity for certain improvements in government programs (but without specific criticism of existing laws or executive policies).

2. Conducting demonstration projects (lodged inside or outside a governmental agency) to explore ways of improving governmental performance in this field.

3. Engaging in newspaper and television advertising which demonstrates, with dramatic photos and slogans, the need to avert the approaching cataclysm (but which does not mention governmental action).

4. Engaging in newspaper and television advertising urging the voting public to consider the "environmental credentials" of all candidates for public office (but not mentioning any particular candidates or contests).

5. Running a program to educate citizens about their rights to register and vote and to encourage them to register and vote (and mentioning the environmental crisis as a reason for electoral participation).

6. Lobbying for changes in environmental control legislation by communicating with legislators and starting "grass roots" letter-writing campaigns.

7. Publishing analyses of the adequacy of current environmental legislation, together with recommendations for new laws.

8. Monitoring and publicly criticizing the work of the executive branch in enforcing existing laws.

9. Organizing (lawful) picketing and demonstrations to call upon the executive branch to enforce existing laws.

10. Initiating litigation (on behalf of a variety of environmental

groups) to compel compliance with existing environmental laws on the part of government agencies charged with enforcement.

The existing statutory, judicial, and administrative precedents do not prohibit items 1, 2, 3, 4, 8, and 9—although the Treasury might well seek to attack item 4 ("environmental credentials" ads) as an indirect violation of the prohibition on support of political candidacies, and it might seek to condemn item 9 (picketing, etc.) as an inappropriate mode of charitable activity and thus violative of the general definition of "charitable" in the Code.[3] Item 5 (nonpartisan voter registration) would have to meet the multi-state and multi-source requirements of Section 4945 of the Code. Items 6 and 7 (direct and "grass roots" lobbying and publishing of analyses) would be permitted only if the activity (a) did not pertain to specific bills —although the scope of this exception is not fully defined;[4] or (b) constituted testimony before a legislative committee upon the express request made in the name of the committee; or (c) constituted "making available the results of non-partisan analysis, study, or research" within the meaning of existing regulations; or (d) constituted a grant to a "public" charity not "ear-marked" for legislative activities although so used by the recipient. Item 10 (public interest litigation) would pass muster if the group conducting the litigation met certain tests announced in 1970 by the Internal Revenue Service (IRS) in order to ensure that the litigation is conducted in pursuit of charitable goals, in compliance with professional ethics, and without unnecessary advantage to private parties.[5]

The precise reach of the existing legal constraints, however, is not our concern. The question before us is whether any of these activi-

[3] If the foundation purported to have an "educational" as well as "charitable" purpose, item 3 (the general ads) might be attacked as violative of the rule that "educational" organizations must present "a sufficiently full and fair exposition of the pertinent facts as to permit an individual or the public to form an independent opinion or conclusion." Reg. Section 1.501(c)(3)-1(d)(3).

[4] The exception is supported by the legislative history and by the text of the Treasury's regulations, although as John R. Labovitz points out in chapter 4 of this volume, the examples set forth in the regulations do not deal with this exception very clearly. I have relied on the regulations, Section 53.4945-2, in writing the rest of the text sentence.

[5] Int. Rev. Serv. News Release No. 1078, Nov. 12, 1970, 4 CCH Standard Fed. Tax Reports, para. 3033.4537.

ties—always assuming that they are undertaken in furtherance of a foundation's chartered purposes—*ought to be* out of bounds, prohibited either by the law or by self-imposed restrictions.[6]

The Full Participation Presumption

In discussing this question, I start with a presumption in favor of full participation, by all individuals and groups in society, in all of the processes by which our public policies are formulated. This presumption is in part informed by the pluralistic premise of the First Amendment—the premise, as Judge Learned Hand stated it, that

> right conclusions are more likely to be gathered out of a multitude of tongues, than through any kind of authoritative selection. To many, this is, and always will be, folly; but we have staked upon it our all.[7]

Moreover, as the political science treatises tell us, our public decision-making process assigns a major role to individual citizens and to the collective institutions they inhabit. The arguments they address to the executive and legislative branches of government, and the positions they take in the more orthodox adversary setting of the judicial branch, shape public decisions at all levels.[8] The process of argument and counter-argument, pressure and counterpressure, may not be the most tranquil way to conduct the public's business, but it has important Constitutional underpinnings and is, in any event, the only system we have. The exclusion of any individual or group from this process will presumably work unfairness by de-

[6] This paper will not deal with the issue of whether a legal prohibition on foundation public affairs endeavors would encounter First Amendment or other Constitutional objections, an issue which has been discussed, with unavoidably inconclusive results, in Note, "Regulating the Political Activity of Foundations," 83 *Harv. L. Rev.* 1843 (1970); Note, "The Revenue Code and a Charity's Politics," 73 *Yale L. J.* 661 (1964); Note, "David Meets Goliath in the Legislative Arena," 9 *San Diego L. Rev.* 944 (1972).

[7] United States v. Associated Press, 52 F. Supp. 362, 372 (S.D.N.Y. 1943).

[8] The political science literature is summarized in Elias Clark, "The Limitation on Political Activities: A Discordant View," 46 *Va. L. Rev.* 439, 445–56 (1960). One commentator contends that "old groups," as compared to "new or nascent groups," are quite ineffective in "activating the mechanisms of formal decision-making," largely because of the tendency of "old groups" to rely on intergroup bargaining. Theodore J. Lowi, *The Politics of Disorder* (1971), pp. 54–58.

priving the individual or group of its opportunity for representation; the exclusion will also inflict damage on the policy-formulating system by depriving it of a part of the counsel and criticism on which it depends.

The argument has been made that the presumption of full participation may once have been valid in this country but has been undermined and discredited by a series of incursions. For example, the Hatch Act excludes federal officials from certain types of electoral participation; military personnel operate under similar constraints; school teachers are typically barred from proselytizing their students. But the prohibition on school teachers does not deny their right to participate fully in political activities when not on duty; in this respect they are no different from other employees who must observe on-the-job regulations. The additional limitations imposed on federal civilian and military personnel represent a more serious restriction on political participation. Does this constitute a *departure* from the presumption, however, or simply a case in which the Congress or the military departments have found that other, more persuasive policy considerations rebut and overcome the presumption? In any event, a recent District Court decision holds that the Hatch Act restrictions are unconstitutionally vague and sweeping;[9] if the decision is sustained, this outcome will reduce the force of any argument that the full-participation presumption is not operative.

The presumption, of course, will not be fully implemented by all citizens all the time. Some individuals and groups may find some modes of participation in public affairs inappropriate or ineffective. Picketing the White House may seem undignified to some and unproductive to others. In many situations, a foundation may well conclude that research or education with a long time frame will promote the foundation's goals—even its public affairs goals—more efficiently than arguments addressed to governmental bodies. But if participation is indispensable to a fair and well-informed decisional process, then what follows as a general premise is that all individuals and collections of individuals must be free to participate in public affairs controversies.

[9] National Association of Letter Carriers, AFL-CIO v. Civil Service Commission, D.C.D.C. (3-judge court), July 31, 1972, 14 U.S. Law Week 2069.

To a visitor from a distant land who had received a general briefing on decision-making in American public life, it would not be immediately self-evident why charitable groups in general, or foundations in particular, should be barred from the public affairs arena. Our visitor might well suppose that these groups represent a set of interests, or at least perspectives, which deserve consideration in the policy-forming process. Whether the charitable organization was concerned with education or with the humane treatment of animals, the group's views, it might be supposed, would be neither more nor less worthy of representation than the views of those who wish to advance the good fortune of the auto industry, or of veterans, or of steelworkers.

The visitor might further speculate about the effectiveness of any charitable organization which turned its back on the public dimensions of its activities, ignoring the governmental aids or impediments to the achievement of its goals. For example, should a community center fail to be concerned about the outcome of administrative proceedings that will determine whether an expressway will tear apart the neighborhood in which the center is located? How can a near-bankrupt parochial school overlook a legislative controversy over tax credits for parents of private school children? How can a private foundation with a commitment to conservation stand aside from litigation or legislative or executive branch activity that will affect the fate of wilderness areas? (Or how can another foundation with a commitment to economic development ignore the implications of *not* developing certain wilderness areas?) To our observer from afar, it might seem that the operating charity or the private foundation which scorns or runs from a public affairs role buries its head, not in the sand, but under the water.

In view of the presumption of full participation in public affairs and the necessitous case to be made for it, what, the guest might ask, can the matter be? What reasons are advanced by those who would rebut the presumption of full participation, who would ask the foundations to be excluded, or to exclude themselves, from public affairs controversy?

Four categories of argument are advanced to limit the role of foundations in public affairs: *Definitional* arguments (relating to the etymological and historical "meaning" of charity); *effectiveness* arguments (relating to the utility and social impact of foundation work in public affairs); *normative* arguments (relating to the fairness and the democratic quality of foundation public affairs activity); and a *prudential* argument (relating to the possibility of reprisals against foundations as a result of their "politicization").

Definitional Arguments

The definitional arguments, more than most of the others, apply to all charities, not only private grant-making foundations. Indeed, the first of these arguments is expressly grounded on the etymology of the word "charity," which derives from the Latin "caritas" ("regard, esteem, affection, love"). Love, it may be argued, implies a giving and supportive role, not legislative, litigative, and other forms of adversarial combat.

A related argument is historical: it asks us to look at the list of charitable purposes set forth in the preamble to the "starting point of the modern law of charities," the Statute of Charitable Uses of 1601:

> . . . some for relief of aged, impotent and poor people, some for maintenance of sick and maimed soldiers and mariners, schools of learning, free schools, and scholars in universities, some for repair of bridges, ports, havens, causeways, churches, seabanks and highways, some for education and preferment of orphans, some for or towards relief, stock or maintenance for houses of correction, some for marriages of poor maids, some for supportation, aid and help of young tradesmen, handicraftsmen and persons decayed, and others for relief or redemption of prisoners or captives, and for aid or ease of any poor inhabitants concerning payments of fifteens, setting out of soldiers and other taxes.

Surely, it is argued, this list does not suggest that it is a charitable purpose to challenge or criticize public agencies or attempt to change the law.

A third variety of definitional argument is simply assertive: Judge Learned Hand (the same Learned Hand quoted a few pages ago!) wrote, in a 1930 decision, that "political agitation as such is outside the statute. . . . Controversies of that sort must be conducted without public subvention. . . ." [10] As Elias Clark has noted in his

[10] Slee v. Commissioner, 42 F. 2d 184, 185 (2d Cir. 1930).

seminal article on the lobbying prohibition, Judge Hand's decision "actually assumes the validity of the restriction without attempting to justify it by argument or authority." [11]

Indeed, I suggest that what I have called the etymological and historical arguments are, like Judge Hand's opinion, little more than assertions. There is, after all, no interior logic which tells us why a group that wishes to implement a love for mankind should foreswear any particular lawful means to that end. If it be thought that combative means negate a loving purpose, then what shall we say of the soldiers who, through the centuries, took arms to defend their countrymen against invasion?

A similar failure to distinguish between means and ends mars the historical argument: The Statute of Charitable Uses of 1601 lists charitable goals, not techniques. Until this century, to be sure, charity usually neglected the public affairs avenues to its stated goals. But with the exception of a few court decisions in Massachusetts (and a somewhat larger array of precedents in England),[12] charity's early avoidance of public affairs controversy was not informed by any normative statements on the part of courts, social scientists, or other commentators. Even when, in 1934, the Congress enacted tax legislation restricting legislative activity by charities, the reason does not appear to have been a determination that political activities were "inherently improper"; Elias Clark has pointed out that the proponents of this restriction expressed, instead, a wish "to restrict political agitation, selfishly motivated, to secure some personal interests of the donor." The American history of charity therefore does not reveal a tradition of reasoned or even intentional opposition to charitable involvement in public policy formation. It is very difficult to say that the long history of noninvolvement represents anything more or less than a failure on the part of charity's managers to perceive the ways in which their institutional goals could be advanced through litigation, lobbying, and other governmental processes—or perhaps a personal distaste for such processes.

In short, there is nothing in the etymology or history of charity

[11] Clark, "The Limitation on Political Activities: A Discordant Note in the Law of Charities," *46 Va. L. Rev.* 439, 447 (1960).

[12] The cases are discussed in Clark, op. cit. supra, at pp. 447–448.

to suggest the inherent inconsistency between charity and "political agitation" asserted by Judge Hand.

Somewhat related to the definitional point is the argument that when a charity engages in "political" activity of any kind, it may be hard to keep sight of the relationship between this activity and the organization's charitable purposes and therefore difficult to determine that the group is implementing a category of charitable purpose for which it has been chartered or which is recognized as "charitable" by the law. This judgmental difficulty was cited by Commissioner Randolph Thrower, in correspondence with the author in 1970, as a reason for the Internal Revenue Service's announced uneasiness about the exempt status of "public interest" law firms. His point was that if such a law firm contended that it was litigating in the "public interest," how could the Service determine in advance whether the litigation would serve a recognized charitable purpose?

The answer to Thrower's concern, and the answer to the more general point we are now discussing, is that it is indeed perfectly proper to compel an organization to announce a crisper public affairs role than "service of the public interest." The group can and ought to be required to specify one or more specific goals recognized as charitable (e.g., health, elimination of discrimination) and to show how its litigation or other public affairs activities relate to those goals. Once this step has been taken, the problem confronting the IRS is no different from the difficulty it faces when it analyzes the *non*public affairs activities of a charitable group, in order to make sure that the activities are consistent with the group's admittedly charitable goals—for example, when the IRS questions the way buildings are used or fellowships awarded.

I conclude that the definitional arguments are nowhere nearly substantial enough to overcome the presumption with which we began—the presumption favoring full foundation participation in public affairs activities—and that we must press on to the next category: the "effectiveness" arguments.

Effectiveness Arguments

THE ARGUMENT OF NONNECESSITY

The first effectiveness point we encounter tells us that this philanthropic trip is not necessary—that conditions in this country (or presumably abroad) are not grave enough to justify foundation involvement in public affairs activities aimed at amelioration. Jeffrey Hart states this position pungently. He asks us to look at the assumptions underlying "the manifestly growing desire, on the part of some of the larger foundations, to play an activist role politically and socially. . . ." The foundations assume, on the basis of riots and "the rhetoric of ethnic suffering," that "the social fabric is in jeopardy, that a national crisis is at hand, and that—something has to be done."

"[A]ll the objective evidence," says Professor Hart, shows this assumption to be wrong. The sole source cited for this conclusion is Professor Edward Banfield's report that "the overwhelming majority of city dwellers live more comfortably and conveniently than ever before" (better housing, schools, transportation, "and so on"), and that although "there is still much poverty and much racial discrimination . . . there is less of both than ever before." Professor Hart says that "conclusions like these, solidly based upon empirical evidence, do not support the assumption that society is in crisis."

Professor Banfield's book, however, makes it clear that "city dwellers" include the vast population of suburbanites and that when we focus on residents of the "inner-central-city" and the "larger-older-suburb," there are "many people who do not share, or do not share fully, this general prosperity. . . ." [13] Certainly we must find it difficult to be relaxed about the "comfort and convenience" of inner-city dwellers when we reflect upon the garrison state measures that these citizens are adopting to defend against violent crime, and when we consider the data relating to unemployment among black youths (exceeding 30 percent in many cities), relating to abandonment of housing in the central city, and relating to the fiscal condition of urban school and mass transit systems. But this is not the forum in which to adjudicate whether my concern or Professor Hart's calm should be the prevailing mood. We will always have

[13] Banfield, *The Unheavenly City* (1970), pp. 4, 11, 12.

these disagreements: one man's crisis is another man's happy hour. Indeed, the very absence of a universal consensus about the nature of our national crises undermines the argument of nonnecessity. In other words, the contention that there is no needful work for foundations to do in public affairs invokes no general norms or common assumptions. The argument therefore cannot be a claim that such foundation work is illegitimate, but only a quarrel with the resource-allocation decisions made by foundations operating in this field— an argument that this is not the best way to spend money, at least not right now. Foundations should listen to such contentions and any other serious objections to their grant-making priorities, but they should not be compelled to accept the wisdom of these objections and abstain from work in the public affairs field. (I hasten to add that neither Professor Hart, whom I have just quoted, nor Professor Moynihan, whom I am about to quote, advance their "effectiveness" arguments in support of a legal restriction on the foundations; instead, these authors appear to call for foundation self-restraint.)

THE DIVISIVENESS ARGUMENT

The second effectiveness argument we encounter contends not that the foundations' involvement in public affairs controversy is unnecessary, but that it excessively polarizes and divides the country and tends to pave the way for totalitarianism. Daniel P. Moynihan is a spokesman for this point of view.[14] Using "the term political in its most general meaning," he concedes that "[t]he activities of foundations are inescapably political, regardless of what Congress might desire or statutes might command." But he states that unless the foundations are "even-handed in the political consequences of these activities, seeking neither to advance nor impede any cause save that of understanding and competence," unless they avoid

> putting the power of their wealth to the service of a particular political interest . . . and, hence, disservice of other political positions of equal plausibility and legitimacy,

they will play a deadly game. In this game, an elite, though rhetorically anti-elitist, group ("whether Eastern liberals or South-

[14] The following quotations are from Moynihan, "Social Welfare: Government vs. Private Efforts," *Foundation News*, March/April 1972, pp. 5–8.

western conservatives") "seeks to bring about social change through essentially extra-political strategies." This process generates "social unrest," together with "fragmentation of democratic forces of the center," helping to weaken the democratic order and usher in a more totalitarian era. I am not sure I fully understand Professor Moynihan's prognosis, and perhaps I do not do it justice. But I think I understand his fear of the consequences that may be brought about by mindlessly provocative confrontation tactics, social change by shock treatment, the irresponsible narcissism of those who do not have to live with the racial or class warfare that ensues. I believe foundations have rarely supported that kind of activity, however, and Mr. Moynihan's book, "Maximum Feasible Misunderstanding," does not convince me that any of the foundations are guilty.

Moreover, avoiding this kind of belligerent agitation does not require a foundation to be "even-handed" or to avoid association with "any cause." In order to resist the role of wrecker, must one stride the center line? Not all advocates pack bombs—or even contribute to the weakening of the fabric of the social order. Indeed, I should think that groups which opposed racial discrimination or pressed to protect neighborhoods against freeways had the effect of repairing rather than damaging this fabric; that the "democratic forces of the center" were in no way shattered when groups with differing land-use philosophies (developmental versus "ecological") were enabled by foundation funds to adjudicate their differences in court. Perhaps this is not the kind of controversy Professor Moynihan meant to caution against, nor the kind of agenda item he meant when he said that

> [t]he creative and general impulses which initiate charitable foundations must not be diverted to the private political agenda of any interest or any group, whether Eastern liberals or Southwestern conservatives. . . .

But if not, then I am not sure what kind of controversy, what "private political agenda," he had in mind.

Normative Arguments

The normative arguments tell us that it is not right for foundations to engage in public affairs activities, for in so doing they offend against (1) a concept of fair play as between users of pre-tax and after-tax dollars (the "unfair competition argument") and (2) a concept that it is undemocratic for "nonaccountable" institutions to use "public" funds to affect the outcome of governmental decisions (the "shadow government argument").

THE UNFAIR COMPETITION ARGUMENT

This contention, which applies to foundations and all other charitable organizations enjoying the right to receive deductible contributions, reflects a Marquis of Queensberry approach. It is not fair, we are told, for a charitable body to advance positions on any side of a public affairs controversy, for its ability to use "pre-tax" dollars (dollars on which the donor received a tax deduction and on which the recipient organization pays no income tax) gives it an unfair advantage over other public affairs advocates who must use "after-tax" dollars (dollars to which the privileges of deductibility and exemption have not attached).[15] The argument has a very slender basis in fact. If the opposing group in a litigation or a controversy over legislation or executive action is a labor union, its income will be tax-exempt, and the dues paid to it are deductible. If the opponent is a veterans' organization, the income is exempt, the contributions deductible. And business organizations deduct the costs of litigation, executive monitoring, and non-grass roots lobbying, when these expenses are characterized as directly related to the needs of the business; they also deduct the expenses of proselytizing

[15] Sometimes referred to as the "tax equilibrium" doctrine, this notion of tax equity between various contesting groups was endorsed by the United States Supreme Court in the context of corporate deductions for lobbying expenses. In Cammarano v. United States, 358 U.S. 498 (1959), the Court, referring to the "sharply defined national policy" against lobbying by charities, declared that it was not a First Amendment violation to prevent business from lobbying with deductible dollars; in this respect, "everyone in the community should stand on the same footing. . . ." 358 U.S. at 513. Congress, however, upset the "equilibrium" three years later by amending Section 162(e) of the Code to permit businesses to deduct their lobbying expenses, on the theory that "taxpayers who have information bearing on the impact of present laws or proposed legislation [should not be] discouraged in making this information available . . . to . . . legislators. . . ." Sen. Rep. No. 1881, 87th Cong., 2d Sess. (1962). The "equilibrium" had already been disturbed with respect to union and veterans' organization lobbying. The present-day situation is that everyone is in "equilibrium" except the charities.

their own shareholders and employees and the expenses of institutional advertising espousing sociopolitical positions, if the advertising is deemed to be for business purposes and does not urge legislative action. (As this was written, the Mobil Oil Corporation published its third advertisement in *The New York Times* on mass transit, this one headlined: "Let's end the Highway Trust Fund.") Moreover, the corporations can also deduct all the expenditures they devote to normal business activities that have a public affairs impact —activities which, for example, inhibit or further the work of the government in promoting jobs for minorities, safety for consumers, a better environment for the public at large. (Corporations can also deduct some expenses in aid of political parties—e.g., MGM's reported payment of $4,000 to fly Sammy Davis, Jr., to the 1972 Republican convention, undoubtedly a "promotional" expense.) Moreover, even political parties now obtain dollars that the contributor can claim as income tax deductions or credits. Accordingly, when it comes to public affairs activities, the noncharitable institutions enjoying "pre-tax" receipts have long since lost their public affairs neutrality. If charity, alone, is to remain neutral, it—and not its opponents—will suffer a competitive disadvantage.

Professor Hart finds this symmetry point unpersuasive for two reasons. One is the fact that the unions, veterans' organizations, and business firms all represent constituencies with "concrete, identifiable interests," whereas the foundations do not—a point which does not relate to the fair-competition argument and which we therefore discuss under the "shadow government" heading. His second caveat is that

> the political activities of labor unions, for example, are the subject of extensive regulation . . . And, in general, the political use of tax-exempt money is the subject of continuing federal scrutiny.

The fact that some tax-exempt groups are excluded from some political areas (for example, unions are barred from contributing to federal election campaigns) may well mean that all exempt organizations (including charities) should be excluded from *those same areas;* but how can it be an argument for barring charities from *all* political areas—including those open to other bodies using tax-exempt and/ or tax-deductible funds?

We must ask, however, whether there are any parties which do *not* enjoy these tax advantages and which might be opposed by a charitable organization in a public affairs controversy. At first blush one might suppose that government bodies and individuals fall into this disfavored position. But the government uses tax revenues and can hardly be considered a disadvantaged competitor. With respect to individuals, those who are engaged in a trade or business are entitled to deductions for business-related public affairs activities. As for other individuals not engaged in business, I have yet to hear of a "public interest" litigation which pitted a charitable body against an individual acting in a nonbusiness capacity. When it comes to nonlitigative public affairs activities (lobbying, public education, etc.), most individuals are unlikely to act on their own, either with or without the benefit of tax deductions; the costs are too high, except for individuals of great wealth, who presumably do not need our compassion on "unfair competition" grounds. These cost barriers require most individuals to participate in public affairs controversies collectively, i.e., through an institution with which they are affiliated. If the institution is a political party, union, veterans' organization, or business corporation, and if the views it presents are congruent with those of the individual member (which is not always the case), he or she benefits from the institution's public affairs activities and from its favored tax status. The individual need not be a member of the organization to benefit from its assertion of a position close to his own. Indeed, in the legislative arena, views congruent with those of many individuals are represented by an institution to which none of the individuals belong: the executive branch. (The Peterson Commission noted that one of its members "who has had extensive legislative experience points out that the executive branch's vast input into the legislative process makes it particularly useful that there be well-conceived and well-organized private contributions to congressional deliberations.")[16]

[16] Commission on Foundations and Private Philanthropy, *Foundations, Private Giving, and Public Policy* (1970), p. 161 (hereafter called "Peterson Commission Report").

What happens, however, when no one of these noncharitable groups deals with, and can therefore give institutional support to, a particular individual's views on legislative or executive matters? Is he out of luck, unrepresented in the public arena, his voice too weak to be heard, while the foundations and other elephantine groups trumpet forth? I doubt it. The overwhelming probability is that any perspective not adequately represented by a noncharitable group—perhaps a concern about health care or the arts or education—will be advanced by some charitable body. In short, it is hard to think of a point of view not embraced by some institution, charitable or noncharitable, governmental or nongovernmental, that enjoys tax-favored treatment. Indeed, since foundations sometimes deal with unpopular causes, it may even be a foundation (or a foundation-funded group) on which the individual must depend to champion his views. (This may be true, for example, for victims of strip-mining or mental retardation, who have found an advocate in organizations funded, respectively, by the Field and Kennedy Foundations.)

And the irony of the present situation is this: the groups on which some otherwise unrepresented individuals must rely—the charities —are legally *less* free than the noncharitable bodies to advance the individual's views if those views relate to legislative matters. As a subset, the foundations enjoy even less freedom than that. Existing law places foundations at a competitive disadvantage relative to other charitable bodies, for the Tax Reform Act deprives foundations of the ability, possessed by other charities, to defend lobbying activities on the ground that they are not "substantial." The "substantiality" test, to be sure, is murky, but it provides at least a colorable justification for the Treasury's apparent failure to look into the Catholic Church's legislative activities on such subjects as birth control and abortion reform. Treasury abstention can be based on the notion that, relative to the overall income or expenditures of the church, nationally or in any one state, such legislative activities are not "substantial." But the private foundation which wishes to enter the arena on the other side of a birth control or abortion controversy can no longer invoke a substantiality defense.

In sum, while charity as a whole, in relation to other tax-favored institutions, is a second-class participant in public affairs, the foundations hold third-class status—and a third-class competitive position —under the existing legal order.[17]

A second, rather different version of the competitive unfairness argument should also be considered (although I have not yet come across it in the existing literature). It has to do with the relative degree of tax "subvention" associated with foundation resources as compared to the resources of other participants in public affairs controversies. The foundations typically derive their resources from the lifetime or testamentary gifts of the wealthiest members of society; the gifts result in contribution deductions taken against the highest income and estate tax brackets—70 percent in the case of income taxes (91 percent during earlier years) and 77 percent for estate taxes. These marginal rates are higher than the marginal rates applicable to the *average* charitable contributor or the average union-dues-payer or veterans-organization-contributor; indeed many contributors do not itemize deductions—or do not have enough income to pay any taxes—and thus do not receive any tax benefit from their gifts. The top individual income and estate tax rates are also higher than the surtax rate (currently 48 percent) against which a corporation deducts its own business expenditures for public affairs activities. Thus, the dollars the foundations use are likely to have resulted in a greater per-dollar tax saving than the resources available to other nongovernmental institutions. The argument, therefore, is that the foundations enjoy a competitive advantage over other public affairs protagonists, not because the foundations alone use pre-tax dollars (they do not), but because the foundations use *cheaper* pre-tax dollars.

This argument has empirical and logical shortcomings. For one thing, it is not uniformly true that the foundation is using cheaper dollars. A few of the largest foundations were created before the age of the income tax and therefore did not receive deductible contributions. Other foundations have received gifts of appreciated property for endowment purposes from living donors since the

---

[17] For a succinct and, in my view, sound critique of the restrictions on foundation activity relating to legislation, see Fritz F. Heimann, "Developing a Contemporary Rationale for Foundations," *Foundation News*, January/February 1972, pp. 7, 11–13. The pending legislation to permit public charities to engage in lobbying under certain quantitative restrictions, H.R. 13720, 92nd Cong., 2d Sess., would not improve the foundations' disfavored position.

passage of the Tax Reform Act, in which case the donors received only half of the normal deduction for these contributions. Some contributors to foundations made gifts during the eight years needed to qualify for unlimited charitable contribution status under the pre-1970 law—a period during which some of the gifts had to be made on a nondeductible basis to meet the required level of giving. It is also true that many of the contributors to *non*foundation charitable organizations have deducted their contributions at the top marginal tax rates.

More important, I do not know what criteria we could employ to assess the difference, in terms of competitive unfairness, between the foundation using a rich donor's "30 percent" dollars contributed to it several years ago, and a business corporation using "52 percent" dollars deducted currently. And how can we measure the difference between a foundation using "30 percent" dollars and a national, state, or local government using 100 percent tax revenues? I single out the business corporation and the government because they are, after all, a foundation's most likely adversaries in public affairs controversies. In view of the resulting difficulty of judging the competitive impact of the present deductibility system, it would seem unfair to use the "cheaper dollars" issue as the basis for imposing an across-the-board ban on foundation involvement in public controversies.

In logical terms, moreover, is competition unfair because one of the parties acquired its dollar resources more cheaply than the other? That might be the case if the differential price enabled the first party to acquire more funds than the other, but that is not true here, for the foundations' principal adversary groups—corporations and government—have vastly greater spending power than the foundations. Alternatively, the use of cheaper dollars might be unfair if the dollars had been obtained in some illegal or corrupt fashion. But the tax advantages accruing to foundation donors, and thus to the foundations, were not improperly obtained; these benefits derive from the settled policy of the tax law to allow charitable deductions along a progressive rate structure. This policy is itself the object of current controversy. If the present deduction system is deemed to work unfairly—in a manner inconsistent with tax progressivity or other egalitarian norms—then the impact of the defect is not confined to the foundations-in-public-affairs context but extends to all aspects of the tax treatment of charitable organizations. If so, the appropriate remedy is not to limit the ability of foundations to deal with public controversy; that would represent fairly superficial symptomatic treatment of an underlying structural defect in the tax system, a shortcoming which would itself be the proper object of reform.

THE "SHADOW GOVERNMENT" ARGUMENT

Apart from the issue of unfair competition, it is also contended that it is fundamentally undemocratic for foundations to participate in public affairs controversies. Professor Hart has set forth what he and others before him have called the "shadow government" objection in the following words:

> [T]he gut issue . . . concerns the role of the larger foundations as a kind of shadow government, disposing of substantial political and social power, and using that power in ways that are in fact highly questionable. Though the foundations to an increasing degree are acting as a political force, . . . they are not responsible to any electorate and so cannot be voted out of office . . . Because of their tax-exempt status, moreover, they are undertaking these activities with public money— money, that is, which otherwise would have found its way into the federal treasury and been used for public purposes.

As mentioned earlier, Professor Hart also points out that foundations represent no "specific, concrete interest in the community"— another way of making Senator Albert Gore's point that foundations enjoy "insulation from control by their beneficiaries" because the beneficiaries "simply cannot be precisely defined as a group, or, needless to say, feared"; as Representative Wright Patman once put it, there are no stockholders—and, we could add, no alumni, parishioners, patients, or other constituents.

In order to analyze the shadow government argument, it must first be parsed:

Foundations
   (i) use "public" funds
   (ii) without having to account
      (a) to the public at large, or
      (b) to any other controlling constituency,

(iii) so as to wield power in "social and political" matters (or in "public affairs," to use our term).

"Public Funds"—While the "public funds" element of the shadow government argument is the least debatable aspect, even that characterization deserves to be received with a bit of caution. As we have already noted, foundations and other charities are not alone in their ability to use otherwise-taxable resources—"public funds"—to play a public affairs role. When Boeing fought for the SST, and Lockheed for its loan, they were using "public funds"—in Professor Hart's meaning of the word—quite as much as a charitable organization. Moreover, I would like to suggest that the "otherwise-taxable" definition of "public funds" may extend even further than the funds held by charities, unions, corporations, and the other varieties of tax-exempt or tax-deducting organizations. For all wealth held by individuals—or at least all individual wealth which has accrued since the adoption of the Sixteenth Amendment in 1913—is "otherwise taxable"; all gain, "from whatever source derived," may constitutionally be taxed. When Congress reduced the top tax rate from 91 percent to 70 percent (in 1964) or from 70 percent to 50 percent on "earned" income (in 1971 and 1972), it acted with the explicit intention of encouraging certain levels of savings, investment, and consumption on the part of individuals. Does this untaxed money constitute "public funds" left in private hands, and, if so, what controls ought to be imposed?

"Accountability"—At this point we encounter the "accountability" theme. Most of us would agree that both our market economy and our traditions of personal liberty require that individuals be allowed to hold, without "accountability," the accretions to wealth which the government chooses not to tax and which individuals thereafter save, invest, and consume. If we do not impose accountability on these individually held funds, what shall we say about the wealth held by foundations, which the government has chosen not to tax? Should the foundations be faulted because they are not "accountable," to the public at large or any other constituency, for the handling of these funds? If so, it must result from some public policy that would be furthered by imposing "accountability" on foundations but not on individuals.

What can that public policy be? It could be a policy of limiting "social and political power"—but that requires us to look at the relative degree of power wielded by foundations in comparison to other organizations and individuals, an examination to which we will return. Another possible reason for demanding of foundations a degree of accountability we do not require of individuals is to enforce the "conditions" for nontaxation. The "condition" for permitting individuals to keep part of their gain free of tax is that they will save it, invest it or consume it; we *know* they will do one of these things; and so we do not need to engage in policing to reassure ourselves that the functions we want individuals to perform with their retained wealth are being performed. But when we allow foundations to retain wealth, or encourage individuals to give their wealth to foundations, it is to carry on certain types of activities called "charitable"—and these need to be policed to ensure compliance with statutory conditions. Accounting to a private constituency or to a public electorate—the two forms of accountability referred to by Professor Hart and other commentators—is one way of achieving this law enforcement function. Thus, in the corporate context, stockholders, as voters or complaining litigants, perform a law enforcement role of policing the fiduciary obligations of the managers and ensuring that they stick to charter purposes. While these private enforcers are perhaps indispensable policemen when it comes to corporations, there are comparable enforcers to whom foundation managers must account for their fiduciary performance and charter compliance: the state attorneys general and their generally more formidable colleagues, the auditors of the Internal Revenue Service. Since the passage of the Tax Reform Act, and in order to honor the regulatory rationale for the imposition of the 4 percent tax on investment income, the IRS has mounted a much more aggressive and ubiquitous enforcement program for the foundations than the shareholders have ever been able to impose on the corporations. In other words, for law enforcement purposes, foundations already live under the functional equivalent of accountability.

A second reason for causing corporate managers to account to their shareholders, and for causing public servants to account to the electorate, is to permit scrutiny and control, not of lawfulness, but of *achievement*. In this respect, foundations do *not* account to constituents—either for the brilliance with which they manage their portfolios (although truly subnormal results would be subject to policing as a breach of fiduciary duty), or for the soundness of their philanthropic decisions.[18]

This lack of constituent control strikes me as logical and even desirable. Compare the foundation with the business corporation. Stockholders, by their insistence on profitability, make management strive to win in the market place, and thus, we are told, insure the most efficient allocation of resources. When judging the performance of charitable trustees, however, the yardsticks of profitability and price are unlikely to be used or not available at all. There is no short-run index of philanthropic success comparable to an earnings statement, and therefore no way in which a constituency could be counted on to exercise rational programmatic control over foundation managers. If there is such a thing as success or failure in this arena, its proofs usually come years later—much more slowly than a corporate outcome and often too late to condemn any philanthropoids still in office.

Indeed—and this may be the most important point—it seems quite clear that not all of the missions of private philanthropy are consistent with the search for a constituency. The goal of experimentation and innovation clearly depends on a congeries of initiatives, some or many of them unorthodox, idiosyncratic, irreverent, absurd. The hard fact is that this process is usually irreconcilable with ongoing constituent control. The dichotomy is sharpest when the constituency is the public at large, the electorate. When the Reece Committee in 1954 asked that the foundations support "what the public currently wishes, approves, and likes," it pointed up the clash. The committee's majoritarian demand flatly contradicted the major premise underlying the role of charity, and particularly the role of foundations: the premise that there is an advantage to the social order which derives from the private, heterodox allocation of some portion of "otherwise taxable" or "public" funds. This

[18] Alan Pifer points out, however, that press comment can theoretically provide public accountability for foundations, and that "internal" accountability is imposed by the organizations in the foundation field, by professional staffs, by trustees, and by the necessity of publishing reports. Pifer, *Report of President of Carnegie Corporation*, 1968, reprinted in Thomas C. Reeves, *Foundations Under Fire* (1970), p. 54.

aspect of the clash between accountability and the mission of philanthropy is illumined in a Yeats poem which I commend to all readers, but for which there is room here only to give the title: "To A Wealthy Man Who Promised A Second Subscription To The Dublin Municipal Gallery If It Were Proved The People Wanted Pictures."

It is not only accountability to a *public* constituency that presents a clash with the role of foundations; the conflict also arises when a foundation is asked to account to the kind of *internal* constituency found in other charitable entities. While one can think of exceptions, it will be an unusual alumni body, a rare congregation or Community Chest distribution committee, which will exercise its voting control to bless outlandish experiments. In other words, if private foundations, as the Treasury wrote in 1965, "enrich the pluralism of our social order," it is largely because the foundations *are* private, freed from the very constituent controls that would provide "accountability." We cannot have it both ways.

To sum up, the functional equivalent of accountability for foundations is present in the area where accountability—or its equivalent—is needed (the area of law enforcement), whereas contemporaneous accountability is missing in the area where it would be unworkable and unhealthy (the area of programmatic control).

If this is a satisfactory (although untidy) state of affairs, does it become unsatisfactory when we move into the public affairs area? One might say so on two rather different grounds. The first (which requires a brief detour from the "shadow government" problem) asks us to review the "presumption of full participation" in the light of the foundation's lack of an operating constituency. The presumption, it may be said, really applies only to individual citizens and the groups that represent them, not to "nonrepresentative" bodies like foundations. This contention seems to founder on either of two theories that underly the participatory presumption.

(a) The *democratic* rationale for the presumption reflects a desire to give every citizen a voice in public decision-making, either individually or through organizations that speak for him. The foundation is not a constituent body but it can and does advance the views of individuals. It expresses, of course, the perspectives of its trustees and officers. More important, it can and does speak for those individuals whose interests are furthered by the foundation's charitable programs—e.g., persons with a stake in conservation or day care or the performing arts, or members of ethnic or minority groups— even though it does not formally "represent" these people. The degree of congruence between a foundation's views and those of large numbers of citizens will, of course, wax and wane depending on the popularity of its positions. But, as we have already noted, the positions taken by a mass constituency organization—charitable or noncharitable—may also bear an uneven fidelity to the views of its members. In either case, foundation or nonfoundation, the organization will serve as the voice for a population of individual citizens larger than its management.

(b) The *pluralistic* rationale for the presumption reflects a desire to improve the governmental decision-making process by permitting it to draw on a multitude of perspectives. Here we are not concerned that these perspectives have constituent support, or even that they emanate from any living human being. The decision-making process is informed by ideas regardless of their source—ideas drawn from constituent bodies, nonconstituent organizations (e.g., foundations), and even the writings of authors long-deceased. Hence, under the pluralistic as well as the democratic explanations of the presumption, foundations are entitled to invoke the presumption despite a lack of "accountability."

The second reason why "accountability" might be demanded of public affairs participants brings us back to the "shadow government" problem. It may be thought that an institution should not be permitted to impinge on public decisions and processes unless it is subject to reining in by a public—or at least an internal— constituency to which the managers must account. But it seems clear to me that contemporaneous accountability is *less* important in the public affairs area than in other fields of foundation endeavor. The key to this belief lies in the word "contemporaneous." A foundation is not currently accountable to the electorate or internal constituencies for the day-to-day or year-to-year quality of its public affairs activities, but ultimately these programs will get nowhere until and unless the foundation's position is embraced by the executive, legislative, or judicial body to which its public affairs activities are addressed. Ultimately, then, the foundation must win or lose its case before the governmental agencies exercising majoritarian control; its public affairs experiments, studies, and positions sooner or later will be judged by the body politic or its agencies. In the long run, the foundation must thus "account" to the larger society for its public affairs efforts. Indeed, this process of being judged by the public takes place more readily within the public affairs field than outside it; for example, it is not so easy to detect the public's role as ultimate arbiter of a foundation's grants to higher education or cultural programs. For this reason, I believe the criticism of foundations on nonaccountability grounds to be particularly weak in the very public affairs area we are discussing.

"Power"—The public's ultimate control bears not only on the "accountability" question but also on the question of foundation power. The most important restraint on the foundation's power, as Fritz F. Heimann has pointed out, is the fact that

> on any matter of public concern, the decision whether a foundation-initiated experiment will receive widespread application is bound to be made by public authorities.

There are, of course, other sources of limitation on foundation power in the political field. For one thing, the foundations cannot really operate in the "shadows": the Tax Reform Act requires them to describe all grants in annual reports available for public inspection. This publicity requirement, coupled with the prohibitions on support of political candidates, means that a foundation cannot exercise secret political control over a mayor or a judge or legislator —the classic kind of political "ownership" that has been so prominent a part of our political history.

Albert Shanker has suggested a more indirect form of political "ownership." Commenting on the New York school decentralization debates of the past few years, he asserts that there was a

> virtual non-existence of debate in academic circles. . . . All the argument there appeared to be on one side. Is it unreasonable to ask whether this seeming unanimity on a controversial idea might have been due in some part to a reluctance on the part of universities and their professors to lock horns with the Ford Foundation, for fear of jeopardizing financial support for other projects? [N.Y. *Times,* Oct. 17, 1971, p. 7.]

In dealing with the particulars of this claim, I suggest that the scholarly literature does not do very much to advance arguments on *either* side of the school decentralization issue; the literature, in fact, seems to me to be surprisingly thin. In any event, I doubt that there are many scholars who really suppose that the projects or institutions with which they are connected would lose foundation backing because of views they express on decentralization or any other subject. I have met a number of the most cautious academic grantsmen, but I have yet to encounter any souls as timorous as those conjured up by Mr. Shanker.

Another limitation on foundation power is the very lack of a constituency—a populous membership which elected officials fear to offend. And in the course of the 1969 legislative proceedings the foundations also found that it was very difficult for them to deploy their *grantees'* constituencies, even for purely defensive purposes. Moreover, the foundations do not have large labor forces which they can threaten to move to the suburbs or across state lines if local governing bodies do not do their bidding.

Another missing ingredient from the foundations' arsenal is the willingness to be harnessed to a common ideology or even a common set of social goals. Among the twenty-six thousand foundations, or the three-hundred-odd foundations with assets of more than $10 million, there is—despite the reputation of Eastern Establishment liberalism—a diversity that is typical of the nation as a whole. Many of the foundations—including several of the larger ones—have no appetite for work in public affairs; some stick to medical research or to support of higher or secondary education. Thus, a survey of approximately two hundred foundations by the Peterson Commission showed that only 0.3 percent of their grants in 1966–1968 supported "studies directly related to public policy issues and . . . dissemination of such studies to the general public. . . ." [19] And those that sometimes or often involve themselves in this work cover a full ideological spectrum. The Pew Memorial Trust and the Ford Foundation march to very different drummers, and Carnegie does not line up with Lilly. Indeed, even the smaller "liberal" foundations mainly based in New York City reflect divergences in approach

[19] Peterson Commission Report, pp. 83, 49. Waldemar A. Nielson's *The Big Foundations* (1972) also points to lack of involvement in this field.

and philosophy that would surprise their more casual observers; the conservative foundations of the Southwest also fail to conform to the monolithic picture drawn by some of their critics.[20] The foundations are, quite literally, far too motley to constitute a concerted striking force on behalf of anyone's political cause.

But the most important limitation, already mentioned in a different context, is the fact that governmental authority lies elsewhere, and foundation experiments and ideas must compete for acceptance in the political market. And this is the basic fact that Professor Hart appears to ignore when he charges that the foundations "intervene in a variety of ways in political and social matters," and when he specifies three instances of intervention in governmental affairs by the Ford Foundation. (Professor Hart actually lists seven cases of objectionable Ford Foundation behavior in the field of "social change," but four of them do not relate to governmental action.)

One of the three cases involves a governmentally related activity that lies outside the scope of the "public affairs" field as I have defined it and, indeed, requires rather special handling. This activity is voter registration work, which, if not properly controlled, can indirectly violate the prohibition against support of political candidates. The first major foundation-sponsored activity in this field was the southern Voter Education Project, which was approved by the Internal Revenue Service in 1962 under detailed restrictions to assure nonpartisanship and to which no "interventionist" scandal has attached. The Tax Reform Act has tightened up these safeguards still further and applied them to the entire foundation field. In picking over Ford's benighted grant to Cleveland CORE (Congress of Racial Equality) in the months preceding the election of a black mayor, Professor Hart does not mention the fact that this form of single-shot voter registration program is now ineligible for foundation support. (He also says that the entire $175,000 grant to Cleveland CORE was for voter work, whereas only $38,750 was so intended. This amount of money in a city of Cleveland's size, expended in what was alleged to be a poorly run drive, could not have done

[20] For an illustration of the tendency of critics to lump alleged left-leaning foundations together and to lump alleged right-leaning foundations together, see, respectively, Rene A. Wormser, "Foundations: Their Power and Influence," and Arnold Forster and Benjamin R. Epstein, "Danger on the Right," in Thomas C. Reeves, *Foundations Under Fire* (1970), pp. 97, 120.

very much for Carl Stokes.) I would agree that charitable groups should not engage in one-time, one-city voter drives, and I generally support the new legal prohibitions to this effect, but I also believe that the vitality of our political system requires a continuation of the kind of voter registration efforts which foundations can continue to support even under the 1969 Act.

Turning to Professor Hart's complaints of Ford Foundation intervention in school decentralization and suburban housing, what these cases demonstrate most clearly is that a foundation may propose, but only the public can dispose. In the schools matter, Professor Hart echoes Albert Shanker's earlier lament about the role of "tax-exempt foundations . . . exempt from accountability" in bringing about a measure of school decentralization in New York. It is not my purpose to defend the Ford Foundation from its critics. But Professor Hart's complaint overlooks two fundamental facts related to the "power" question under discussion. First, the New York City movement for community control did not originate with the Ford Foundation; it originated at least two years before the Ford Foundation entered the scene (upon the invitation, incidentally, of public officials—the mayor and the superintendent of schools); and it began where any movement that leads anywhere must begin—with indigenous popular sentiment: in this case, the frustration and anger of the parents at Intermediate School 201 in Harlem. Second, the translation of this movement into state policy was carried out not by the Ford Foundation but by the state legislature in Albany. Paying at least as much heed to Mr. Shanker's union as to the Ford Foundation's demonstration program, the legislature enacted a highly restrained decentralization measure that was widely viewed as at least a partial defeat for the community control forces—and for the point of view attributed by Mr. Shanker to the Ford Foundation.

As for exclusionary land-use practices in the suburbs (if that is what Professor Hart means by " 'open housing' in the suburbs"), I must comment on the extraordinarily summary fashion in which Hart dismisses what Secretary of Housing and Urban Development George Romney was reported to have called America's most serious domestic problem, a problem which the Kerner Commission identified as a major source of racial polarization and economic deprivation—and, indeed, a major threat to domestic peace—in the decades to come. The very few foundations that deal with the problem of exclusionary land-use policies are concerned with the issue of whether this country will deny its poorer and darker citizens access to the nation's growth centers—the suburban areas where the jobs and the developable land are to be found. But it is an issue that will not be decided by the foundations at all. It will be decided in part by municipalities (some of which, such as the Dayton, Ohio, suburbs, have decided to accept lower-income housing on a voluntary "fair share" basis, while others have refused to do so); it will be decided in part by the courts (some of which—both state and federal—have already declared certain exclusionary practices unlawful under state or federal law, while the United States Supreme Court has hinted at a more cautious approach); it will be decided in part by the state legislatures (the Massachusetts legislature has attempted to establish "inclusionary" standards for local zoning, while the New York legislature has made an effort—vetoed by the governor—to deprive the state's Urban Development Corporation of its zoning override powers); it will be decided in part by the federal executive branch (the Department of Housing and Urban Development has established criteria to encourage the dispersal of federally assisted housing, while the President has argued against a strong federal role in this field); and it may be decided in part by the Congress (a number of bills would condition the availability of federal housing and other aid on the reduction of exclusionary practices, while it was a congressional committee that cut back on the availability of rent supplements when it heard that they might be used in the suburbs).

Within the limits imposed by the present law, foundations have supported research, litigation, and public education programs that relate to all of the above-mentioned approaches to the problem of exclusionary land-use practices. But it is also clear that various foundations, intentionally or not, have made grants that cut in the opposite direction—principally grants to environmental defense groups opposing residential or industrial development that might generate lower-income housing. Indeed, some foundations have made grants that support *both* approaches. This contrapuntal movement within the land-use field illustrates the point that foundations do not have a monolithic position on public questions.

Despite all the limitations on foundations which we have discussed, the possibility remains that a substantial-sized foundation might intervene in a small polity—for example a modest-sized town or school district—and engage in a massive effort to effect a particular governmental result. It might finance public education, citizen activity, litigation, and (within the present or modified statutory restrictions) lobbying activity, all to a single end—for example, the prevention of an industrial development in the cause of environmental protection. And although its methods and goals were lawful and fully disclosed, the foundation might simply swamp the public processes of the town with so much communication and citizen activity that rival forces could not get a fair hearing. This is the only version of the "shadow government" scenario which strikes me as remotely plausible. But I believe it has to be considered a very faint contingency. I have yet to hear of any such smothering effort by a foundation, successful or otherwise.

For those who are concerned about this possibility, however, an attempt to hobble the participation of all foundations in public affairs is not a fair way to deal with the problem. It constrains twenty-six thousand foundations in order to eliminate the odd (and so far hypothetical) bully.

In the long run, of course, the most effective way to protect local polities from "excessive" foundation power is to strengthen the processes and structures of local government. The most important check and balance on the power of any institution is a democratic governance system vital and resilient enough to learn and profit from, rather than be overwhelmed by, the large groups that surround it. Accordingly, as foundations play their part in improving the governmental apparatus at all levels, they decrease still further any conceivable threat they may pose to the democratic order.

The shadow government point, therefore, seems to me to add up to very little. But I do not wish my disparagement of foundation power to carry with it the notion that foundations have no useful role to play in the area of public affairs. Proposing is not disposing, to be sure, but proposing is crucial; it is essential that the public disposers take account of the issues that foundations may help to develop, the views that may have no champions except those funded by foundations. To be specific, I do not know where—except for the foundations—those who wished to experiment with public school community control could have obtained financing; I do not know where—except for the foundations—those who wished to explore the possibility of opening the gates of suburbia could have found the funds they needed.

A PARTIAL SUMMING UP

The answer to all the arguments considered under both the "normative" and the "effectiveness" headings is, to some degree, empirical. For example, the answer to the "divisiveness" argument questions the factual accuracy of the suggestion that foundation-financed projects have had a polarizing or fragmenting effect; the answer to the "unfair competition" argument admits the possibility of litigation or other controversy between an exempt organization and a nonexempt individual, but suggests that such a clash is in fact highly unlikely; and the answer to the "shadow government" objection concedes that a foundation might be able to swamp the decision-making processes in a small polity—but contends that this is a fairly remote possibility. It is not entirely satisfactory to rest a major policy conclusion on fairly impressionistic factual conclusions and prognoses. But we must recall the presumption of participation with which we began; assuming that this starting point is accepted, those who would limit the foundations' role have to present fairly persuasive evidence—and fairly strong policy arguments—to justify a result that overrides this presumption. Accordingly, if the factual conclusions and prognoses I have set forth appear to be correct or at least plausible—and if my answers to the policy arguments also appear to be correct or at least plausible—then the logical outcome is this: that the "effectiveness" and "normative" arguments fail to overcome the presumption in favor of full foundation participation in public affairs, and therefore these arguments do not justify a governmentally imposed or self-imposed proscription on foundation work in this area.

I do not for a moment suggest that the absence of general proscriptions obviates the need for self-restraint and thoughtfulness on a case-by-case basis. All institutions (and all individuals) must police the fairness and the social consequences of their own acts, and foundations are not exempted. (I will shortly propose a few cautionary guidelines on this subject.) But in the foundation public affairs field, as in so many other areas of government regulation, we will slide into over-regulation if we attempt to ban an entire field of activity in order to prevent occasional excesses; here, as elsewhere, we will have to rely, for the elimination of abusive behavior, on a modicum of institutional common sense, on the counsel of respected institutional peers (occasionally one foundation will tell one of its brethren to take it easy), and, finally, on that powerful engine of self-regulation: fear. Fear of a bad press, fear of a hostile auditor, fear of an angry Congress will probably take care of most of the abusive conduct. The difficulty, of course, is that it will take care of much more than that. And this point leads us to our final category of arguments against foundation public affairs involvement—the "prudential" argument, which suggests that *all* such involvements be eschewed in the interest of self-defense—which suggests, in other words, that the counsel of fear be adopted as a general exclusionary rule shaping the conduct of foundations.

The Prudential Argument

The distinction between this argument and the other arguments we have considered—the fact that the prudential objection is wholly expedient and does not purport to invoke questions of principle— becomes clearer if we consider the position of Robert Paul Wolff, a Columbia philosopher who is "a self-proclaimed radical." Considering the question whether universities ought to remain "neutral" on political questions, Professor Wolff contends that neutrality is impossible because of the university's deep involvement in the surrounding economic and cultural order; he asserts that this is so even with respect to such apparently nonideological matters as deadlines for student papers; "neutrality" is therefore a "myth." Turning, however, from definitional or normative considerations to prudential concerns, Professor Wolff argues that universities should continue to sustain the myth, simply because in the absence of apparent "neutrality," "conservative forces in society at large" would seize upon the loss of apparent "neutrality" to rush in with various repressive measures aimed at unorthodox or radical teachers. "Let the university once declare that it is a political actor, and its faculty will be investigated, its charter revoked, and its tax-exempt status forthwith removed." [21] In other words, the university's aura of apparent neutrality buffers it from hostile forces.

1969 AND ALL THAT

A similar point is made with respect to foundations and their non-"neutral" (or, in Professor Moynihan's term, non-"even-handed") involvement in public controversies. Those who warn foundations away from this activity sometimes point to the Tax Reform Act of 1969 in support of their position. Look, they say, what happened to you in 1969, and look what got you into trouble—in particular, the "political" actions of the Ford Foundation. But it is not at all clear to me that what I have here called "public affairs" activity—activity related to the executive, legislative, and judicial decision-making processes—had much to do with what happened to the foundations in 1969. To be sure, a fair amount of congressional (and editorial) anger focussed on certain "political" actions, but these targets of abuse were, for the most part, the following:

1. Activities that appeared to represent a violation, at least in spirit, of the prohibition against intervention *in electoral campaigns*—i.e., Ford's grant for CORE's voter drive in Cleveland on the eve of the Stokes-Taft mayoralty campaign (discussed above), and the complaints about the Frederick W. Richmond Foundation's alleged assistance to the candidacy of Frederick W. Richmond for Congress—a matter about which Mr. Richmond's successful opponent, Congressman John Rooney, testified with some vigor at the 1969 House hearings. (I note that, despite the CORE incident, Congress did not seem to be excessively disturbed about voter registration as a field of foundation activity, for the Congress ended up by rejecting a Treasury proposal that it ban all such activity; it substituted a provision which authorizes foundations to continue to support registration drives on a multistate, multisource basis.)

2. The travel-study grants to the former Robert Kennedy associates (also discussed above), a series of grants which were *sui generis* and do not fit into the pattern of foundation work we are considering.

In sum, the objects of Congressional ire were not the "public affairs" activities under discussion here.

Moreover, there were plenty of other reasons for congressmen to

[21] Wolff, *The Ideal of the University* (1969), p. 75.

hate the foundations, reasons having nothing to do with political conduct: self-dealing, control of business enterprises, insufficient payout to charity, speculative investing, and, more generally, the feeling that foundations represented a special kind of tax-free plaything for rich folks, pockets of untaxed and unaccountable wealth not doing very much for the common weal—in short, bastions of privilege. As Professor Moynihan has put it in a talk to foundation representatives:

> To many of the Congressmen involved, it was clear at the time that the foundations represented nothing more than one further manifestation of the protean and wicked forces of Giant Eastern Capitalism. *They* were Main Street; *you* were Wall Street.[22]

Most of the provisions of the Tax Reform Act specifically relate to one or another of these nonpublic affairs concerns. It is true that the one section dealing with political matters [Internal Revenue Code (I.R.C.), Section 4945] deprives foundations of the "substantiality" defense in legislative-influencing cases (and thereby, as we have noted, creates a third-class status for the foundations on this point).[23] But the rest of the statutory language, coupled with the legislative history of this section, mitigates this discrimination, permitting the Treasury to write regulations that incorporate what has been the more *permissive* interpretation of the pre-existing law covering all charitable organizations [I.R.C., Section 501(c)(3)]; under this interpretation, foundations will be allowed to take and publicize a position on a pending bill if the position results from "nonpartisan analysis, study or research." Moreover, the Ways and Means Committee backed away from its tentative proposal, mentioned above, that "[n]o private foundation is to be permitted to directly or indirectly engage in any activities . . . intended . . . to influence the decision of any governmental body. . . ."; the rejection of this position leaves foundations free to fund litigation and the monitoring and criticism of executive branch behavior.

[22] Daniel P. Moynihan, "Social Welfare: Government vs. Private Efforts," *Foundation News*, March/April 1972, pp. 5, 8.

[23] Even this move seems not to have been intended to do more than to avoid the fact that "a large organization, merely because of the substantiality test, may engage without consequence in more lobbying than a small organization. . . ." House of Representatives Report No. 91-413, Aug. 2, 1969, p. 32.

The events of the following fall (1970) provided another opportunity to test the intentions of Congress with respect to public affairs activity. When the Treasury announced that it was reconsidering the tax-exempt status of organizations engaged in various forms of "public interest" litigation (on environmental, civil rights, consumer safety, and similar matters), it drew a great deal of opposition from individual members of Congress and, in a preliminary fashion, from one congressional committee. One obvious compromise would have been to distinguish between foundation-conducted or foundation-supported litigation activities and those undertaken without foundation participation. It would not, of course, have been the first time that such a distinction in favor of nonfoundation charities had been made in the scheme of charitable regulation. (Professor Boris Bittker has catalogued these distinctions in chapter 5.) Accordingly, if there had been a pent-up feeling that foundations should stay out of "public interest" litigation, the 1970 uproar would presumably have brought it forth, and someone in Congress would have proposed that the controversy be settled with a compromise disfavoring the foundations. But this did not happen.

The brief history I have just set forth is not substantial enough to permit a confident assertion that Congress or the public at large approves of the public affairs activities we are considering, and it is true that at various points in time—notably when the Reece Committee issued its report in 1954—one heard congressional expressions of discontent with foundation involvement in public controversy. But this review does indicate that the events of 1969–70 do not provide support for the prudential argument we are now considering, and it suggests that when it comes to legislation, as compared to fulmination, congressmen are less hostile to public affairs involvement than many have thought.

A MATTER OF GUESSWORK

Beyond that cautious finding, however, the rest is largely guesswork. The prudential argument, after all, is a prediction: it warns of retaliation following what Professor Hart calls "any unduly risqué political initiative." Without some kind of intensive and detailed interviewing of the members of Congress, we have no solid basis for making the necessary forecast of the degree of "unduly risqué" behavior that will loose the storm. The Peterson Commission's survey of 885 "opinion leaders" disclosed that 69.2 percent of them favored foundation "grants to study public policy issues and influence public opinion or government action through dissemination of the study." But "opinion leaders" do not necessarily reflect legislators' predilections, and so we are thrown back upon our own notions about the predispositions of our legislators.

My own notions are, first, that legislators' reactions to public affairs activity will in part reflect their attitude toward the foundations' work as a whole and that this outlook can reasonably be expected to improve as the Council on Foundations and individual funds continue their program of explaining the activities of the foundations to local and national audiences. (One hopes that individual foundations will avoid some of the aggressive special pleading that irritated certain members of the Senate Finance Committee in the final weeks of the 1969 deliberations.) Second, I assume that most legislators believe that their own decisions, and those of the other branches of government, will be improved by exposure to—and need not be shielded from—a wide variety of views, and that these legislators, if not needlessly provoked, therefore will accept the participation of foundations in public affairs. (Indeed, I wonder if such an attitude does not explain congressional rejection, in 1969, of proposals for flat prohibition of public affairs activity.)

SOME CAUTIONARY GUIDELINES

My caveat about "needless provocation," of course, hedges this optimistic prognosis. Indeed, this vague caveat could be misinterpreted to rule out *all* forms of public affairs activity. Accordingly, I offer, with some hesitation, my own limited definition of needless provocation, which also serves as a counsel of caution to foundations embarked on public affairs programs:

1. *Avoid all research or public education activities which, because of their timing or their topical or geographical focus, will assist, or will appear to assist, a particular candidate for public office*—and thus appear to violate the letter or spirit of the prohibition on support of political candidates. This injunction should not prevent foundations from funding supplementary staff or research assistance to executive or other officials to permit them to do a better job—

often an especially productive use of foundation resources. But the timing and nature of such a program have to be carefully regulated to make sure that it does not directly serve as campaign assistance. (Obviously anything that helps the officeholder to work more effectively may indirectly assist his reelection chances, but that is not a reason for failing to support programs aimed at improving government operations.)

2. *Avoid participation in or support of what appear to be belligerently sloganistic or manipulatively propagandistic public media campaigns aimed at the legislature, the executive, or public opinion in general,* whether or not permitted by statute. (The Code now forbids a "grass-roots" campaign to influence action on specific legislation unless the activity constitutes "making available the results of nonpartisan analysis, study, or research.") In many ways this is the hardest of my prudential guidelines to justify on logical grounds. If the American Cancer Society and the Heart Association can launch TV propaganda against cigarettes, partly with foundation funds, and if religious groups can dot the subway walls with tolerance posters, partly with foundation funds, why should not the foundations support no-holds-barred publicity campaigns urging people to put pressure on government officials? In other words, why should a grass-roots campaign aimed at governmental action stand on any different footing from a program urging private action? I cannot provide any principled ground for this distinction, and all the answers I have given to the various arguments disclosed in this chapter suggest that the foundations should not be so limited as a matter of law. And yet I suggest this self-imposed limitation because congressmen and Treasury officials may continue to feel that there is some inconsistency between "charity and politics," or that there is some problem with foundations "throwing their weight around," and because these residual feelings might be catalyzed by the "political pressure" atmosphere of unrestrained "grass-roots" campaigning.

3. *Wherever possible, engage in public affairs activities not by directly engaging in foundation-directed projects, but by supporting the program of an operating charity with a constituency and a specific stake in the public affairs controversy*—e.g., a voluntary hospital interested in increased appropriations for mental health research

or a conservation organization interested in litigation affecting water resources. This suggestion, like the preceding one, does not invoke principle, but simply honors the apparent congressional preference for publicly supported or what Professor Bittker calls "publicly patronized" charities, as compared to private foundations. (A friend says that, on principle, he finds this suggestion troubling, for it encourages foundations to insulate themselves from the "static" their controversial activities might otherwise generate. His point is a good one, but I would respond—also in terms of principle—by noting that my recommendation has a countervailing virtue: it permits foundation views to be put to the external test—albeit limited —of acceptance by another group with a constituency of its own.)

4. *Avoid acting like a gun-slinger.* Choose projects on the basis of a careful analysis of the relation of the project to the foundation's goals (which themselves should be explicitly reconsidered from time to time) and on the basis of a thorough investigation of the integrity and competence of the grantee, using outside advice where possible. And be prepared to document the fact that the foundation went through this process. Apart from the obvious importance of thoughtful decisions, the point of this recommendation is to avoid the allegation of impulsive and arbitrary action, the charge Professor Hart has leveled at the Ford Foundation when he says that its "money was poured in on whim."

5. Within the limits of personnel and funds (and these limits may be severe), *follow through carefully and critically on the grantee's work,* even where this measure is not required by the "expenditure responsibility" requirements of the Tax Reform Act. In addition to its intrinsic merit, thorough postauditing should avoid the charge that the foundation acted irresponsibly in a hit-and-run fashion.

6. *Avoid grants to groups that seem to prefer heat to light, confrontation to resolution.* Many organizations with a serious commitment to any social goal will and ought to have some pretty sharp edges and may have to be contentious and noisy in order to be heard. That also may be true of foundations themselves, and, accordingly, I believe that it will be unfortunate if the "nonpartisan analysis, study or research" condition on legislative activity causes foundations to soften the positions they adopt. (The Treasury regulations do not necessarily require such softening so long as the underlying

analysis is balanced and comprehensive, but many foundations will probably act on the premise that blandness is the safer course.) But there is a spectrum of bellicosity, and occupation of the far end of this spectrum will neither advance the goals of any foundation I have encountered nor protect the foundation world from reprisal.

7. *Make sure that none of the foundation's grants subsidizes an unfair contest.* A foundation ought not (even if the law permitted) finance a mammoth legislative campaign in a small community which has the effect of swamping opposing points of view; similarly, the foundation ought not support a vexatious litigation or one which singles out, from among a number of potential defendants, the one least able to finance a defense. Once more, both principle and prudence support this guideline.

THE RESIDUAL RISK

Even if foundations follow the foregoing prescription for avoiding "needless provocation," they may not head off trouble. My prognosis may be unrealistic; it may violate the late Paul Mus's comment that "rational actions mean measures in harmony with the structure of facts, rather than with logical arguments." In other words, it is conceivable that further public affairs involvement on the part of the foundations, no matter how carefully handled, may bring on a period of persecution. At best, this might result in harassment of the foundations; at worst, it might not only outlaw further work in the public affairs field but generally limit the foundations' freedom of action and impose further taxes on their resources and further limits on their ability to acquire new funds.

For the reasons I have given, the odds against this result seem very long to me, the hazard quite limited. But if even a slight risk remains, one may ask: is the game worth the candle? Should all the other good works foundations perform ("the game") be jeopardized even for a second in order to permit foundations to operate in the realm of public affairs ("the candle")?

What leads me to suggest an affirmative answer is the belief that, in large part, the game *is* the candle. It is in the public affairs area that all the old clichés about foundations—they represent "venture capital," "take risks," "leverage other resources," encourage "institutional change," illustrate the "synergism" between the private and public sectors, and, generally, contribute to "pluralism"—bear the closest approximation to reality. It is here, no less than in other areas of endeavor, that foundations can make a unique contribution to improving the human condition. For this reason, the foundations should, with all deliberate vigor, press for the removal of existing restrictions on certain types of person-to-person or "grass-roots" legislative activity. For the same reason, the foundations should not give up, without a struggle, that public affairs work which they can undertake under present law and which, in so many ways, justifies their existence.

"It is the business of [charitable] trusts," an officer of the Carnegie United Kingdom Trust said a few years ago, "to live dangerously." I doubt that public affairs activities are perilous. But if danger does lie that way, then it is the business of the foundations to grasp the nettle.

John R. Labovitz

4

1969 Tax Reforms Reconsidered

Taxation is only obscurely or indirectly the subject of most of the foundation provisions of the Tax Reform Act of 1969. Although buried deep in the Internal Revenue Code, enforced by the Internal Revenue Service (IRS), and resembling other tax legislation in their complexity, these provisions are in fact primarily regulatory in character. They impose a series of prohibitions and limitations on foundation activities. Stated oversimply:

> Foundations are prohibited from engaging in direct or indirect financial transactions (so-called self-dealing) with donors or other related parties, whether the transactions benefit the foundation or not.
>
> The assets of a foundation may not be invested in risky or speculative ventures that jeopardize its charitable purposes.
>
> The use of foundations to control closely held or family businesses is restricted through a provision limiting the permissible combined stock holdings of a foundation and related parties to 20 percent. Elaborate phase-out provisions are prescribed for existing excess business holdings owned by foundations.

JOHN R. LABOVITZ, *formerly an assistant director of the Commission on Foundations and Private Philanthropy, was in 1970 associate editor of the report of the President's Commission on Campus Unrest. He is currently associated with the American Bar Foundation project to monitor the impact of the foundation provisions of the Tax Reform Act of 1969. Although this paper draws upon information obtained in the course of that project the opinions herein are those of Mr. Labovitz and not necessarily of the Foundation.*

Foundations are required to spend an amount for charitable purposes each year equal to their current income, excluding capital gains. If a foundation's income is less than a prescribed rate of return on its investment assets, it is required to pay out this minimum investment return (initially set by the statute at 6 percent, with a phase-in period for preexisting foundations).

Foundations are prohibited from making expenditures to attempt to influence the outcome of a specific election. Grants for voter registration are permitted only in limited circumstances intended to insure nonpartisanship.

Foundations are forbidden to make any payments to elected or appointed government officials except for reimbursement of domestic travel expenses.

Individuals who receive foundation grants for travel, study, or similar purposes must be selected in accordance with objective and nondiscriminatory procedures approved in advance by the Internal Revenue Service.

Foundations must exercise "expenditure responsibility" over grants to other organizations that are themselves private foundations or do not qualify for tax exemption as charities. Expenditure responsibility requires the foundation to make reasonable efforts and establish adequate procedures to see that the funds are expended by the grantee for the prescribed purpose, to obtain complete financial reports from the grantee, and to submit detailed reports to the IRS.

Foundations are prohibited from making expenditures to attempt to influence legislation either by seeking to affect public opinion or by communicating with government officials who may participate in the formulation of legislation. Exceptions are provided for "making available the results of nonpartisan analysis, study, or research"; providing "technical advice or assistance" to a governmental body or committee in response to its written request; expressing opinions on legislation affecting the foundation's own tax or legal status.

Foundations are prohibited from making expenditures for noncharitable purposes.

To enforce these restrictions, Congress enacted a series of "excise taxes" designed to serve as penalties for violations. Some of these sanctions—for excess business holdings and failure to meet the prescribed payout—are levied against the foundation itself. Others—for jeopardy investments and various categories of impermissible expenditures—are enforced by taxes both on the foundation and on knowingly involved foundation managers. The penalty taxes for self-dealing and payments to government officials are imposed against the self-dealer or government official and against knowingly involved foundation managers. Failure to correct a violation after notice results in a second, much higher level of taxes. For repeated or willful and flagrant violations the taxes may be doubled, and ultimately a "termination tax" may be imposed on the foundation. This tax consists of the foundation's total assets or, if less, the total tax benefits received by the foundation because of its tax exemption and by substantial contributors because of the tax deductibility of their contributions to it.

The Act also encourages states to enforce the new restrictions by requiring foundations to amend their governing instruments to include its provisions. It increases public disclosure of foundation activities by requiring foundations to prepare annual reports and advertise their availability for public inspection.

The 1969 law includes provisions indicating the less-favored status of private foundations in comparison with other charitable organizations. First, it imposes an annual excise tax of 4 percent of net investment income (including capital gains) on each foundation. This tax is said to reflect a congressional determination that "private foundations should share some of the burden of paying the cost of government, especially for more extensive and vigorous enforcement of the tax laws relating to exempt organizations." Second, the law includes provisions making the tax advantages for contributions to private foundations less attractive than for contributions to other charitable organizations.

Central to these provisions is the new legislative definition of "private foundation," a term that previously had no precise legal meaning. The Act defines foundations negatively, by excluding various classes of charitable organizations from private-foundation status. The essential characteristics of the excluded organizations is that they receive their financial support from the general public or a large number of donors. Congress found that these publicly supported charitable organizations, unlike private foundations, tend to be more responsive to public opinion and therefore require less stringent regulation by the federal government.

Foundation Reactions to the Tax-Reform Law

Foundations and their legal advisors were initially stunned by the regulatory structure Congress had enacted, although the final law was less sweeping than the early recommendations of the House Ways and Means Committee. The consensus among major foundations ultimately came to be that parts of the law were beneficial (such as the prohibition of self-dealing) and parts of it atrocious (primarily the tax on investment income). They considered the law as a whole to be tolerable, if unwelcome. Indeed, some felt that the introspection produced by the legislative process was quite valuable. Few major foundations found any important grant programs that had to be discontinued or substantially altered because of the new restrictions.

A few large foundations, and especially some with extensive holdings of low-yield corporate control stock, thought the 6 percent payout too high. Two such foundations, Kellogg and Pew, pressed for an amendment to the law to reduce the percentage to 5 and to lengthen the phase-in period. Criticism of the 4 percent tax on investment was more nearly universal; most foundations resented the reduction it caused in the amount they could distribute to charity. Some activist foundations were initially quite concerned about the restriction on legislative activities by foundations and discussed possible challenges to the provision on First Amendment grounds.

For the most part, however, reactions to the new law were more tentative and uncertain. As was natural, the Act produced a period of confusion for foundations, since it was an extremely comprehensive set of federal regulatory provisions imposed on organizations that had been subject to little regulation in the past. And it was an exceptionally complicated piece of legislation, with a number of ambiguities and sufficient play in the joints that its precise meaning would not be clarified until the Treasury Department issued interpretive regulations and IRS enforcement began. Much depended on how charitable the Treasury draftsmen were and, thereafter, how zealous IRS agents were in their enforcement work.

Regulation-drafting proved to be a time-consuming task. Three years after the Act went into effect, final regulations on many of its provisions had still not been issued. Proposed regulations covering many of the sections had been issued, but the draftsmen were still tinkering with them and no timetable could be projected for their completion.

Uncertainty and complexity had a number of consequences. Some foundations continued to operate as they always had, occasionally in ignorance of the new requirements. One foundation, for example, continued its practice of paying a modest consulting fee to the head of a state agency to review applications and make recommendations on those that should be approved for funding. The executive director of the foundation was genuinely surprised to learn that the hiring of expertise from a government official might lead to penalty taxes. The legal profession, with the exception of the growing fraternity of specialists in the field, did not always pay attention to the new law either. Trust instruments and charters for new foundations continued to be drafted as they had been before the Act was passed, even though the provisions had immediate (and in some cases retroactive) application.

For foundations that attempted to adapt their procedures to the new restrictions, a lengthy review process was required. The day-to-day involvement of legal counsel in the operation of foundations increased dramatically—hardly an unmixed blessing. Many foundations began to ask their lawyers to review each grant they were considering and sought opinion letters on a wide variety of other transactions.

Greater reliance on legal advice was certainly a prudent course for foundations to adopt, but it has proved to be expensive. Legal fees paid by foundations have almost certainly increased substantially since 1969; the paperwork the lawyers recommended has led to higher clerical costs and has in some instances required added staff.

There were other, less tangible costs, such as the diversion of management time to questions of compliance with the law. Many foundation administrators reported that they had to spend substantial time trying to come to grips with the new provisions, time that otherwise would have been devoted to questions of programs or to review of grant applications. Whether, or how much, this has affected the quality of foundation grant decisions is difficult to judge.

A number of foundation executives reported that the Act had a pervasive influence on their activities; they were constantly aware of its negative injunctions—and the personal financial sanctions they faced for violation of these injunctions. This may be a short-run or idiosyncratic phenomenon, however. Other foundation executives considered the law to be merely an irritant, requiring some paperwork but little more, and a few bragged of how painlessly they had made the adjustment to it.

Evaluation of Some Specific Provisions of the 1969 Law

To offer an opinion on each of the foundation provisions would take far more space and immerse the reader in far more technical minutiae than is warranted here. Instead, I will concentrate on a few provisions that seem ill-conceived or overdone, a few that are creating problems, and one that warrants a defense. Not necessarily in that order, the provisions are those concerned with self-dealing, the tax on investment income, the payout, excess business holdings, expenditure responsibility, and the restriction on influencing legislation.

SELF-DEALING

Some foundations are having difficulty in adjusting to the self-dealing provision. Two types of situation cause particular problems: first, where the foundation's business affairs have traditionally been closely linked with those of related parties; and, second, where the foundation's board consists of leading citizens, especially in a small city. The Act prohibits transactions between the foundation and substantial contributors, foundation managers, members of the families of these persons, and businesses controlled by them or their families. The proposed regulations extend the prohibition to transactions between disqualified persons and organizations controlled by the foundation. Whether the disqualified person benefits, or the foundation loses, from the transaction is immaterial. The penalty for violation of the prohibition is a personal tax on the self-dealer (disqualified person) and on knowingly involved foundation managers. To prevent its imposition, foundations are required to keep careful records of who is disqualified at any particular time and to guard against direct and indirect transactions between these persons and the foundation.

The record-keeping may be extremely complicated. As one lawyer for an operating foundation in a medium-sized city put it, "There will be questions coming up whenever the foundation buys a piece of equipment. It may be difficult or impossible to insure compliance, since we are unsure of who owns what." Another foundation official, also a lawyer, reacted more heatedly: "The individual penalties are in the nature of criminal tax penalties. That is how they are viewed by men whose reputation in the community is at stake. A group of distinguished citizens shouldn't have to put up with this crap."

The self-dealing questions that can arise are sometimes anomalous, as the following examples from interviews indicate. Where do visitors to the foundation stay when the only decent hotel in town is owned by a disqualified person? How does a foundation advertise the availability of its annual report for public inspection (an advertisement required by the law) when a board member owns the local newspaper? Where will a foundation that leases office space from a disqualified person house the additional staff it needs to meet the record-keeping requirements of the law? (Under an exception to the self-dealing prohibition, pre-existing leases may be continued until 1979, but additional space apparently may not be rented from disqualified persons.) Conversely, who will rent the relatively undesirable space in the foundation's building that a board member, who rented it partly as a favor to the foundation, is required to give up?

Given its intricacy, it is not surprising that the self-dealing provision is described in the legal literature in such terms as "the greatest trap for the unwary of all the private foundation provisions."

While hardly a matter of momentous concern from the standpoint of public policy, the self-dealing provision illustrates the technical shortcomings of the Tax Reform Act. There is no question that there were some abuses before 1969—transactions that unfairly benefited a donor at the expense of a private foundation—and that the existing law, which permitted "arm's-length" transactions, had proved inadequate. How much abuse there was, and whether any even approached the ingenuity of some of the schemes covered by the new provision, was not known.

The only sanction available under the prior law was removal of a foundation's tax exemption, but no serious consideration was given by Congress to changing the sanction without altering the substantive rule. It is conceivable that an arm's-length or fairness test, coupled with monetary penalties against the wrongdoer, would have been sufficient. The difficulty of proving violations that was the supposed justification for the absolute prohibition does not seem so great when the punishment to be inflicted is scaled to the transgression.

Even if the difficulty does justify the absolute prohibition in some circumstances—for example, for direct transactions between a donor or foundation manager and the foundation—it does not seem to warrant the draftsmen's zeal in inventing ways to mulct foundations and extensions of the rule to prevent them. There are a great number of unwary (or simply unaware) disqualified persons abroad in the land; booby-trapping their path with an overreaching rule hardly seems a reasonable policy to pursue.

THE TAX ON INVESTMENT INCOME

If the self-dealing provision is a good idea carried too far, the 4 percent tax on investment income of private foundations is a bad one that threatens to be carried further. The tax has no policy justification. Even an assertion that it is in the nature of an audit fee raises more questions than it answers. For example, income is not a very reliable indicator of the cost of enforcement and therefore is not the best measure for an audit fee. If the tax is actually for auditing, it is excessive in amount and defective in form, since it raises far more money than is needed and the proceeds are not earmarked for this purpose. Finally, it is a debatable proposition that particular types of organizations should be required to pay the cost of enforcement of the tax laws against them; such payments do not meet the usual definition of user fees. Nevertheless, most foundations claim that they would accept the idea of an audit fee, if it were measured by assets and scaled to the actual cost of enforcement. Their view is grounded in prudence, not principle; the audit fee might at least prevent higher taxes as a result of future display of congressional pique at foundations.

The more serious objections to the tax are that (except for operating foundations) it generally punishes the wrong parties—potential recipients of grants, not foundations—and that, in the process, it erodes the traditional tax exemption of charitable organizations. The question of tax exemption perhaps should be reexamined, but on its own merits, not by indirection.

THE PAYOUT PROVISION

Many foundation officials are critical of the payout provision in the law. Most of them accept the notion that foundations should be required to distribute to charity an amount equal to their current income. Their objection is to the minimum investment return established in the Act—the requirement that foundations distribute at least 6 percent of the value of their assets if they do not have current income of a greater amount. They generally blame the Commission on Foundations and Private Philanthropy (the Peterson Commission) for the inclusion of this excessive figure in the statute.

Both the Treasury Department and the House Ways and Means Committee agree with the critics of 6 percent. They have endorsed a reduction of the minimum investment return to 5 percent, which was the figure in the original version of the legislation.

What is involved in this dispute is basically a conflict about the objective of the minimum investment return. It was included in the payout provision, according to the Ways and Means Committee report on the original bill, "to prevent avoidance of the 'current-benefits-to-charity' purpose of this provision by investments in growth stock or unproductive land." Five percent was selected as a reasonable surrogate for the current yield from a foundation's investments in 1969, and the Secretary of the Treasury was to adjust the figure periodically to reflect changes in money rates and investment yields.

The Peterson Commission was not concerned about plugging a loophole in a mandatory income-distribution requirement. It was seeking an appropriate measure of the return society had a right to expect from private foundations. It pointed out that foundations represented "a huge capital investment in philanthropy," which had been "jointly funded by the donor and by society through a full and immediate tax deduction." A majority of the commission advocated a mandatory payout of from 6 to 8 percent because it considered this to be a reasonable level of total return, with an appropriate allowance for inflation. And, the commission said, "we believe the only correct yardstick for measuring investment performance is the *total rate of return*"—including interest, dividends, realized capital gains, and unrealized appreciation. The commission urged that the payout requirement refer only to a percentage of the foundation's assets. This, it said, "would put the emphasis where it belongs: on the overall investment performance of the foundation, not on the form of the return it receives."

The Peterson Commission's recommendation was not adopted by Congress; instead, the 6 percent figure advocated by the commission was simply inserted in the loophole-plugging minimum-investment-return provision. This had two ancillary consequences. First, the Secretary of the Treasury is required to adjust the figure to reflect changes in current investment yields, rather than the overall performance of investment funds comparable with foundations. Second, and less important, foundations that earn current income above the minimum investment return are required to pay out more than the percentage rate.

More significantly, the form of the payout provision Congress adopted makes it that much harder for many foundation officials to accept it. They are correct in their contention that 6 percent is an excessive figure for current investment yield. Foundation portfolios have traditionally had a far lower yield, and not only because foundation investment performance has been mediocre. Figures for 1967 for a sample of private foundations, stratified by asset size, illustrate the point:

Foundations by Asset Size	*Income (Excluding Long-Term Capital Gains) as a Percentage of Beginning-of-Year Assets, 1967 (Mean)*
Under $200,000	3.8
$200,000–$1 million	3.9
$1 million–$10 million	4.4
$10 million and over	3.5

Figures for total return for the same foundations (and the same year), however, give quite a different impression:

Foundations by Asset Size	*Investment Return as a Percentage of Beginning-of-Year Assets, 1967 (Median)*
Under $200,000	5.1
$200,000–$1 million	8.2
$1 million–$10 million	13.1
$10 million and over	13.7

It appears that 1967 was an exceptionally good year, especially for larger foundations, and the data are subject to some nitpicking. Nevertheless, it is probably fair to conclude that 6 percent is not an unreasonable level of total return to expect from a foundation's portfolio, even though it is more than foundations can be expected to realize in current income. In fact, attempts to realize a current yield of 6 percent would probably result in an overemphasis on investment in debt obligations and a sacrifice of long-run capital appreciation for immediate income. If this should occur, then the House Ways and Means Committee is right in its assertion that 6 percent "may well have damaging effects on the continuing vitality of many foundations."

The Peterson Commission hoped its payout recommendation would produce better investment management by foundations, including more diversification and a greater turnover of investments. Obviously, if 6 percent is to be realized and paid out, not simply obtained on paper, assets must be sold or distributed after they gain in value. This objective is difficult for a foundation to achieve if its portfolio is locked into control stock of one corporation, especially when the stock has a low dividend yield. The payout requirement, probably more than the still-distant threat of the provision limiting holdings in a business, has already led to secondary offerings by such foundations as Kresge, Dana, Lilly, and Johnson. It has also, unfortunately, led in some instances to the conversion of stock to 6 percent debentures.

In short, it appears possible for foundations to survive with a 6 percent payout requirement if it is viewed from the perspective of total return and investment decisions are made accordingly. It need not lead to the erosion of the foundation's size nor leave it defenseless against inflation.

The Amount of Foundation Distribution to Charity—Whatever effect the payout has on foundation investment performance and the morale of foundation administrators, there is little question that, when fully effective, it will lead to a substantial increase in foundation distributions to charity. Figures for the 1967 sample also illustrate this point:

Foundations by Asset Size	*Distributions for Charitable Purposes as a Percentage of Beginning-of-Year Assets, 1967 (Median)*
Under $200,000	17.6
$200,000–$1 million	7.7
$1 million–$10 million	4.9
$10 million and over	4.3

Only one-third of the largest foundations and two-fifths of those in the $1 million–$10 million group met or exceeded a 6 percent payout rate. While the payout rate for the smaller foundations was significantly higher, this is primarily attributable to "pass-through" contributions—funds received and distributed during the same year. More restrictive rules governing the tax deductibility of these contributions may lead to a reduction in the payout by these foundations; in total amount, however, this should be more than offset by the increased payout of larger foundations.

Payout and Limited Life for Foundations—When the Senate Finance Committee considered the Tax Reform Act of 1969, it added an amendment that would have limited the tax-exempt life of a private foundation to 40 years. The committee reasoned that permanent tax-exempt foundations could grow to acquire such economic power as to have an undue influence on the economy and government decisions; that eventually the original contributions that gave rise to immediate tax deductions, rather than just the return from them, should actually be used for charitable purposes; and that, in 40 years, a foundation should have been able to attract enough public support to become a public charity or to find appropriate ways to use its assets directly for charitable purposes. More simply put, the committee was not enamored with foundations.

The committee's amendment was excised from the bill on the Senate floor, but not before a rationale was offered as to why a substantial payout was an answer to at least some of the concerns reflected in the limited-life proposal. The Peterson Commission was the chief proponent of this argument.

The commission asserted that a high payout requirement

> means, in effect, that the right to perpetual life must be earned and will not be conferred as an automatic privilege. A foundation's ability to continue to make a high payout to charity—and not the fact that it has reached its twenty-fifth or fortieth birthday—provides one rational basis for distinguishing between those foundations which should be permitted to continue and those which should be phased out of existence.

Wherever the merits lie in the debate about perpetuity (a debate that itself had a very limited life), one may suggest that the Peterson Commission's argument based on a high payout is not wholly convincing. (In fairness, it should be noted that the commission also raised a number of other arguments against limited life.) While investment performance may be "one rational basis" for determining whether or not a foundation should continue to exist, it is hardly the most rational. If it were possible, foundations should be judged on the quality of their charitable giving (or operating programs), not just their ability to spend a prescribed quantity of funds. To condition continued existence on sound investment decisions is not necessarily to reward the foundations whose charitable performance is the best. Indeed, there is a quantitative inconsistency in the argument, for a foundation that regularly exceeds the high payout will gradually wither away; the more devoted a foundation is to doing its small part toward meeting what the commission called "the charitable crisis of the 1970s," the less likely it is that it will ever see the year 2010.

This is not to argue against high payout—or at least a 6 percent payout. It is instead to suggest that its objectives are limited—to produce an adequate social return from endowment contributions for which immediate tax benefits were given and to serve as a prod for the more productive investment of foundation assets. Even if the tax exemption of foundations were limited in duration, these would still be valid objectives and the provision would make sense.

On the other hand, the arguments for limited life are not adequately answered by the imposition of a payout requirement. In the main, these arguments do not revolve around a dead or listless hand of the past but rather a too active hand in the future. That concern must be answered more directly should limited life again become an issue.

EXCESS BUSINESS HOLDINGS

The case for the provision limiting the use of foundations to maintain control of a closely held business rests on four major points. First, foundations with such holdings have generally produced less benefit to charity than others. Their income has often been low, since other stockholders had little interest in receiving dividends and the foundation did not require any particular level of return. Second, the corporate business may have an unfair competitive advantage. Third, the managers of the foundation may be diverted from their charitable duties in order to manage and improve the business. Finally, and more amorphously, there is something unseemly about the use of a charitable organization to maintain control of a business.

Opponents of the provision generally argue that the concern about benefit to charity is met by the minimum-investment-return provision, as is the point about unfair competitive advantage insofar as it relates to the ability of the company to pay low dividends. Other unfair business advantages, such as the company's ability to borrow from the foundation, are met by the self-dealing rule. The contention that the managers of the foundation are diverted from charitable duties is not supported by any tangible evidence; to the contrary, they may devote too little attention to the business. That business and charitable interests are merged in one entity does not create any more potential for diversion than exists when foundation managers have outside business connections. As to unseemliness, those opposed to the restrictive provision contend that the arrangement also has two public-policy virtues: it increases the flow of funds to charity and it provides an alternative to takeovers of closely held businesses by outsiders at the death of their founders. Without the availability of the foundation device, the assets the founder devoted to charity would have been taken in estate taxes, and the business might have had to have been sold to a conglomerate or other outside interests to meet this tax burden.

Some statistical points should be taken into consideration. The Peterson Commission found that, as of 1968, 41 percent of all contributions to foundations and fully 70 percent of the contributions to foundations with over $100 million in assets consisted of stock in which the donor and his family owned at least a 20 percent interest. When foundation holdings were combined with those of substantial contributors and their families, 8 percent of the foundations, with nearly half of all foundation assets, had at one time or another held control stock (that is, the combined holdings exceeded 20 percent of the voting stock). Six percent of the foundations, with two-fifths of all foundation assets, still had such holdings at the time of the commission's survey in mid-1969. While the commission's figures are subject to a number of caveats, the basic finding is confirmed by other studies. The contribution of control stock in a closely held business was an extremely important source of foundation assets before the enactment of the 1969 law.

It is widely agreed that in the future private foundations will not figure prominently in the estate planning of the founders of closely held businesses. Some gifts of control stock may continue, but only as wills predating the Act are probated. Any provision for a private foundation in new estate plans will probably not include contributions of control stock.

The wisdom of the provision as it applies prospectively, therefore, turns on the balance between the reform it achieved and its effect on the creation of new foundations and the growth of existing foundations. This "birth rate" question is discussed later in more general terms.

"Outliving the SOB's"—For most existing foundations, the birth rate issue is academic. If they are concerned about the excess-business-holdings provision, it is its possible effect on their own holdings, not the future of the private foundation field, that is bothering them. The phase-out provisions, which give these foundations from ten to twenty years to begin divesting, have attenuated even this

concern in many cases. A more sympathetic Congress or corporate expansion may make divestiture unnecessary. The divestiture plans for some foundations were bluntly expressed by a lady in the Southwest. "We just hope to outlive the sons of bitches," she said.

The Ratchet Effect—Some foundations with pre-existing holdings (generally those with combined holdings of more than 20 but less than 50 percent) face a more immediate problem. The phase-out rule applied to these foundations permits them to maintain but not increase their 1969 level of holdings. If the combined holdings decline for any reason, the new level becomes the maximum permitted holdings.

This requires these foundations to keep careful records of their disqualified persons and the amount of stock each holds. A purchase of stock by a grandson of a board member, transfers as part of the administration of an estate, and a variety of other transactions engaged in by disqualified persons, even without the knowledge of the foundation, could lead to penalty taxes on the foundation. One foundation administrator speculated, not entirely in jest, on the opportunities this created for the children of a wealthy entrepreneur to "screw the old man's foundation."

It does not seem unreasonable to suggest, as did one foundation executive confronted by this situation, that there should be "a cushion on the ratchet," giving the foundation some time to adjust to the changes in its permitted holdings occasioned by transactions to which it is not a party. (The IRS, through some creative legislative interpretation, is reported to have reached the conclusion that penalty taxes will not be imposed as a result of transactions by disqualified persons, but this conclusion has not been formally announced.)

PROGRAM RESTRICTIONS

Only two of the program restrictions imposed by the 1969 laws— expenditure responsibility and the prohibition on expenditures to attempt to influence legislation—will be considered here. Some other program restrictions, including the limitations on grants to individuals and the restriction on payments to government officials, had affected particular foundations among those interviewed, but for the most part in relatively minor ways. One foundation, for example, had replaced its direct scholarship program with grants to colleges for scholarships, because it could not develop procedures that would satisfy the law's requirements while preserving its ability to respond quickly in hardship cases that came to its attention. Another foundation, which was supporting an international conference, had to find individual donors to pay the expenses of public officials, since overseas travel was involved. Generally, however, foundations expressed an ability to live with these restrictions, as well as with the prohibition on involvement in elective politics.

Expenditure Responsibility—This provision probably leads to more foundation paperwork than any other in the law; one official of a large foundation described it as "a doggone hassle and a lot of hooey." The provision requires that a private foundation institute reasonable procedures to insure that grants to organizations that are not public charities are spent for the intended charitable purposes.

There are two ways of dealing with this requirement—by instituting the procedures or by avoiding all grants to organizations other than public charities. Most foundations have chosen the latter course; they simply do not make a grant to any organization that cannot show that it qualifies as a public charity.

This imposes a burden on applicant organizations, which must produce an IRS determination or a lawyer's opinion letter supporting their claim to public-charity status. It is a particular burden on new organizations or those that are just seeking tax exemption. The regulations defining public charities have been in a state of flux since the statute was enacted, and at least five thousand charitable organizations probably will not know whether the IRS considers them public charities or private foundations until well after the final regulations are published. The IRS is holding the status of many new charitable organizations in suspense until there are final regulations.

The burden on private foundations may also be considerable, for potential grantees must be told of the requirement to document their public charity status and how to comply with it: "We have to make sure every little applicant is straight with the IRS." A few foundations, moreover, interpret an ambiguous provision in the instructions for their tax returns as requiring them to ascertain the precise statutory provision under which grantees qualify for public-charity status. Some, through an abundance of caution, reconsideration of their grant management practices, or a misunderstanding of the law, exercise the equivalent of expenditure responsibility for all grants, including those to colleges and other institutions whose public-charity status is unquestioned.

Some of the foundations willing to make grants requiring the exercise of expenditure responsibility find that it takes a considerable effort to impose on a grantee the accounting system it necessitates. A few foundations, with small staffs and a commitment to innovative programs (often involving new organizations), feel that they are seriously hampered by the provision. One foundation administrator said in the spring of 1972 that her foundation was "settling into a routine that is not all that healthy." As executive director, she found that she was spending most of her time preparing reports, checking files, and seeking financial statements from grantees—"worrisome things, once again telling you the easiest grant to make is a general purpose grant to a public charity carrying out a traditional program." She asserted that "hundreds of millions of dollars a year are going into the status quo" in order to avoid the burden of expenditure responsibility.

The figure is certainly subject to question. Most of the foundation grant dollars that go to public charities were not diverted to these recipients because of the expenditure-responsibility provision. Nevertheless, even foundations that did not have a policy against expenditure-responsibility grants often considered them less desirable than grants to public charities:

> All being equal, we would choose a nonexpenditure responsibility grant over expenditure responsibility.
>
> There are so many organizations that can comply, why give to private operating foundations?
>
> Any organization that we'd be interested in funding should have enough sense to set itself up as a public charity.

These quotations are from executives of relatively conservative foundations; expenditure responsibility may provide them with an added rationalization for favoring established organizations, but it hardly creates the favoritism.

On the other hand, a number of more activist foundations were not deterred by expenditure responsibility:

> It's increased our paperwork about a third, but it's no real hassle. It hasn't had any dramatic effect.
>
> Expenditure responsibility is a nuisance; it requires paperwork we wouldn't otherwise have to do. It slows us down just a little bit.

If anything, some of these foundations became more activist after the passage of the Act, and expenditure responsibility did not impede their programs. Only one instance was found where a foundation gave up a major category of grants (in this case for projects carried out by non-exempt organizations) because of expenditure responsibility: "It is just too much for anyone in this small foundation to do to the extent of protecting trustees from potential liability."

The disinclination of many foundations to make expenditure responsibility grants primarily affects the fund-raising prospects of community organizations. Even if a foundation is willing to make the grant, it may take a considerable effort to convince the community organization to accept the strictures it imposes. Some knowledgeable observers suggest that the full impact of the expenditure-responsibility provision has not yet been felt: "The Tax Reform Act came at a time when new community institutions were not being spawned as they once were. If it had been in the 1964–1967 period, there would have been hell to pay."

In principle, expenditure responsibility is not an unreasonable idea. Foundations should assume some obligation to assure that their grant funds are used for their intended purposes, especially when the grantee is not itself a tax-exempt charitable organization. Yet it is disconcerting that the provision should have the effect of reinforcing the tendency of most foundations to avoid new or untried endeavors and troubling that it should discourage grants to minority, ghetto, and poverty groups. As one foundation executive commented: "Congress or the IRS would never have dared suggest that this type of grant was improper."

The question is the extent to which the provision has indirectly had the effect of suggesting that there is impropriety in making grants to these organizations. If it has had this effect, it is difficult to conceive of a remedy. Neither the extension of the requirement to cover all grants nor its repeal seems a satisfactory solution. Perhaps all that can be hoped is that foundations become more proficient in making their way through the maze of paperwork imposed by the current provision.

Attempts to Influence Legislation—Most foundations traditionally have avoided making grants for projects that involved public-policy issues or smacked of lobbying. For these foundations, the prohibition on expenditures to attempt to influence legislation was a matter of no great moment. Indeed, they may have welcomed it as a reaffirmation of their existing practices and a justified slap at those foundations whose involvement in the governmental process had heightened Congressional animosity toward foundations in general.

Foundations that did support public-policy studies or demonstration programs were initially quite concerned about the prohibition. They hesitated on some projects and requested a spate of legal memorandums because of their uncertainty about the scope of the provision. Their primary effort, however, was directed at insuring that the Treasury Department's regulations left them as unhampered as possible. They largely succeeded in this enterprise, and they afterward generally took the position that the provision was tolerable. Some minor areas of doubt remained, and a few foundations were troubled by the prospect of enforcement of the provision by IRS agents less understanding than the draftsmen of the Treasury. Most foundation administrators, however, seemed satisfied that the prohibition would not disrupt the legitimate activities of their organizations.

That the prohibition is proving bearable in practice does not mean that it makes sense in principle. In fact, the very regulations that the foundations applaud seem to offer evidence that the provision is ill-conceived. Consideration of the regulations governing attempts to influence "any legislation through an attempt to affect the opinion of the general public or any segment thereof" will serve to illustrate the point:

1. *What is "any legislation"?* The regulations state that legislation includes an "action by the Congress, by any state legislature, by any local council, or similar body, or by the public in a referendum" or similar procedure. "Legislation" comes into existence for

this purpose when it is "being considered by," or is "to be submitted imminently to," a legislative body for action, including introduction, enactment, defeat, or repeal. The regulations indicate that a proposed treaty required to be submitted to the Senate for its advice and consent becomes legislation "at the time the President's representative begins to negotiate its [sic] position with the respective parties to the proposed treaty"—an interesting rule to contemplate with respect to disarmament, among other matters. On the other hand, legislation does not include efforts to persuade an executive body to form, expand, or acquire property for a public park or equivalent preserve so long as the private foundation does not propose a specific budget for the park to be submitted to the legislature or to persuade the legislature to pass the necessary authorization. Imminence, apparently, is not the same in every field. Put differently, peace is more imminent than parks, at least in the tax law.

2. *What "influences" legislation?* The regulations, as well as the legislative history of the provision, distinguish between "examinations and discussions of broad social, economic, and similar problems . . . of the type with which government would be expected to deal ultimately," which are permissible, and attempts to affect public opinion on particular legislation, which are not. "Public discussion, the general subject of which is also the subject of legislation before a legislative body," is acceptable, "so long as such discussion does not address itself to the merits of a specific legislative proposal." Environmental pollution and population growth are mentioned as illustrations of general subjects of this type.

The provision also exempts "nonpartisan analysis, study or research" from the prohibition on attempts to influence legislature. The regulations define this term as "an independent and objective exposition of a particular subject matter," which may advocate a particular position or viewpoint "so long as there is a sufficiently full and fair exposition of the pertinent facts to enable the public or an individual to form an independent opinion or conclusion." The "mere presentation of unsupported opinion" does not qualify.

If one believes, as the author does, that a test requiring a "full and fair exposition of the pertinent facts" may be difficult to administer, especially in areas where complicated scientific or technical issues are involved, then the scope of the exception for studies of a "general subject" and the point at which discussion of legislation may be said to be an attempt to influence it are important questions. Unfortunately, the regulations on the provision offer little guidance on these questions, and what is said hints that any mention of legislation is an attempt to influence it and that the general subject exception is generally meaningless. The practical import of the regulations seems to be that a full and fair exposition is required whenever a foundation is commenting on an issue that is relevant to a legislative controversy and sometimes, perhaps, even when it is not.

The examples given in the regulations concern the issue of what is "nonpartisan analysis, study, or research," but they implicitly define the scope of the exception for studies of a general subject and when attempts to influence legislation may be said to begin. In one example, a private foundation established a research project "to collect information concerning the dangers of the use of pesticides in raising crops for the ostensible purpose of examining and reporting information as to the pros and cons of the use of pesticides in raising crops." A published report resulting from the project analyzes the effects and costs of the use and nonuse of pesticides under various conditions and the advantages, disadvantages, and cost of allowing the unabated use of pesticides, controlling their use, and developing alternatives to them. It concludes that their use is more detrimental than nonuse and recommends prompt legislative regulation. The project is deemed to be permissible "since it is designed to present information on both sides of the legislative controversy" and is sufficiently full and fair. The important point for present purposes is that it is considered to relate to the legislative controversy and apparently is not protected by the exception for studies of a general subject, even though it includes no comment on pending legislation, as opposed to that suggested in the study itself.

Another example—again dealing with the pesticide issue—involves a foundation-published bimonthly newsletter that reports on "all published materials, ongoing research and new developments with regard to the use of pesticides," including objective summaries of proposed legislation on the subject. Again, this study is deemed to be nonpartisan, full, fair, and educational, and it is therefore held to be permissible. But, again, it is apparently considered to be related to the legislative controversy, not the broad subject of pesticides. More important in this instance, the implication is that such a newsletter is an attempt to influence public opinion on legislation, although all it does with respect to legislation is to describe pending bills. The net result seems to be that the "nonpartisan analysis, study or research" test will be the overriding criterion when a foundation study is relevant to a legislative determination or includes any comment on legislation.

The Peterson Commission contends that a line cannot be drawn between the fields of interest of foundations and those of government. "Practically every area of significant foundation activity," the commission said, "is one in which federal, state, and local governments are also active, generally on a much larger scale." It is inevitable, therefore, that many foundation studies will touch on legislative issues in ways similar to the pesticide examples. Does it make sense to require that these studies always present a full and fair exposition of the facts on both sides of the legislative controversies to which they are relevant, even though the legislative issue is not the primary concern of the study and there is no intention to attempt to influence the outcome of the legislative process?

The pesticide examples used in the regulations also point up a more basic flaw in the statute. Whatever the strictures on foundation attempts to regulate the use of pesticides through legislative action, there are virtually none on foundation expenditures to seek the same objective through administrative proceedings or court action based on existing law. Why permit foundations to advocate a particular policy position by supporting litigation in the judicial branch, participation in rule-making and adjudicatory proceedings before administrative agencies, and attempts to influence executive branch decisions while prohibiting them from advocating legislation?

This is not to suggest that a more sweeping prohibition should be written; that would only compound the illogic of the existing provision. It may not be too far-fetched to suggest that the current provision reflects congressional irritation at foundations and their grantees and that its basic purpose was simply to keep them away from Capitol Hill. Insofar as one can find a policy justification for the provision, it must be that involvement in the government decision-making process is not an appropriate charitable activity for private foundations. This rationale is obviously broader than the provision that was adopted. It appears to be an amalgam of two different ideas: first, that charity is distinctly separable from government; and, second, that private foundations are used by the wealthy or an intellectual elite to disseminate their public-policy ideas on a tax-free basis. The first idea reflects an antiquated notion of charity, and it suggests the need for a careful redefinition of the term as it affects all tax-exempt organizations, not just foundations. The second idea is part and parcel of the more general suspicion of foundations. It will be discussed in the concluding section.

Birth, Death, and Transfiguration

THE EFFECT OF THE 1969 LAW ON THE CREATION OF NEW FOUNDATIONS AND THE EXPANSION OF EXISTING ONES.

Some critics of the Tax Reform Act contend that its most serious effect will be a reduction in contributions to private foundations, leading to a gradual decline in the diversity of the foundation field and a relative or absolute diminution of flexible charitable assets available to meet social needs. A number of provisions of the law make the tax benefits from contributions to private foundations less attractive than those from contributions to public charities. This is especially true of contributions of appreciated stock or other capital-gains property, which accounted for a preponderance of past gifts to foundations. As mentioned previously, the excess-business-holding provision is also expected to affect the birth rate of foundations. Other provisions—and the regulatory framework as a whole—further discourage gifts to foundations. The following comments by foundation trustees and lawyers are illustrative:

> There will be far fewer new foundations. It's too goddamned complicated. To create an *inter vivos* foundation will require real push, merit and desire.

> A wealthy person who looks at the law and sees the punitive levies against trustees will say, "What the devil, why bother?"

> Some trustees of our foundation wonder whether it is worth it. I doubt that any of the trustees will leave anything to the foundation now.

The climate is different. People think of "foundation" as a dirty word, and a little suspicion is directed at foundation people.

The appreciated property provision has seriously affected life-time giving to foundations, which is extremely important because wealthy people like to see the results of their giving. And because people are a little afraid of what may happen, testamentary giving is also affected. The complexity of the law is causing some foundations to be abandoned.

No figures are yet available on the reduction of giving to foundations, and the consequences for estate planning will not be fully evident for some time to come. Assuming, however, that there is a substantial continuing decline in contributions to foundations, one must ask another question: have those who once gave to foundations simply begun to contribute directly or have they reduced their total charitable giving?

Where a foundation served only as a status symbol or a convenient method of evening out annual contributions, there may be no reduction in total giving to charity. The amount received by operating charities may even have increased, reflecting the elimination of the transaction costs of interposing the foundation between the donor and the ultimate recipients. Where the separate existence of the foundation was important—for control of a business, the achievement of charitable objectives, or less tangible reasons—giving may decline. To determine the overall effect on total giving requires detailed analysis of contribution deductions claimed on individual tax returns, a task that only the IRS can undertake.

A reduction in total giving to charity does not necessarily support the contention that the foundation provisions are ill-advised. Before 1969 the tax law provided in effect that a donor who established a foundation could have the benefit of controlling the charitable organization in addition to the tax deductions he obtained from his contributions. This provided an extra incentive to give to charity and extracted more contributions, generally from the wealthy. The 1969 law may be regarded as a congressional determination that the terms of this bargain were over-generous to the contributor and the bargain itself tainted. The appropriateness of this determination is ultimately a question of opinion. In an era when tax reform is a moral crusade as well as a political issue, the numbers alone are not an adequate response.

TERMINATION OF FOUNDATIONS

One of the anticipated consequences of the Tax Reform Act was that a substantial number of private foundations would simply contribute all their assets to public charities and go out of business. It was considered especially likely that the thousands of very small foundations run out of a donor's vest pocket or his lawyer's desk drawer would be terminated. In fact, one of the claimed advantages of the complexity of the foundation provisions was that it would help insure that these foundations were killed off. No one would mourn the passing of these organizations. They did little that the donor could not accomplish without the foundation and their rapid proliferation had helped give the entire field a reputation as tax dodges.

Many of these foundations may well have been abandoned after the law went into effect; again, no reliable numbers are available yet. Most observers suggest, however, that termination has occurred more slowly than predicted.

The reason, ironically, is primarily the complexity of the law. Until the final regulations are issued clarifying the terms under which foundation assets may be given to community foundations and other public charities, few foundations seem willing to terminate. Many donors or surviving relatives are waiting to see the extent to which the foundation's resources can keep their separate identity within the public charity and what vestiges of control or influence over the spending of its funds can be retained. One does not give up a personal charity easily.

While the termination rules are being clarified, the foundations have to abide by the new law. They may be discovering that it is not as formidable as they originally feared; familiarity may breed contempt, but it also brings routinization.

Finally, it is not that simple to terminate a charitable organization, especially one that is a trust. A court decree may be required, and the state attorney general may have to approve the public charity that is to receive the assets. The process can be both expensive and time-consuming.

Despite the complications, a substantial number of foundations have probably either terminated or become moribund, achieving the same result more simply by distributing their assets while maintaining formal existence. When the legal situation is clarified, far many more will presumably go out of business.

CHANGING AN ORGANIZATION'S STATUS
FROM PRIVATE FOUNDATION TO PUBLIC CHARITY

The statute prescribes procedures for organizations that desire to continue their existence as public charities rather than private foundations. In some instances, organizations that look like foundations, have the word in their names, and always thought of themselves as foundations were pleasantly surprised to learn that one or another of the quirks in the definition permitted them to qualify as public charities. One organization was even classified as a public charity although it appeared to lack all the required characteristics. Its administrator admitted that he did not fully understand the definition of a public charity, but he thought the organization should qualify. He checked a number of boxes on the IRS classification form, since no one of them seemed exactly applicable, attached the most recent report of the foundation's activities, and submitted it. Some months later, the organization received a favorable ruling from the IRS.

At the other extreme is an operating organization that sought to become publicly supported the first year after the law took effect, one of the permitted escape routes from foundation status. It broadened the membership of its board and initiated a fundraising campaign. The organization did not need more operating capital, since it has an adequate endowment. New contributions were critical, however, to its claim that it had become a public charity. The fund-raising effort did not begin until the last few months of the year, but by year's end the foundation had raised an amount totaling roughly 3 percent of its endowment income. In 1971, with the help of a fund-raising firm, the organization raised 10 percent of its total support, although the cost of the solicitation absorbed two-fifths of the amount raised. In addition, according to the executive director, counsel fees, mostly in connection with the attempt to change status, were "damned expensive." (The legal costs were especially high because the IRS contended that the organization had failed to raise sufficient public support in 1970. The IRS relied on a proposed regulation issued in May 1971 that redefined public support, imposing a 10 percent floor for the first time. It argued that this minimum level of public support had always been an implicit requirement under the law.)

Some operating organizations in similar circumstances are reluctant to seek contributions in order to become public charities. If the organization were destitute, one administrator said, local philanthropists would provide support. But they are not prepared to make up the tax on investment income, the major cost of foundation status for this organization. "They would resent fund-raising by an organization as well-endowed as we are."

Another way museums and other organizations maintaining facilities open to the public may achieve public-charity status is by charging admission fees. Most have apparently rejected this course because the receipts from admissions would have to substantially exceed their income from investments, an extremely difficult requirement for an endowed organization. Some are also concerned that charging admission would require them to provide additional facilities for visitors and would lead them to emphasize attendance levels rather than quality.

Many operating organizations simply do not know how they can qualify for public-charity status. Some may not even be aware that they are private foundations. More than two years after the law went into effect, one museum director estimated that a majority of his colleagues did not know that their organizations had to pay a tax.

Other operating organizations may be in a situation similar to that of one I visited. Although the organization may qualify for public charity status (or perhaps could with some minor changes in its operation), the executive director had no idea what was required. He kept asking the organization's attorneys whether it could become a public charity, but, he said, "They just aren't interested in trying to get us qualified."

Conclusion

Maybe Congress felt there were too many half-assed charities and was trying to cut them back. But you shouldn't be put out of business simply because of the burden of having to live under the law.

After everyone spins his wheels and consults his lawyer, he'll be able to live with it.

These two quotations are from lawyers with far different perspectives on the foundation provisions of the Tax Reform Act of 1969. The first lawyer represents a number of smaller foundations; he has terminated some of them and hardly regards their disappearance as a social loss. Yet he was sharply critical of the necessity under the new law for a charitable organization to "be well-lawyered and well-accountanted."

The second lawyer was specifically referring to the effect of the law on independent research organizations, but his comment had broader applicability. It describes the effect of the new law on those foundations that are well-lawyered and well-accountanted and have substantial staff resources. These foundations participated most actively in the legislative process and have been most involved in regulation-drafting. They can live with the product largely because it is in language their lawyers understand and may even have written. Compliance may not be inexpensive, but it will not change the essential character of the foundations.

The foundations that are least able to live with the law in any semblance of comfort are those with small staffs who take their charitable endeavors and the law's requirements quite seriously. "You find yourself becoming more and more conservative," one administrator said. "You turn to your lawyers more and more often, every time the slightest question comes along." Among those questions are such improbable matters as the extent to which members of foundation staffs should be permitted to participate in politics in their communities. The lawyers upon whom foundations rely are not always fully conversant with the new provisions. Foundations located in smaller communities may have particular difficulty obtaining the expert assistance they need.

Eventually, of course, foundations will achieve a new, more

bureaucratic normality. In the meantime, one may legitimately wonder whether all the wheel-spinning was a necessary accompaniment to their regulation.

More fundamentally, one may question whether the fuss has all been worth it. The 1969 law was intended to curb a variety of abuses in which foundations were known or thought to have been involved, and it apparently achieved this objective, although not without some side effects. The 1969 law, however, was also a manifestation of congressional and public suspicion of foundations. It is too early to say that it has allayed that suspicion, and the possibility remains that the regulatory scheme will be extended further. While foundations are acting with more sensitivity to public opinion, the basic reason for suspicion of them remains. Indeed, to the extent that the law is considered bearable by foundations it may be attacked as ineffective by their critics.

The major reason for suspicion of foundations is precisely their stated justification for existence—that they are pools of social capital, extracted from the wealthy and made available for flexible use without outside pressure or control. To some, the source of the funds and the mixed motivations of their donors are enough to taint the organizations. To others, permitting the wealthy or an independent elite to exercise virtually complete discretion in budgeting public (or partially public) moneys condemns the enterprise.

The usual defense of foundations, depending upon the audience, either attempts to wrap them in the flag of all charity or to point to one or another of their accomplishments. The Tax Reform Act makes the first defense more difficult, for it separates foundations from safe, more solid charitable organizations. The definitional line the Act draws illustrates the vulnerability of foundations, for it explicitly focuses on their independence and implicitly recognizes that their function cannot be stated precisely.

The second line of defense—that foundations support useful endeavors—is a shaky one in politically volatile times. The very diversity of foundation activities may guarantee that some achievement of some foundation will appeal to anyone; it also guarantees that each person can find a greater number of misguided, ill-conceived or simply unimportant foundation activities. What is perhaps even more troubling is that the pragmatic defense relies essentially on an act of faith—that those who run foundations will prove to be both wise and benevolent.

The ultimate success of the Tax Reform Act of 1969 may therefore depend on what one assumes its basic objective to have been. If it was intended to recognize the suspicion of foundations and bury it in obscurantism, it appears to have been a short-run success. If it was intended to highlight the fundamental public-policy issue, it may yet pose a more substantial danger to foundations.

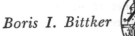

Boris I. Bittker

5

Should Foundations Be Third-Class Charities?

Under the Internal Revenue Code, private foundations are subject to a bewildering array of restrictions and burdens that are not imposed on other charitable organizations. This is true whether we compare the treatment of foundations with that of so-called 50 percent charities (certain publicly supported organizations and—regardless of the extent of their public support—churches, schools and colleges, hospitals, governmental units, and a few other organizations) or with that of "publicly patronized organizations" (organizations that are excluded from the private-foundation category if they can show that they normally derive more than one-third of their support from gifts, dues, service charges and the like from legally eligible persons and that they normally receive not more than one-third of their support from gross investment income).[1]

A specialist in the field of taxation law, BORIS I. BITTKER *is Sterling Professor of Law at Yale University. He has a wide background in government service and in legal scholarship and is the author of five books on taxation, the latest being the fourth edition of* Income, Estate and Gift Taxation, *in Collaboration with Lawrence F. Stone.*

[1] In summarizing complex statutory provisions, I have tried to guard against both inaccuracy and intolerable prolixity by using such caveats as "ordinarily" and "in general." Perhaps, however, I should state explicitly that every description of existing and prior law is intended as an outline, never as a complete exposition.

Lest this tripartite classification suggest that the Internal Revenue Code's map of exempt organizations is divided, like ancient Gaul, into only three parts, I should point out that an ingenious cartographer (Norman A. Sugarman) has identified fourteen—not merely three—categories of charitable organizations, which he has arrayed in a chart showing the impact of 34 different legal requirements on each of these groups.[2] Though the chart contains 476 cells —diversity enough, one might think, for the most finicky of legal draftsmen—Sugarman warns us that "full detail is not included" and that his chart is only "a guide or starting point." No more detail is needed, however, to demonstrate that private foundations do not all participate in the same benefits and burdens and that one might debate the precise class to which a particular category of foundations has been assigned by Congress—whether third-class or even less attractive accommodations. I will return to these distinctions later in this chapter, but for the moment I will use the label "third class" as a way of roughly summarizing the burdens that are imposed by the Internal Revenue Code on private foundations but not on other charitable organizations. These include the 4 percent excess tax on investment income; the punitive taxes on self-dealing, improper investments, and excess business holdings; and restrictions on their donors' right to deduct contributions.

What All Charities Have in Common

If one turns directly from this network of rules that are applicable to private foundations to the task of unearthing and evaluating the theories on which the distinctions rest, one may overlook the important fact that all tax-exempt charitable organizations, including foundations, have much in common. (I will use the term "charitable organization" as a generic label for all organizations that qualify for the tax-exemption under Section 501 (c) (3) of the Internal Revenue Code, whether their functions are educational, religious, scientific, or strictly charitable.) Indeed, a good case can be made for the proposition that their differences are minor when compared with their similarities, and that Congress displayed more

[2] Sugarman, A Tax-Treatment Table for Charitable Organizations under the Tax Reform Act of 1969, 16 Practical Lawyer, No. 3 (March 1970), p. 85.

wisdom from 1913 to 1950, when all charities enjoyed substantially
the same tax status, than in subsequent years, when it introduced
one distinction after another, culminating in the intricacies of the
1969 rules.

These similarities stem from the following statutory requirements,
which apply to all Section 501(c)(3) organizations:

*1. The organization must be organized and operated exclusively
for religious, charitable, scientific, or educational purposes.* Critics
who assert or imply that private foundations can be organized and
operated for political or idiosyncratic purposes disregard this bed-
rock statutory requirement, which is made as concrete as most non-
mechanical legal rules by legislative history, Treasury regulations,
administrative rulings, and a host of judicial decisions, as well as
by the burgeoning supervisory authority vested in state courts and
administrative agencies. If a substantial number of private foundations in fact serve noncharitable functions, one would expect a
spate of litigation challenging their exemptions or the deductibility
of their donors' contributions. One will search in vain, however, for
litigated cases or even for administrative rulings sufficient in volume
to support the assertion that this statutory requirement is widely
ignored or unenforceable.

*2. No part of the net earnings of the organization may inure to
the benefit of any private shareholder or individual.* Here again,
all Section 501(c)(3) organizations are subject to a prohibition that
cannot be dismissed as inconsequential or unenforceable. An analo-
gous statutory rule applicable to transactions between two business
corporations under common control (Section 482, permitting income
and deductions to be recomputed to reflect the results of a hypothetical arm's length bargain) is routinely employed by the Internal
Revenue Service and has given rise to hundreds of litigated cases
and to thousands of administrative adjustments. It is easy to assert
that private foundations or other types of charitable organizations
can safely ignore Section 501(c)(3)'s prohibition on the diversion of
earnings to private gain, but these allegations should induce skepticism rather than immediate acceptance. Even after allowing for
administrative sluggishness and for the Internal Revenue Service's
limited enforcement budget, one is struck by the paucity of cases
in which the Service has asserted—let alone proved to the satisfac-

tion of a court—that an exempt organization allowed its net earnings to inure to the benefit of private persons.

3. All Section 501(c)(3) organizations are forbidden to engage in a wide range of political activities. Far from being a dead letter, this statutory prohibition, elaborated if not actually expanded by the Treasury regulations, is sufficiently stringent to have elicited in 1972 several proposals for legislative relaxation. The impetus for these amendments, moreover, came not from the idle rich but from persons associated with the cause of tax reform.

4. All Section 501(c)(3) organizations are taxed on their unrelated business income (subject to a transitional exception for churches). If anything, a private foundation is less likely than other charitable organizations to be able to prove that its business income is related to its exempt functions, and hence it is especially vulnerable to this tax liability.

5. All Section 501(c)(3) organizations are subject to extensive reporting requirements (except churches and certain groups with less than $5,000 of annual gross receipts), and their exemption applications are ordinarily open to public inspection.

The "Income" of a Charitable Organization

Two other aspects of all charitable organizations also suggest that their shared characteristics are of more importance than their differences, viz., (a) the concept of "income" was developed in a business context and is not easily adapted for use in measuring the financial results of a charitable organization's operations; and (b) even if this definitional hurdle is vaulted, it is impossible to fix a tax rate commensurate with the principle of "ability to pay" that is central to the major contemporary theory of income taxation.[3]

THE DEFINITION OF "INCOME"

From its inception, the federal income tax has been imposed not on gross receipts or gross income, but on an adjusted net amount—roughly speaking, gross income less business expenses. As a guide to

---

[3] I have developed these ideas in greater detail in Churches, Taxes and the Constitution, 78 Yale L. J. 1285 (1969), from which the comments in this section of this chapter are adapted.

the concept of "net" or "taxable" income, there exists an extensive body of legal and accounting principles derived from business and financial practice, but it is awkward to apply these principles to non-profit organizations.

An illustration may help. Assume that a church's receipts and expenses for the year are as follows:

Receipts:	*(Thousands)*
1. Investment income (dividends, interest, etc.)	$100
2. Gifts and bequests	75
3. Total receipts	$175
Disbursements:	
4. Salaries of clergymen, maintenance of buildings, etc.	$100
5. Medical and social welfare program for indigent persons	50
6. Total disbursements	$150
7. Net receipts (line 3 minus line 6)	$25

How should the taxable income of this organization be computed? At first blush, the computation of gross income seems simple: it is $100,000, the investment income on line 1; Section 102 of the Internal Revenue Code excludes the gifts and bequests of $75,000 (line 2). Perhaps, however, Congress did not intend this statutory exclusion to inure to recipients who actively solicit gifts and bequests as a regular and indispensable activity; if begging is a business, the "gifts" and "bequests" it generates may not be the type of "gifts" and "bequests" that Section 102 embraces. Maybe, then, the church's gross income is $175,000, rather than $100,000.

Turning now to its deductions, are the salaries and other disbursements of line 4 deductible under Section 162 of the Internal Revenue Code, which speaks of "all the ordinary and necessary expenses paid or incurred during the taxable year in carrying on any trade or business"? The activities of a church or other nonprofit organization do not constitute a "trade or business," it will no doubt be argued, so that it is impermissible to deduct the line 4 expenses. On the other hand, the "business of religion" has for centuries evoked despair from the pious, jeremiads from reformers, and sneers from unbelievers; perhaps churches should be allowed to pluck an advantage from this criticism by treating the salaries of clergymen, the maintenance of houses of worship, and the like as business expenses under Section 162.

The next issue is the proper classification of the medical and social welfare program for indigents, costing $50,000 (line 5). If the church must rely on the statutory allowance for the deduction of charitable contributions (Section 170), it would encounter an obstacle, in that Section 170 permits contributions to be deducted only if they are funneled through a nonprofit organization. (Natural persons and business organizations cannot deduct charitable contributions made directly to individuals, and since philanthropic organizations are themselves tax-exempt, there has heretofore been no need to allow them to deduct such benefactions.) Even if Section 170 is twisted into an allowance for direct contributions in the case of churches, our hypothetical court would then have to decide whether the church should be subjected to the percentage restrictions imposed by Section 170 on the charitable deductions of other taxpayers. If the court imposes a limit, should it be 50 percent of adjusted gross income (as with natural persons) or 5 percent (corporations)? Or should it be the unlimited charitable deduction that is granted to trusts by Section 642(c) of existing law? As will be suggested shortly, this focus on Section 170 may distort our vision; perhaps the cost of the medical and social welfare program, like the salaries of clergymen and the maintenance of religious buildings, should be deductible as a business expense because it serves the church's primary objectives in the manner that Section 162 expenses advance the functions of a profit-oriented business. Since the "taxable income" of a business organization is defined in terms of its function (the conduct of profit-oriented activities), it would be reasonable to define the "taxable income" of a charity by reference to its objective, the betterment of mankind's moral, spiritual, and physical condition. This would lead to a deduction for all amounts distributed to achieve these ends, in the form of gifts to the needy, below-cost education for students, and so on.

If this step is taken, however, we are close to the theory that all amounts irrevocably earmarked for charitable purposes, even if not distributed, have been set aside with sufficient definiteness to justify a deduction. To be sure, a business organization may not deduct reserves for estimated future expenses. This, however, is for a reason not applicable to charitable organizations, viz., that if circumstances change and the anticipated liabilities do not materialize, the reserves will inure to the benefit of the shareholders or partners of the enterprise. By contrast, a nonprofit institution's income is, at the very moment of receipt, irrevocably dedicated to nonprofit purposes, with no possibility of reversion to the donor, directors, or other managers. For this reason, it would be logical to allow an immediate deduction in computing the organization's tax liability, rather than wait for an actual distribution. If this suggestion is adopted, however, this residual deduction will always offset the nonprofit organization's income, leaving nothing to be taxed.

Depending on what answers one gives to these questions, the church's "net income" or "loss" is one of about a dozen different amounts. As a teacher of taxation, I am not surprised by this conclusion, nor would I suggest that there are never any difficulties in computing the taxable income of profit-oriented groups; but I am prepared to testify that the very concept of "taxable income" for a charitable or religious organization is an exotic subject, more suited to academic speculation than to practical administration.

These difficulties in computing the "income" of a charitable organization are implicitly acknowledged by the Internal Revenue Code. The 4 percent excise tax imposed on private foundations in 1969, for example, is levied on the organization's "net investment income," not on taxable income. While the stated purpose of the tax—reimbursement of governmental expenses incurred in auditing the tax returns of private foundations—might suggest that all foundations, not merely those operating at a "profit," should pay the tax, these expenses are not likely to be related, even in a rough way, to the organization's net investment income. One suspects therefore that this measure was used instead of gross receipts or gross expenditures because it seemed to be a substitute or proxy for taxable income, the latter being rejected as the appropriate measure for the reasons suggested above. Even more suggestive is the elaborate definition of "undistributed income" in Section 4942 (imposing a tax on the undistributed income of private foundations), which is a very different breed of animal from the undistributed income of business organizations.

THE APPROPRIATE TAX RATE

Charitable organizations resemble each other not only in their resistance to conventional measures of income, but also in the difficulty of fixing a tax rate reflecting their ability to pay. Even if the taxable income of a charitable organization is somehow computed (most likely, by arbitrary answers to the prickly questions posed above), whose "ability to pay" should determine the appropriate tax rate? In the case of a church, for example, should we look to the economic circumstances of its parishioners, to those among them who contribute to its financial needs, or to a worldwide assemblage of persons who, now and in the future, subscribe to its creed? If a college operates at a profit, does this redound to the benefit of its trustees, faculty, students, alumni, contributors, or the public at large? It is obviously impossible to attribute the "income" of charitable organizations to a definite group by requiring every probable beneficiary to report his estimated share on his own tax return, in the way that income of a partnership is attributed to the partners in proportion to their respective percentage interests, reported by each partner on his individual return, and aggregated with his other income in computing his personal tax liability. It is equally almost impossible to engage in a hypothetical pass-through of the organization's income to its potential beneficiaries in order to compute an average tax rate that will be imposed on the organization itself. Because of these obstacles, any tax rate will be arbitrary and, given the fact that many of the beneficiaries of Section 501(c)(3) organizations are indigent, there is no assurance that a particular rate will be fairer than a zero rate.

ARE PRIVATE FOUNDATIONS DIFFERENT?

Perhaps it will be argued that the foregoing arguments, even if valid when applied to most charitable organizations, are less persuasive in the case of private foundations. A private foundation, it may be asserted, is nothing more than an incorporated pocketbook used by its founder to sprinkle largess among charitable applicants as the mood strikes him. If this view of private foundations is accepted, a corollary might be the attribution of the foundation's undistributed income to the founder, who would be taxed on these amounts in the years they are accumulated by the foundation, and allowed offsetting charitable contribution deductions only when they are distributed to a charitable organization that is independent of his whims. Limited to private foundations that are in fact controlled by their founders, such a system would not be irrational; and with certain qualifications, it could be made to harmonize with other provisions of the Internal Revenue Code, under which trust income is taxed to the grantor of the trust if it can be accumulated for beneficiaries to be designated by him. Even in this area, however, Congress has relieved the grantor of taxation if his right to sprinkle the trust's income and corpus among the beneficiaries is hedged about by limitations and if the trust is to last for more than ten years. Moreover, while there is a formal parallelism between a trust for members of the grantor's family and a foundation for the benefit of charitable donees (and possibly a psychological parallel for a person who remembers Alma Mater as fondly as his parents), there are also differences that, over the years, have impelled Congress to treat charitable trusts very differently from trusts for the benefit of the grantor's friends and relatives.

As will be seen, I find the "incorporated pocketbook" theory of private foundations sufficiently persuasive to justify tax provisions that encourage foundations to distribute their income currently and require accumulations to be explained. Except for these requirements (embodied in Section 4942 of existing law), however, private foundations share so many of the normal characteristics of the most admirable charitable organizations—including the awkwardness of defining taxable income and the impossibility of fixing a tax rate commensurate with the financial circumstances of their beneficiaries—that statutory distinctions among them seem to me to rest on unpersuasive assumptions.

The Origins of Differentiation

The first major departure from the practice of treating all Section 501(c)(3) organizations alike came in 1950, when the Internal Revenue Code was amended to strip their exemptions from charities that engaged in "prohibited transactions" (specified acts benefiting substantial contributors), or whose undistributed income was unreasonable in amount or duration, used to a substantial degree for nonexempt purposes, or invested in a manner jeopardizing their exempt purposes. Without offering any explicit rationale for doing so, Congress exempted churches, schools and colleges, hospitals, and certain publicly supported organizations from these rules. By asserting that the new self-dealing rules were applicable to "organizations which are manipulated to the private advantage of [their] substantial donors," the 1950 committee reports implied that charitable organizations subjected to these rules were more prone to this type of abuse than those exempted. This suggestion, however, was concomitantly watered down by the comment that "similar criteria" might be used to determine whether other charitable organizations "are operated exclusively for exempt purposes." Although a similar disclaimer of exclusivity was not issued for the new rules on accumulated income, the Internal Revenue Service from time to time successfully asserted that unreasonable accumulations and similar acts were inconsistent with Section 501(c)(3) status even if the organization was not subject to the statutory rules.

Thus, the 1950 legislation—which planted the seed of today's full-grown statutory distinctions between private foundations and other charitable organizations—was based on a vague impression that foundations were somewhat more susceptible than other organizations to the abuses diagnosed by Congress, not on a firm conviction that disease was rampant in one group but unknown to the other. The distinction, in short, was hardly more than a statutory presumption, or a congressional instruction to the Internal Revenue Service to be especially alert to the possibility of misfeasance or nonfeasance by private foundations but not to overlook similar behavior by other charitable organizations. Moreover, since the new rules were replete with such words as *reasonable, adequate,* and *substantial,* the legislation, when translated into administrative action, may have added little to the long-standing and overarching requirements, applied by Section 501(c)(3) to all charitable organizations, that they must be "organized and operated exclusively" for the exempt purposes specified in the statute and must not allow any part of their net earnings to inure to the benefit of any private shareholder or individual.

The process of distinguishing among charitable organizations, begun on this modest scale in 1950, was accelerated in subsequent years. In 1954, when the ceiling on an individual taxpayer's deduction for charitable contributions was raised from 20 percent of adjusted gross income to 30 percent, the extra 10 percent allowance could be used only if the donee was a church, school or college, or hospital. The announced reason for raising the ceiling for gifts to these institutions was "to aid [them] in obtaining the additional funds they need, in view of their rising costs and the relatively low rate of return they are receiving on endowment funds." It is difficult to believe that other operating charities were not feeling the same pinch; and in 1964, Congress acknowledged this by enlarging the charmed circle to include "publicly supported" charities:

> Greater uniformity in the availability of this additional 10-percent deduction is desirable because of the many beneficial activities that are carried on by various philanthropic organizations not now eligible for the 30-percent deduction. This is especially true of many cultural and educational organizations and major charitable organizations not now eligible for the 30-percent deduction.
>
> The additional 10-percent deduction is limited to organizations which are publicly or governmentally supported, however, and this additional deduction is not made available in the case of private foundations. These latter types of organizations frequently do not make contributions to the operating philanthropic organizations for extended periods of time and in the meanwhile use the funds for investments. The extra 10-percent deduction is intended to encourage immediately spendable receipts of contributions for charitable organizations. [S. Rept. No. 830, 89th Cong., 2d sess., 1964-1 C.B. (Part 2) 502, 562.]

Charitable organizations qualifying for the extra 10 percent allowance were simultaneously favored by two other provisions of the 1964 legislation: contributions to them in excess of the donor's percentage ceiling qualified for the newly enacted carryover of excess contributions of Section 170(b)(5) (now Section 170(d)), and the unlimited charitable deduction of Section 170(g) was amended to favor contributions to the same donees.

The 1954 and 1964 legislation seems to embody two distinctions, resting on different rationales. The first is a division between operating and nonoperating charities, based on the premise that those in the former category needed special assistance in maintaining their activities at accustomed levels (or expanding them) in the face of increased costs and low yields on their endowments. Presumably it was thought that nonoperating charities, with fewer ongoing commitments, can retrench or postpone their activities more easily. The second distinction was between public and private charities, evidently resting on a judgment that publicly supported charities satisfy more pressing social needs than private charities, or that public support constitutes an informal referendum conferring an endorsement on public charities that private charities have not elicited. These separate rationales coincide in the case of many charitable organizations. Hospitals, for example, are burdened with continuing commitments that are not easily reduced, and are also often supported by the public; while family foundations, conversely, are usually free to retrench when income is low and they lack explicit public endorsement in the form of contributions. There are also, however, cases in which the rationales conflict: some privately supported charities engage in day-to-day operations that are comparable with those of publicly supported charities, and they may even have a regular public patronage; conversely, some publicly supported charities are grant-making institutions. Churches, schools and colleges, and hospitals, it should be noted, were favored whether publicly supported or not; the nature of their activities, not the source of their support, put them into the charmed circle.

The 1969 Changes

These pre-1969 ventures into differentiation were eclipsed, both in importance and in intricacy, by the 1969 legislation. In evaluating the main theme of this legislation, viz., that "private foundations" are in some sense less deserving than other charitable organizations, I will discuss the principal burdens imposed by the 1969 legislation on private foundations, in an effort to assess whether their actual record or potential for abuse justifies special treatment. Since other charitable organizations are not subject to the statutory burdens to be discussed, this approach necessarily entails judgments about their practices—as compared with those of private foundations—in the area that elicited congressional action against private foundations. My discussion will be unavoidably speculative, since detailed information is not available in many instances; but, as will be seen, the congressional committees responsible for the 1969 legislation suffered from the same disability.

This comparative approach requires repeated comparisons between "private foundations" and other charitable organizations qualifying for tax exemption under Section 501(c)(3). The term "private foundation" is defined by Section 509 by a process of exclusion to mean all Section 501(c)(3) organizations except (a) churches, schools and colleges, and hospitals (i.e., charities that qualified for the extra 10 percent allowance enacted in 1954), (b) publicly supported charities (i.e., the category that was added to the former group in 1964), (c) a newly defined group of "publicly patronized" charities (described in the opening paragraph of this chapter), and (d) a few other groups of minor significance to this discussion.

TAX ON INVESTMENT INCOME

Section 4940 imposes a tax (described by its statutory heading as an "excise tax") of 4 percent of every private foundation's net investment income. As proposed by the House Committee on Ways and Means, the rate of this tax was 7.5 percent. The rationale for it was twofold:

> Your committee believes that since the benefits of government are available to all, the costs should be borne, at least to some extent, by all of those able to pay. Your committee believes that this is as true for private foundations as it is for taxpayers generally. Also, it is clear that vigorous and extensive administration is needed in order to provide appropriate assurances that private foundations will promptly and properly use their funds for charitable purposes. This tax, then, may be viewed as being in part a user fee. [H. Rept. No. 91-413 (Part 1), 1969-3 C.B. 200, 213.]

Parting company with the first part of this rationale, the Senate Finance Committee recommended not a tax to help cover the general costs of government, but an "audit fee" to reimburse the government for "the cost of examining the finances and activities of the [private] foundation to see that it continues to qualify for exemption." Its "audit fee" theory led the Senate Finance Committee to propose a tax "measured by the value of the assets to be supervised and examined rather than . . . a charge on income which some, however inappropriately, might view as a beginning in the removal of [the] income tax exemption." Without explicitly choosing between the "ability to pay" and "audit fee" rationales, the conference committee recommended the 4 percent tax that was actually enacted.

Viewed as a method of financing the costs of government by taxing "all of those able to pay," as proposed by the House, the tax is open to two objections: (a) there is no reason to believe that the rate is appropriately related to the economic status of the beneficiaries of foundation assistance (whose grants, directly or indirectly, will presumably bear the burden of the tax), and (b) there is no reason to believe that these persons have a greater ability to pay taxes than those who benefit from the activities of charitable organizations that are exempt from the 4 percent excise tax, such as churches, schools, hospitals, and publicly supported organizations. Indeed, the ultimate beneficiaries of both types of organizations are ordinarily the very same persons, since private foundations probably make most of their grants to charitable organizations that are exempt from the new tax. To this extent, the tax imposes an economic burden on the ultimate beneficiaries when income gets to them by one route rather than another.

If the tax is viewed not as a method of imposing the general costs of government on persons according to their ability to pay but as an "audit fee," its status is somewhat more complicated. All Section 501(c)(3) organizations are subject to statutory restrictions, as described earlier in this paper, that entail supervisory and auditing expenses. No reason was given by the congressional committees for requiring private foundations, but not other Section 501(c)(3) organizations, to reimburse the government for these expenses. Perhaps it was thought that the cost of auditing and supervising churches, schools, hospitals, and publicly supported or publicly patronized organizations should be defrayed by the general public because they provide benefits to a wider group of beneficiaries than do private foundations. This theory rests on a dubious factual assumption, and it is even more flimsy when extended to the many other classes of exempt organizations that are not subject to the 4 percent excise tax, such as chambers of commerce, labor unions, fraternal societies, and mutual societies that are free (unlike private foundations) to operate solely in the interest of their members. Perhaps—to suggest a rationale that is not even mentioned in the committee reports—the cost of supervising private foundations is enough greater than the cost of supervising other exempt organizations to justify the 4 percent excise tax imposed by Section 4940. Given the intricacy of the restrictions on private foundations that were enacted in 1969, it is entirely possible that the cost of auditing their returns will be very high. But if the restrictions themselves are needlessly complex, or if private foundations are no more prone to abuses than those charities that are not subject to the new rules, a tax to defray the swollen cost of auditing their returns is less easily justified.

PROHIBITIONS ON SELF-DEALING

From 1950 to 1969, the Internal Revenue Code stripped certain Section 501(c)(3) organizations of their exempt status if they engaged in a "prohibited transaction," a term embracing a variety of transactions favoring a substantial contributor or related person. This sanction on self-dealing, which came into play only if the transaction accorded preferential treatment to the insider, was replaced in 1969 by an absolute prohibition on almost every conceivable transaction between a private foundation and a "disqualified person" (broadly defined), enforced by a graduated set of penalties on the disqualified person and any foundation manager who knowingly participated in the forbidden act. The change is explained as follows by the Senate Finance Committee:

> Arm's-length standards have proved to require disproportionately great enforcement efforts, resulting in sporadic and uncertain effectiveness of the provisions. On occasion sanctions are ineffective and tend to discourage the expenditure of enforcement effort. On the other hand, in many cases the sanctions are so great, in comparison to the offense involved, that they cause reluctance in enforcement, especially in view

of the element of subjectivity in applying arm's-length standards. Where the Internal Revenue Service does seek to apply sanctions in such circumstances, the same factors encourage extensive litigation and a noticeable reluctance by the courts to uphold severe sanctions. . . .

To minimize the need to apply subjective arm's-length standards, to avoid the temptation to misuse private foundations for noncharitable purposes, to provide a more rational relationship between sanctions and improper acts, and to make it more practical to properly enforce the law, the committee has determined to generally prohibit self-dealing transactions and to provide a variety and graduation of sanctions, as described below. [S. Rept. No. 91-552, 1969-3 C.B. 423, 442-3.]

Despite the superficial plausibility of these comments, it is entirely possible that the arm's-length test of a prior law was, in fact, as effective a prohibition as the more draconic 1969 rules. It is not unusual for taxpayers to respond to an arm's-length test by steering clear of danger, lest their judgment be challenged by a suspicious revenue agent in the light of hindsight. For this reason, as well as because the new rules use some ambiguous terms that will provide defenses for the disqualified person who is prepared to take chances, the 1969 changes may prove in practice to be less than revolutionary.

Moreover, the cases cited by the 1965 Treasury Report on foundations to illustrate "the types of self-dealing cases which are being entered into and the difficulty which the Internal Revenue Service has in applying the arm's-length test contained in existing law"— a complaint that was endorsed by the Senate Finance Committee— are far from impressive. The first such example (Clay Foundation v. United States)[4] involved a $10,000 loan by a foundation to a corporation controlled by the foundation's creator. The Treasury argued that an oral promise by a corporate officer to execute a mortgage to secure the loan on the foundation's request was not adequate security for the loan. The court concluded, to the contrary, that the transaction created a valid and enforceable lien in favor of the foundation. The Treasury's residual fear that the lien would be dissipated if the corporation sold the property seems adequately refuted by the fact that the corporation had a net worth of several hundred thousand dollars—ample security, one would

[4] 233 F. Supp. 628 (N. D. Tex. 1964).

think, for a loan of $10,000. The Treasury's second example is another case lost by it in the courts (Griswold v. Commissioner)[5] involving some $200,000 of loans by a foundation to the donor and other related persons. The court found that the donor was able to borrow more than twice as much from banks, with no more security and at lower interest rates than the foundation loans, that the loans to one of the donor's relatives were secured by real property worth twice the amount of the loans, and that the remaining loans (10 percent of the total) were repaid with interest and, even if assumed to be on more favorable terms than the borrowers could have obtained from banks, did not evidence an intent to divert assets from charity to the donor's family. The third example in the Treasury Report is a contribution of $65,000 by the donor to his charity, followed immediately by a loan of the same amount by the charity to the donor's corporation. No suggestion that the security or other terms of the loan were unfair to the foundation is made, and there is therefore no reason to think that the loan was not an entirely satisfactory way of investing the donated funds, or that a loan by the donor to the corporation followed by a contribution of the corporate note or bond to the foundation would not have justified a deduction under Section 170 for the full face amount of the loan.

These cases are augmented by nine other examples, not one of which, unless augmented by additional facts, supports the conclusion that the arm's-length standard of pre-1969 law cannot be enforced; if such additional facts existed, they were inexplicably omitted from the Treasury Report. As described, indeed, several examples affirmatively suggest that the standard was quite capable of effective enforcement and that the Treasury's complaint, viewed realistically, was that its mere assertion of impropriety was not automatically accepted as valid. This attitude is similar to the allegation of some students that "no one listens" when they really mean that "those who listen won't do what we demand."

In any event, it is far from clear that private foundations are more inclined to engage in improper self-dealing than other charitable organizations. The overwhelming bulk of "50 percent charities" are probably governed by persons who are not subservient to their substantial contributors, are conscious of their fiduciary obligations,

[5] 39 T. C. 620 (1962).

and are responsible to the attitudes of such constituencies as alumni, members, professional staffs, faculties, students, and the general public. Even so, self-dealing is not unknown in religious, educational, medical, and publicly supported institutions. As to private foundations, a Treasury questionnaire described in the 1965 Report on private foundations said that the average number engaging in six types of self-dealing between 1950 and 1964 ranged from 0.2 percent to 1.6 percent for five types of self-dealing and was 4.2 percent for the sixth type (purchasing securities or other property from a contributor or similar persons). While these responses may have understated the frequency of self-dealing, it should be noted that the questionnaire was not limited to transactions favoring the contributor but embraced those that were favorable to the foundation as well. Indeed, it seems quite likely that purchases from contributors were far more prevalent than other acts of self-dealing because of the "bargain sale" technique for transferring appreciated property to charities, in which the contributor recovers his cost but contributes the appreciation to the charitable donee. This tax device may have been unduly generous to the donor, but it brought funds to the foundation rather than milking it for the benefit of the donor, and the restriction imposed on it by the enactment of Section 1011(b) in 1969 almost certainly has reduced the flow of funds to charitable purposes. Moreover, public charities have frequently advertised the bargain sale as a favorable mode of making contributions, and I know of no evidence that they were less successful than private foundations in attracting this type of contribution. Despite a few spectacular instances of improper self-dealing reported by the Treasury or revealed by congressional hearings in recent years, I am far from persuaded that the problem was very common or that the arm's-length standard of pre-1969 law was as unsatisfactory as the committee report quoted above asserts. I am even more skeptical of the implied assumption that the difference between private foundations and other charities is so great (either in the frequency of self-dealing or in its resistance to discovery and correction) as to justify a flat prohibition on self-dealing by private foundations, when other charities are not even subject to the pre-1969 prohibitions on self-dealing that favors their contributors and other insiders. On the other hand, this discrimination (as I would regard it) is ordinarily unlikely to impinge seriously on the legitimate activities and social values of private foundations. We may, in short, be witnessing a tempest in a teapot.

EXCESS BUSINESS HOLDINGS

Section 4943 imposes a tax of 5 percent of the value of private foundation's "excess business holdings in a business enterprise," excess business holdings being defined as, ordinarily, stock in excess of 20 percent of the voting stock of a business corporation less the amount owned by disqualified persons (as defined). (An additional tax of 200 percent is imposed if the foundation persists in retaining its excess holdings after a prescribed correction period.) The foundation is allowed five years to dispose of holdings acquired by gift or bequest after May 26, 1969, and ten, fifteen, or twenty years to dispose of excess holdings acquired before that date. The explanation given by the Senate Finance Committee for this legislation is:

> Those who wish to use a foundation's stock holdings to acquire or retain business control in some cases are relatively unconcerned about producing income to be used by the foundation for charitable purposes. In fact, they may become so interested in making a success of the business, or in meeting competition, that most of their attention and interest is devoted to this with the result that what is supposed to be their function, that of carrying on charitable, educational, etc., activities is neglected. Even when the foundation attains a degree of independence from its major donor, there is a temptation for the foundation's managers to divert their interest to the maintenance and improvement of the business and away from their charitable duties. Where the charitable ownership predominates, the business may be run in a way which unfairly competes with other businesses whose owners must pay taxes on the income that they derive from the businesses. To deal with these problems, the committee has concluded it is desirable to limit the extent to which a business may be controlled by a private foundation. [S. Rept. No. 91-552, 1969-3 C.B. 423, 449-50.]

In support of these allegations, the Senate report refers to the Treasury's 1965 Report on private foundations, which briefly described six "striking illustrations of foundation participation in business." Not one is described in enough detail to permit the reader to judge whether the foundation's trustees were diverted from their charitable responsibilities by the burden of running its businesses, whether the businesses grew or declined in size while controlled by the foundation, whether the businesses were aggressively managed or not, or even whether the foundation's ownership was long-standing or temporary. Quoted in full, one of the Treasury's examples is:

> Example 4. The D foundation owns a crude oil refining company to which it assigns a book value in excess of $32 million.

Other readers of the Treasury Report may be deeply impressed by this "striking illustration," but my reaction is a suspension of judgment, coupled with doubts about the validity of the report's sweeping generalizations if this type of evidence is the best that a team of talented and diligent investigators could unearth.

The theory espoused by the Senate Finance Committee that foundation managers will devote their time to business rather than to their charitable responsibilities disregards the fact that the corporations in question require business management whether their stock is owned by foundations or by other investors. Conversely, the foundation's investments must be managed by its officers (or by advisors paid by the foundation), whether the portfolio consists of all the stock of three corporations or 10 percent of the stock of each of 30 corporations. No evidence is offered to sustain the view that the aggregate number of man-hours required to manage the corporations and to manage the foundation's portfolio is altered by the concentration of the foundation's holdings in a few corporations, and it is hard to believe that any such evidence could be found. It is equally difficult to comprehend why the foundation's charitable functions are more likely to be impaired by its trustees' desire to make "a success of the business" than by their desire to increase the yield of a diversified portfolio. Success in either endeavor will increase the funds available to finance the foundation's charitable functions. It should be noted, moreover, that the restriction imposed by Section 4943 is in no way dependent on a showing that the same persons actually manage both the business and the foundation. The foundation's managers, officers and directors are, of course, ultimately responsible for deciding whether to hold or sell the foundation's investments, but this is equally true whether the portfolio is diversified or concentrated.

Along with the "distraction" theory, the Senate Finance Committee alleged that foundation-owned businesses "may be" excessively aggressive in competing with other enterprises. True, they "may be," but no evidence is offered to support the conclusion that this possibility has come to fruition. If the trustees of a private foundation think that its assets will be most productive if invested in companies that are aggressively competitive, a prohibition on its ownership of controlling blocks of stock will not cure this propensity; the trustees can simply diversify their portfolio, while continuing to invest in aggressive companies. (Whether they own all of the company's stock or only part, it will of course be subject to normal corporate taxes.) If the Senate Finance Committee's theory is that the foundation's return on its investment, being untaxed, will permit it to expand its ownership in the aggressive sector of the economy, that is of course true; but once again, this possibility will not be terminated by discouraging the ownership of controlling blocks of stock, since diversification is an adequate alternative strategy. The "unfair competitor" theory, then, is quite unpersuasive; and, perhaps more pertinent to the main theme of this paper, it is no more applicable to private foundations than to other charitable organizations.

Something should be said here about another criticism that is often directed against the ownership by private foundations of stock in family corporations, since it is part of the context in which Section 4943 was enacted even if it is not the announced rationale. This is the assertion that private foundations are frequently devices to perpetuate family control of a business from generation to generation by warding off state and federal death taxes. There is a kernel of truth in this claim, but it is easily exaggerated to the point of fantasy. To begin with, the transfer by a living person of voting or nonvoting stock to children and grandchildren is a simple and cheap way to accomplish the same result; by systematically using the annual gift tax exclusions and the lifetime exemption, and by following the widespread practice of placing a value on the stock that is low but sufficiently plausible to avoid or survive a gift tax audit, the founder of the family business can pare down the amount that will appear in his estate, without sharing any of his wealth with charity. A restrictive agreement permitting the remaining shares to be purchased by the surviving members of his family will usually permit the stock to be valued at a modest amount (e.g., book value) at his death or, at worst, lead to a compromise valuation. (It is common knowledge among experienced lawyers that closely held stock is almost always valued for death-tax purposes much below the price at which the family would be willing to sell it.) The death tax that is payable after these simple precautions have been taken can often be defrayed in whole or in part by redeeming stock of the family corporation (and by using appreciated property for this purpose without recognizing gain at the corporate level), or deferred for payment over a ten-year period under a statutory provision enacted for the benefit of closely held businesses. These opportunities mean that a private foundation is rarely needed by the tax-conscious family. Of the 17,303 foundations classified by asset size in the 1967 *Foundation Directory,* there were 10,500 "very small" foundations with assets averaging $35,000 and 5,339 "small" foundations with assets averaging $260,000. It is difficult to believe that any of the former group or many of the latter played a significant role in perpetuating family control of closely held businesses. At dollar levels this low, the death tax saved by a charitable contribution can rarely have threatened the family with a loss of control. In such circumstances, the foundation (to borrow a phrase used by Randolph Paul in another context) is no more than a handkerchief thrown over something already covered by a blanket.

For a few great fortunes, of course, the private foundation has been the key to continued inside control of a family business. Building on this fact, the authors of estate-planning manuals and tax letters sometimes try to convince every local automobile dealer that a private foundation is necessary to protect his children from penury or to enable him to pose as a latter-day Henry Ford; but this kind of puffing resembles the patter of a pitchman at a country fair. It is understandable that these exaggerations should be quoted with glee to support restrictive legislation,[6] but repetition does not make them valid.

INVESTMENTS JEOPARDIZING THE FOUNDATION'S CHARITABLE OBJECTIVE

Section 504 of the pre-1969 law, enacted in 1950, provided for a loss of tax exemption if a foundation invested its accumulated income "in such a manner as to jeopardize" achievement of the charitable, educational, or other objectives constituting the basis of its exemption under Section 501(c)(3). Because it applied only to accumulated income, this provision did not prevent the investment of the foundation's principal in speculative ventures (e.g., stock warrants, commodity futures, margin accounts); it was expanded by the 1969 Act to reach the "jeopardy" investment of any amount. The penalty was simultaneously changed from a loss of tax exemption to a tax of 5 percent of the amount involved (imposed on the foundation itself and, in the case of "knowing" action, on its managers as well), plus additional amounts if the investment is not "removed from jeopardy" within a prescribed correction period. The new provision (Section 4944) is applicable to all private foundations but not to other charitable organizations.

No explanation was given for distinguishing among charitable organizations in penalizing "jeopardy" investments in 1950, nor was this lacuna filled by the committee reports on the 1969 Act. Perhaps it was thought that organizations with widespread public support must function in a glass bowl that will discourage speculative investments, and that the trustees of educational, religious, and medical institutions are so dedicated to their exempt functions that they will avoid excessive risks in the investment of their resources. By contrast, it may have been thought that the exempt functions of private foundations might be overshadowed, in the hearts and minds of their trustees, by the exhilaration of the stock market and the commodity pit. If these are the psychological underpinnings of

---

[6] E.g., "The real 'causa mortis' of the small foundation lay in its having been discovered by the tax and estate planners. The 1969 Act is only the belated effort of Congress to take the foundation device back from them and restore it to philanthropy." Surrey, The Tax Reform Act of 1969—Tax Deferral and Tax Shelters, 12 Boston Coll. Indus. and Comm. L. Rev. 307, 318 (1971).

Section 4944's distinction between private foundations and other charitable organizations, it would be as hard to prove as to disprove their validity. But the same could be said of a precisely contrary hypothesis, viz., that the day-to-day demands of a college, hospital, or church may tug so insistently at the heartstrings of its trustees as to cause them to throw prudence to the winds in a desperate effort to maximize the return on the organization's resources, whereas the trustees of grant-making foundations, having no obligation to meet a weekly payroll, will be inclined to avoid undue risks. I see no a priori basis for choosing between these conflicting hypotheses, and the specific instances that are occasionally cited in support of Section 4944 do nothing to resolve this uncertainty in my mind. I conclude, therefore, that the case for distinguishing among charitable organizations in the application of Section 4944 is unproved.

TAX ON FAILURE TO DISTRIBUTE

Under pre-1969 law, a private foundation was subject to a loss of tax exemption if income was accumulated in an amount or for a period that was unreasonable in the light of the foundation's exempt functions. According to the committee reports on the 1969 Act, this provision was unsatisfactory because it failed to reach foundations whose assets did not generate current income, the concept of an "unreasonable accumulation" was too subjective, and the loss of tax exemption was either ineffective or unduly harsh. To correct these alleged deficiencies, Congress enacted Section 4942, which imposes a 15 percent tax on a private nonoperating foundation's undistributed income—defined (roughly speaking) as the foundation's actual income or a specified percentage of the value of its investment assets (whichever is higher), less its qualifying distributions for the year, amounts set aside for specified projects with the approval of the Treasury, and "excess" distributions carried over from prior years. A second tax, at the rate of 100 percent, is imposed if the foundation's failure to distribute is not remedied during a prescribed correction period, and there is a third level of penalties for flagrant violations. Transitional rules for organizations created before May 27, 1969, reduce the mandatory payout rate during the years 1972–74, exempt accumulations to meet certain pre-existing commitments, and allow time for judicial reformation of charters requiring income to be accumulated or forbidding the invasion of corpus.

The committee reports on Section 4942, like the reports on the pre-1969 provision which it superseded, do not explain why a mandatory payout rule should be imposed on private foundations but not on other charitable organizations. The distinction presumably rests on the implicit assumption that the operating budgets of schools and colleges, hospitals, and churches compel them to use their income currently and to avoid nonproductive investments, except when the prospect of overriding future needs dictates the accumulation of reserves. This rationale is consistent with the exemption of private operating foundations from the payout rules of Section 4942. It is also consistent with the rule that other private foundations can accumulate income for specific projects with Treasury approval, a mechanism that can be regarded as a substitute for the internal pressure on operating charities to use their funds currently unless there is an overriding reason to accumulate them. The exemption of publicly supported charities from Section 4942 may be based on the assumption that many of them are under the same pressure as schools and colleges, hospitals, and churches to use their funds for current needs, and that the others will not be able to attract public support if they invest in nonproductive assets or accumulate their income without good reason.

I know of no hard evidence to support this distinction between the private foundations that are subject to Section 4942 and the charities that are exempt, and indeed am skeptical of the possibility of measuring their comparative propensities to accumulate income without justification. There are grant-making private foundations with a strong commitment to programs and objectives, impelling them to use their resources currently rather than postpone the day of distribution. Conversely, there are operating charities and even some publicly supported organizations with programs that are modest in proportion to their assets, so that they are able to accumulate their income with impunity. Even so, the distinction drawn by Section 4942 is persuasive enough to serve as a general principle. Of all the 1969 distinctions between private foundations and other charitable organizations, this one seems to me to rest on the most solid base.

TAXES ON CERTAIN EXPENDITURES

Section 4945 imposes a 10 percent tax on a private foundation's "taxable expenditures," defined as amounts paid or incurred for: (a) specified political activities; (b) grants to individuals, unless awarded on an objective basis (under a procedure approved in advance by the Treasury) as a scholarship, fellowship, prize to a person selected from the general public, or grant to achieve a specific objective or to improve the grantee's capacity or skill; and (c) grants to other private foundations (and certain other groups), unless the granting foundation assumes "expenditure responsibility" by specifying the purpose of the grant, obtaining reports from the grantee on its use of the grant, and reporting the facts to the Internal Revenue Service. The initial 10 percent tax on taxable expenditures is buttressed by a tax on foundation managers for willful violations, and by second and third level penalties if corrective action is not taken within a prescribed period.

The imposition of a tax on a private foundation's expenditures for certain political activities (primarily attempts to influence legislation, grass-roots lobbying, and voter-registration drives in limited areas) reflects a distrust of the general statutory prohibition on political activity, fueled by the failure of this prohibition to prevent a few activities that were distasteful to a few members of Congress. These activities were financed by a small group of private foundations, and there is no evidence that similar activities were supported by any of the exempt organizations that are not subject to Section 4945. This is probably enough to explain why private foundations, but not other exempt organizations, were subjected to the political activity restrictions of Section 4945; I doubt that it would be profitable to search for a principled or universally valid justification for the distinction. Colleges and hospitals are not likely to finance voter-registration drives, but one could have said the same, with equal confidence, of the overwhelming bulk of private foundations, even if Section 4945 had not been enacted. As for churches, those with a strong commitment to the social gospel seem as likely as private foundations, if not more so, to interest themselves in voter-registration activities.

Section 4945's restrictions on "individual grants" by private foundations are also best viewed, if one wants to be realistic, as a bit of legislation whose general form belies its specific origin. If the Ford Foundation had not made its famous grants to members of Senator Kennedy's staff when they left their federal jobs after his assassination, it is not likely that the Senate Finance Committee would have concluded that

> existing law does not effectively limit the extent to which foundations can use their money for "educational" grants to enable people to take their vacations abroad, to have paid interludes between jobs, and to subsidize the preparation of materials furthering specific political viewpoints.

It is probable, however, that a diligent search would disclose instances in which colleges have made room for lame-duck congressmen, ex-cabinet officers, and other governmental officials (as "consultants," "politicians in residence," etc.), without requiring them to run the normal academic gauntlet before appointment or to discharge more than nominal duties thereafter. Indeed, hospitality to such governmental "in-and-outers" is more often praised than criticized.

An impartial extension of Section 4945's requirement that individual grants be awarded "on an objective and nondiscriminatory basis," under a procedure approved in advance by the Treasury, to cover all potential sanctuaries for public servants who are temporarily at liberty, however, would be attacked as an invasion of academic freedom in the case of colleges and religious liberty in the case of churches. Private foundations may have no greater propensity than other charities to make the kind of grants that stimulated Section 4945's restrictions, but their defenses were weaker. In this respect, the 1969 restrictions on individual grants are reminiscent of the Reece Committee's warnings that foundations were financing un-American activities and Congressman Patman's recent complaints about foundation grants for "esoteric research subjects." Both objections could have been aimed, with no less (but with no more) accuracy, at educational and religious institutions. Congressman Patman's favorite target—a Bollingen Foundation grant for the study of medieval Bosnian tombstones—could have been enlarged to embrace university seminars in Byzantine art, the purchase of ikons by churches and art galleries, and even the scrutiny of colonial tombstones by New England historical societies and the D.A.R. (One wonders what rhetoric would have been employed if a foundation had financed the study of acupuncture before President Nixon's 1972 trip to Peking.) Foundations were not selected for criticism because they are more likely than other exempt institutions to engage in "the development of trivia into nonsense" (Congress Patman's label for "esoteric" research), but because restrictions on their activities are not so readily perceived as inconsistent with the spirit of free inquiry and cultural pluralism.

Conclusion

As promised, this assessment of the comparative propensity of charitable organizations to engage in the activities that are taxed or penalized by the Tax Reform Act of 1969 has been founded—like the legislation itself—more on speculation than on solid evidence. Despite the abundance of congressional hearings and Treasury investigations, the Ninety-first Congress had little more before it than isolated instances of actual, alleged, or suspected misconduct by a few foundations, coupled with a plethora of suggestions that these cases were typical and that existing law "could" or "might" or "probably would" lead to abuses. Even more conjectural was the unarticulated premise that foundations were more likely to succumb to temptation than other charitable organizations. If the need to justify a distinction between private foundations and other charities rose to the conscious level, it was probably satisfied by contrasting the sins of the most errant foundations with the reputations of the most scrupulous religious, educational, and publicly supported charities. Yet it is common knowledge that preachers sometimes divert church funds to personal ends, that the nonprofit façade of a school or college can mask a proprietary operation, that some hospitals serve primarily to enrich their physician-entrepreneurs, and that some publicly supported charities allow most of their contributions to be siphoned off by grasping fund-raisers. It is equally clear, however, that these instances did not—and should not— impel Congress to extend to the vast body of charitable organizations the labyrinth of statutory restrictions, navigable only by lawyers and accountants and guarded by penalties far exceeding the civil penalties for deliberate tax fraud, that was prescribed in 1969 for private foundations.

One wonders, therefore, whether it is quixotic to seek an explanation for the "third-class" status of private foundations, as I have done, in the congressional announcements that accompanied the legislation. Perhaps it would be more realistic to attribute these restrictions to skepticism or distrust of the very characteristics that are often extolled as the virtues of the private foundation—its capacity to experiment because it is usually free of permanent commitments and is controlled by trustees answerable primarily to their own sense of responsibility. In the words of the 1965 Treasury Report on private foundations:

> Private foundations play a significant part in the work of philanthropy. While the foundation is a relatively modern development, its predecessor, the trust, has ancient vintage. Like its antecedent, the foundation permits a donor to commit to special uses the funds which he gives to charity. Rather than being compelled to choose among the existing operating organizations, he can create a new fund, with its own areas of interest and emphasis. His foundation may encourage existing operating organizations to develop in new directions, or it may lead to the formation of new organizations. Even if it does neither, it reflects the bents, the concerns, and the experience of its creator; and it thereby increases the diversity of charitable works. In these ways, foundations have enriched and strengthened the pluralism of our social order.
>
> Private foundations have also preserved fluidity and provided impetus for change within the structure of American philanthropy. Operating charitable organizations tend to establish and work within defined patterns. The areas of their concern become fixed, their goals set, their major efforts directed to the improvement of efficiency and effectiveness within an accepted framework. Their funds are typically consigned to definite—and growing—budgets. The assets of private foundations, on the other hand, are frequently free of commitment to specific operating programs or projects; and that freedom permits foundations relative ease in the shift of their focus of interest and their financial support from one charitable area to another. New ventures can be assisted, new areas explored, new concepts developed, new causes advanced. Because of its unique flexibility, then, the private foundation can constitute a powerful instrument for evolution, growth, and improvement in the shape and direction of charity. [pp. 12–13]

The Treasury—in this extract—speaks favorably of "the bents, the concerns and the experience" of the foundation's creator; but the other side of this coin bears a portrait that the Treasury finds less admirable: a rich man getting a tax deduction for a gift of stock of a family corporation that will be used to finance such charitable activities as his "bents" may suggest. A similar conflict can be percieved in the Treasury's reference to the foundation's "unique flexibility" in moving from one focus of interest to another: on the other face of this coin, the Treasury finds the distasteful picture of a private person spending "governmental funds" (i.e., the value of tax deductions and exemptions) on programs that have not been approved by the appropriations committees of Congress. Finally, "the pluralism of our social order" is a value that must not be attacked head-on, but expenditures for the study of Bosnian tombstones, registration of minority voters, or litigation against welfare agencies reflect a diversity of preferences that evokes less approbation than the choice between cancer research and flood relief.

But, however unwelcome these manifestations of the private foundation's independence, flexibility, and originality may have been to some critics of the institution itself, they were not so patently offensive or widespread as to induce a full-scale attack. Instead, they created, I suggest, administrative and legislative misgivings that crystallized in the conviction that a series of propensities toward misconduct, plausibly illustrated by the specific acts of some foundations, were endemic to the whole species. Since other types of charitable organizations were viewed with less suspicion, their bad apples were either overlooked or regarded as exceptional. The net result was a strategy of isolating the private foundation from other charities, which began in 1950 and culminated in 1969.

The foundations, for their part, could not successfully respond to this strategy by arguing that they were no more prone to engage in the misconduct attributed to them than are other charities. The foundations had neither the inclination nor the tools to uncover acts of misconduct by others; even if it had been otherwise, a sense of political realism would have taught them that throwing mud is no way to keep clean. Nor was a strategy of asserting that misconduct was confined to a small segment of their company likely to succeed: the classic legislative response to this defense is a com-

bination of "where there's smoke, there must be fire" and "if you
don't do it anyway, a prohibition won't hurt you." Understandably,
therefore, many foundations accepted the legitimacy of the legislative objectives and, at least arguendo, the validity of the illustrative cases of abuse, concentrating their efforts on mitigating the
severity of a restrictive program that seemed inevitable. Others, be-
lieving that their best defense was to lobby for a tailor-made escape
hatch, had even less reason to debate the basic issues. These decisions were probably wise, given all the circumstances, but a consequence of continually focusing on palliatives is that every criticism
of the private foundation becomes sanctified and every statutory
restriction becomes a plateau; the only remaining issue is whether
another step will be taken, not whether the ratchet should be re-
leased because the original assumptions were fallacious. In the final
analysis, then, a convergence of these strategies was more responsible
for the statutory network that relegates private foundations to
"third-class" status than either the evidence or the arguments
offered by the legislative committee reports.

Richard E. Friedman

6

Private Foundation-Government Relationships

Advocates of private foundations often assert that the strength of foundations lies in their flexibility, their ability to act quickly in response to new situations or new kinds of problems, and, above all, in their ability to innovate and take risks. But not all knowledgeable commentators agree with this view. The dissenters point out that these positive qualities are really latent or potential ones, not actual existing attributes. In sharing this point of view, I will direct my comments toward enhancing the status and improving the operation of private foundations.

I will discuss the relationship of foundations to government with particular reference to human-services programs, and in so doing I will draw a great deal from my own experience. There are several interrelated questions concerning the foundation-government relationship. What do private foundations do? What does government do? What is their relationship, if any, in the delivery of human services? Should there be a relationship? If so, what should it

RICHARD E. FRIEDMAN, *regional director of HEW Midwest Region V, has practiced law in Chicago, run for political office (U.S. House of Representatives and mayoralty of Chicago), and served as assistant to the state treasurer and as first assistant attorney general of Illinois. This chapter was written by Mr. Friedman in his private capacity. No official support or endorsement by the Department of Health, Education and Welfare is intended or to be inferred.*

163

be? In answering these questions, we must also look into the constraints, real or imaginary, that impede a full and productive relationship between private foundations and government. And we must decide whether foundations are performing the primary duties that have entitled them to special tax status.

In examining these questions, this paper will review the change in private-foundation versus government spending in the field of human services, the need for an exchange of information between private foundations and government, and the problem of determining the allocation of their relative resources in delivering these services. The second thrust of the paper is future-oriented—a discussion of innovative programs to be undertaken by private foundations, including a program for evaluating the way federal agencies and private foundations spend their money on human-service needs. The paper concludes with a discussion of the role of the Internal Revenue Service (IRS), the status and proliferation of small foundations, and a procedure for the dissemination of information about private-foundation activities.

Government in this paper refers to the federal government, primarily the major socioeconomic agencies providing human services: the Department of Health, Education and Welfare (HEW); the Office of Economic Opportunity (OEO), and the Department of Housing and Urban Development (HUD) through its Model Cities Program. State government has addressed itself to philanthropy primarily in the areas of regulation, registration, and reporting of charitable trusts and charitable organizations. *Private foundation* here has the broadest definition (community trusts are included).

Present Trends

CHANGING RATIO OF PRIVATE FOUNDATION
TO GOVERNMENT SPENDING

In the field of human services, private foundations have operated independently of government. The directions taken by private foundations and government have sometimes been parallel, sometimes divergent. There is no evidence that foundations and government have ever taken any significant, long-lasting joint approaches to their responsibilities for the delivery of human-service programs.

Until the 1950s, much of the initiative for social change and innovation in the delivery of human services came from private foundations, though even before this period numerous small human-service agencies had been established and were functioning successfully within government. Consolidating several federal human-service agencies, HEW was created in 1953; OEO and the HUD Model Cities Program began in 1964 and 1965, respectively. Through these agencies, government has rapidly increased the amount of its expenditures in the area of human services.

Private foundations make about 60 percent of their annual grant expenditures on human services—activities coming within the categories of health, education, and welfare as defined by the Council on Foundations. The welfare category includes community development, housing, and transportation as well as social services. Except for operation of the Food and Drug Administration and for Social Security Administration payments, HEW's expenditures, as one might presume, are mostly in the area of human services. For purposes of definition and clarity, welfare payments, social insurance, and veterans' payments are excluded from the following statistics, so that we can make direct comparison between HEW expenditures for health, education, and social and rehabilitation services, and similar expenditures of foundations.

In 1961, private foundations spent $218 million on human services. In the same year, government spent $3.5 billion on the same kinds of services—about 16 times as much. In 1971, private foundations spent $673 million on human services; in that year, government spent $15.3 billion. Government's spending on human services was thus 23 times that of private foundations. Although it is anticipated that private foundation spending will increase, the difference in spending on human services by government and private foundations is sure to become even greater over the next five years.

As these developments in spending patterns make clear, government has overshadowed private foundations in the social services area. On a dollar-for-dollar basis, private foundation expenditures are actually insignificant when compared to government spending. In order to maintain any relevance, private foundations must accordingly analyze their role in terms of the significance and impact achieved by their expenditures. At the beginning of this century, the roles and expenditures of private foundations and government were substantially different, as F. Emerson Andrews, former president of the Foundation Center, illustrates: "In 1913 the federal government's total expenditures for education amounted to $5 million. Carnegie Corporation of New York in that year spent $5.6 million, so that if it had devoted all its funds to the field of education, it could have more than equaled the federal government total." In 1971, however, federal programs for education cost $6.5 billion, while foundations spent only 6 percent of this amount, a total of $343 million.

Less than 6 percent of private foundations have assets of over $10 million, yet they spend 50 percent of all the money made available through foundation grants. The remaining 50 percent is divided among numerous small foundations. More than 85 percent of all grants are made by private foundations with assets of less than $10 million.

A small foundation probably makes most of its grants in the community where it is located, and it probably has only limited contacts with other private foundations making human-service grants in the same community. Although some efforts have been made to coordinate the objectives and resources of small and medium-sized foundations (notably the Co-ordinating Council of Foundations in Hartford and the Inner City Fund in Chicago), it is not likely that a small or medium-sized private foundation is part of a grand strategy directed toward resolving human-service problems in the community.

For purposes of discussion, let us assume that a hypothetical private foundation has assets of $10 million and spends about $400,000 annually on human services, in a community of three hundred thousand. In the same community, HEW may spend $800,000 on health, $1,300,000 on education, $7,750,000 on social and rehabilitation services, and $125,000 on other services such as child development—a total of about $10 million. As OEO may spend $200,000, and HUD Model Cities may spend $1,800,000, total government spending on human services may approach $12 million annually in the community. (This of course does not include state- and local-government expenditure on education and other human services.)

The individual private foundation is outspent by the federal government by a ratio of 30 to 1. One branch of one federal agency could alter the proportion by deciding to terminate or modify one or two of its projects in the community, to a total of $400,000, and the impact on the community would be negligible, provided adequate substitute programs were introduced. But this modest shift (by government standards) might equal the total annual expenditure of our hypothetical private foundation.

A private foundation executive must recognize these changed circumstances and seek to adapt affirmatively, lest his foundation simply become irrelevant. Whatever they may have been in the past, private foundations today are not on the "cutting edge" of social change. In fact, some observers have questioned whether the social services provided by private foundations merit the continuance of their special tax status. Lane Kirkland, secretary-treasurer of the AFL-CIO, in his dissenting opinion in the report of the Commission on Foundations and Private Philanthropy, makes the point that a serious cost-benefit analysis of foundations (involving tax loss versus social benefits achieved) is rare. It is therefore difficult, in his view, to substantiate the commission's assumption that there is a trade-off between public and private funds for social programs.

The point at issue is whether an appropriate balance between public and privately controlled funds can be achieved. In the field of human services, private foundations have a unique potential which deserves encouragement. If foundations do not realize this potential, their efforts in this area may properly be construed as pale imitations of government activities, because of the relatively insignificant scale of their programs when compared with government programs. This really means that private foundations either achieve their potential or abandon the human-services area in which approximately 60 percent of their present spending is now centered.

INTERPLAY OF INFORMATION

Private foundations and government need to share information. An interchange between the two would reinforce the efforts of each and help them allocate their individual resources.

Foundation executives remain largely uninformed concerning the planning of the federal human-service agencies. This lack of information may keep them from understanding government objectives and thereby may cause them to plan less effectively than they otherwise might. By the same token, government could benefit from advice and counsel provided by foundations. The disjointed planning process which now exists points up the need for foundations and government to cooperate in their planning for the delivery of human services. Government needs this input to ensure that its efforts are consistent with national priorities and the preferences of a specific community.

It is especially in the fields of community organization and planning that private foundations can promote the development of information that is not readily available from other sources. For example, many of the advocacy planning organizations, such as Urban Planning Aid in Cambridge, Massachusetts, were originally and primarily funded by foundation grants. These groups studied the needs and desires of urban neighborhoods and presented their findings in the form of alternatives to proposed projects, such as highways and schools. They gave the residents of the community a chance to be heard in cases where government planning commissions seemed to be unresponsive to their needs.

The private-foundation executive probably does not know the government administrator who plans, manages, or decides upon federal programs for his community. He probably does not know the specific nature of the federal grants made in the community in prior years; he does not know the nature of the grants about to be made or those being considered for the next year; he is unaware of the budgeting cycle of the federal agencies, the nature of their internal decision-making criteria or methodology or the nature of the five-year federal planning process. It is also likely that the only information a private-foundation executive receives about current federal funding in a community is what he can glean from newspaper stories.

Although HEW funding is complex, there are several points of entry for individuals or organizations. HEW administers about 280 different programs. There is wide latitude in developing guidelines for programs and in the selection and funding of individual projects. Although much of the decision-making within HEW occurs in Washington, OEO and HUD have decentralized many of their programs to the ten regional offices, and HEW is moving rapidly towards similar decentralization of many of its programs. A foundation executive who is reluctant to become involved in the maze of an agency's Washington headquarters will be welcome in the regional office. A foundation executive is an excellent source of information that would be welcomed by an enlightened federal agency administrator.

The Federal Regional Council is another point of entry into the federal system. The FRC is composed of the heads of the major federal socioeconomic agencies (HEW, OEO, HUD, Environmental Protection Agency, Law Enforcement Assistance Administration, Department of Labor, and Department of Transportation). It has been in existence since 1969 and was greatly strengthened in March 1972 by presidential executive order. The purpose of the FRC is to coordinate the grant-making of the individual federal agencies by countering the fragmentation of government, and to give the public a common point of entry into the federal system. A private foundation should be aware and make use of this new instrument of government.

The regional administrator of a federal agency actively seeks information on priorities and preferences of states, cities, and communities within a region. Since the entire country is divided into only ten "standard regions," it is very difficult for the regional administrator to learn what he needs to know in order to make the proper allocation of the resources available to him. For example, Region V covers six Midwest states—Illinois, Indiana, Michigan, Minnesota, Ohio, and Wisconsin. Forty-five million people, constituting 22 percent of the total population of the United States, reside in this region. There are 27 major urban areas in this region. Clearly, centralization of information at the regional level is most important and, when it is achieved, is a valuable resource for nongovernmental as well as governmental institutions.

A private foundation can gain access to a great variety of information from the regional office. For example, a private foundation interested in day-care facilities can learn details of all the current funded projects in the community, including their location, staff, number of children served, level of funding, and in some cases an evaluation of their performance. This information can be used by a private foundation in a variety of ways in developing plans for the allocation of its resources.

The information is developed by the regional office from new or pending grant applications, from discussions with state planning agencies, and from the agency administrators. An example of co-operation in this area is the effort of the Michigan Office of Criminal Justice to redesign its state planning process so as to bring about effective exchange of information among federal, state and local agencies, private foundations, and interested corporations.

With this kind of information, a private foundation can more objectively decide whether to alter or modify its present program. A private foundation funding programs providing services to unwed mothers, for example, may find that while the total number of unwed mothers in the area it serves is reduced, the rate of pregnancy for women under fifteen years of age has multiplied five times in the last twenty years, creating a markedly different set of human-service problems. The private foundation's response may be to shift its objectives to child-care and sex-education programs.

Federal agencies spend a significant amount of money on research and demonstration projects. It sometimes takes several years for a successful project to be adequately reported and the information widely disseminated. The lead time required for the replication of important new programs can be shortened considerably if the private foundation learns about the project at the regional level. This kind of communication provides the private foundation with an opportunity to respond more quickly to a target in its own community.

Community trusts traditionally fund a wide range and number of community undertakings. When government changes its goals only slightly, a community organization may not be refunded. The community trust must be aware of this possible change so that it can prepare a contingency plan that would cover the community organization suddenly confronted with financial difficulty.

Overall, it is clear that there is a common ground between private foundations and government and that lines of communication are available but seldom used. Both foundations and government would operate more effectively if they shared information. However, this does not go to the heart of the problem, which is how a private foundation can utilize its grants in relationship to government spending so that, taken together, government and private foundation expenditures provide the greatest benefit to those in need of human services.

COOPERATIVE FUNDING BETWEEN PRIVATE FOUNDATIONS AND GOVERNMENT: A DANGER

Private foundations must carefully weigh the kinds of joint or cooperative undertakings that might be initiated with government. Although many such projects would clearly be desirable, some could be opposed to the objectives of private foundations. Let us take a look at a possible instance.

In 1967, Title IV-A of the Social Security Act was amended to provide for federal matching grants on a three-for-one basis for purchase of social services. These grants were to be made available on an unlimited, open-ended basis to grantees undertaking to provide human services to people at or near the poverty level. Private foundations were made eligible to receive the grants, provided the objectives of their projects were covered under the provisions of a state plan.

It took a while for the program to become well known, but when the word got out and the guidelines were clarified, the number of grant applications and awards significantly increased. In 1967, the federal share of Aid to Families with Dependent Children, which is about 75 percent of total Title IV-A expenditures, amounted to $181 million. In 1970, this figure increased to $539 million. By fiscal year 1972, it was estimated to reach $1,598 million, a three-fold increase every three years.

The IV-A program has produced many benefits, but some of the dangers presented to private foundations have been overlooked. A private foundation, like many individuals looking after their own financial security, may find that it can resist everything but temptation. It is certainly a great temptation to turn $1 of private foundation money into $4 of funding by obtaining a three-for-one matching federal grant. The additional funding scans well on a year-end balance sheet, but its negative effect may be that the private foundation has altered its priorities and perception of human-service needs for the inappropriate reason that the federal cookie jar is open. The kinds of programs which can be funded under IV-A are limited, and not all private foundation programs can qualify. In fact, a great deal of skillful juggling of foundation objectives may take place in order to obtain additional federal money. Instead of approaching the problem by first determining needs and then seeking funds, one may identify available money first and determine needs later. If there is not outright alteration of a foundation's purposes, there is certainly a great risk of rearranging priorities to take advantage of a special situation.

There is, of course, a compelling financial argument used to justify this alteration of private-foundation objectives. However, if private foundations are to remain a positive social force, they must resist being engulfed by government. There is no surer way for this to happen than for a private foundation to become ineffective while its balance sheet grows fat artificially. If private foundations decline in this manner, their fall will have occurred not through government action or interference but through their voluntary pursuit of government funding for the wrong purposes.

Future Direction: Innovation

The Peterson Commission estimated that only 3 percent of all the grants by private foundations could be classified as innovative. By innovative we mean both experimental approaches to familiar problems and pioneering efforts in areas previously untouched by private foundations. The data also indicate that private foundations allocated an even smaller percentage of their grants to projects considered politically controversial. It is a fair assumption that grants that have as their purpose "social change" probably represent only a very minor fraction of total private-foundation grants or expenditures.

An Urban League study completed in 1971 shows that grants for human services made by private foundations to black and Spanish-speaking communities were disproportionately low when measured in terms of the per capita needs of the minority population. Vernon Jordan of the League, for one, has pointedly criticized the lack of private foundation involvement in social change. And Professor

Alvin Schorr, dean of the School of Social Work at New York University, in his paper entitled "The Tasks for Voluntarism in the Next Decade," has demonstrated that most of the changes that have occurred in the field of human services in the United States in recent years have come from government rather than from private voluntary social-welfare agencies.

The evidence indicates that private foundations are not performing the role of innovators. This is unfortunate in view of the often-cited potential that private foundations have for pioneering new programs through the use of "risk capital." It is crucial for the field of human services as well as for private foundations themselves that this type of program become a major part of their activities. Projects undertaken in conjunction with government could greatly facilitate this change of priorities.

The decision-making process in government is grounded in part on the realities of politics. Neither congressional legislation nor administrative decisions can get too far ahead of what is politically feasible. Government needs assistance in responding to changed priorities, and one of the few social institutions equipped to meet this challenge is the private foundation.

In theory, as foundation advocates say, one of the great strengths of private foundations is their flexibility. The decision-making process of a private foundation should be relatively simple and quick. A foundation is likely to have a small administrative staff rather than a bureaucracy with its own set of vested interests. Unlike government, private foundations usually do not allocate funds for more than one year in advance. They are free to develop new programs without being locked into prior funding commitments.

DEVELOPING CONSTITUENCY RELATIONSHIPS

In practice, however, there are several barriers to the utilization of this flexibility. The private-foundation grant-making process is unstructured, and standards are subject to many variations. Moreover, much of the process is either secret or at least not public. Perhaps one of the reasons for private-foundation support of routine rather than innovative projects is that private foundations do not have a constituency to which they are accountable or from which they receive support.

The average American is only dimly aware of the existence of private foundations and their function as a social institution. Most people do not care one way or the other about private foundations, except when they do something which is regarded as sufficiently extreme to draw attention from the media. When this occurs, the public attention is usually critical rather than laudatory. In a time when every subculture regards itself as a constituency to be reckoned with by political leaders, it is remarkable that private foundations, which are American social institutions with distinguished historical antecedents, continue to be inconspicuous and lack spokesmen who articulate what they mean to America.

Private foundations have overlooked their natural constituency, the people they serve, the recipients of a large array of human-service programs found in virtually every urban center in the country. Most private foundations fund social-service agencies which deal directly with the ultimate recipients. Government funding is similar in that it deals with states, local government, or local social-service agencies rather than the ultimate recipient. The critical difference is that the general public and human-service recipients form judgments about government programs; judgments are rarely formed by the public or recipients about private-foundation programs because private foundations are rarely identified with the services they support. An appropriate public-relations program would be the first step in developing an enthusiastic foundation constituency—provided, of course, that foundation programs achieve positive results. It may seem odd to form a coalition of people at or near the poverty level with private-foundation executives and donors who are at the other end of the socioeconomic ladder, but if the motivations and objectives of private foundations are valid, then the coalition is needed and should follow.

OVERCOMING THE OBSTACLES TO INNOVATION

A broad range of innovative programs can be aided and advanced by private foundations. At the far end of the spectrum, a program designed to promote social change would undoubtedly attract conflict and criticism. Certainly foundation administrators are not enthusiastic about taking risks, and if risks are taken, there may be repercussions, either political or financial. However, much of the anxiety about risk-taking is imagined and the assumed consequences are unreal.

Some private-foundation executives justify as prudence their continued emphasis on the funding of routine projects and their failure to become involved in innovative activities. While the feeling is that it is not prudent for private foundations to take risks, the consequence of this policy may inadvertently lead them to take an even greater risk—they may become irrelevant as social institutions.

Over the past twenty years, court cases have greatly enlarged the "prudent man" rule which limits the investment of trust funds. Legal barriers to innovative financial investment have been broken; barriers to social investment can also be breached. This hesitancy and anxiety can be dispelled when the alternatives and potential support for private foundations are carefully examined. These social-investment barriers are not actually legal ones but are mainly the result of timidity and lack of imagination.

COOPERATING WITH GOVERNMENT

The key to overcoming reluctance, I suggest, is development of a pattern of joint undertakings with government. Targets can be identified and private foundations can assume a leadership role. By an appropriate kind of mutually reinforcing arrangement, the federal government can provide operational and sustaining funding to a project that has proved its merits, thereby extending the needed support for an innovative role on the part of private foundations. If the pilot project fails, however, private foundations can point to the encouragement they have received from government and perhaps to their prior successes which became institutionalized with large-scale government funding. Private foundations can then afford to fail on occasion without dangerous results; government can afford to fail only rarely.

Apart from hard risk-taking and social-change ventures, there is an intermediate objective that may induce private foundations to discontinue funding routine activities and to allocate significantly more of their resources to innovative programs. This objective is the meeting of the great need for an intensive, programmatic examination of existing human-service delivery systems. Good programs fail because individual projects fail, and projects often fail for relatively minor reasons. This type of program monitoring is innovative only in the sense that it is not being done. This intermediate step can serve to point private foundations in the direction of more fundamentally innovative undertakings.

Most innovative programs are initially conceived as short-term demonstration projects, but many become entrenched and elicit continued support from government and private foundations. The innovative phase of these programs is usually completed in two or three years. If these programs deserve permanence in the community, they should be able to attract their own constituency for funding after four or five years. Continued government or private foundation funding of an innovative program after five years may present a problem of resource allocation to both government and private foundations.

In saying that private foundations ought to greatly alter their present funding priorities, one should note that innovation for the sake of innovation is not always a good thing. A series of unplanned innovative programs may be like a profusion of slender reeds which can choke a healthy plant growing in their midst. There are many good programs which have a marginal financial base. It may be a better investment of private-foundation and government funds to support tottering programs than to invest in a similar, yet newer, program in the same community. Government encouragement and assistance to private foundations in their necessary transition to a more innovative role can help ensure that their new activities will be efficient and constructive.

LAYING THE GROUNDWORK FOR COOPERATION

In November 1971, a meeting was held in Chicago to examine possible points of contact between HEW and private foundations in the six midwestern states of Region V. The purpose was to enable officials of HEW and private foundations to learn more about each other personally and institutionally, and to attempt to develop a joint undertaking. The one-day meeting was presented in the form of a series of workshop sessions and was modestly successful in providing information about each group to the other. The risk-taking or exposure to repercussion was minimal. The unstated achievements of the meeting were the relief experienced by the private-foundation representatives when no IRS agents came pouncing out from behind the draperies and the discovery that the government-agency delegates represented a great deal of available expertise in many areas of concern to private foundations. Further, the foundation representatives learned that the government human-service people had had nothing to do with the drafting of the 1969 Tax Reform Act. Indeed, very few government representatives had ever heard of the Act before. The stated accomplishment of this unique meeting was the agreement to develop a joint project between private foundations and government on a subject of importance to both.

As a result of the November 1971 meeting, a conference entitled "The Youthful Offender: The Reach for Alternatives" was held in Cleveland in the early summer of 1972. The purpose of the meeting was to examine the various social institutions that have impact on juvenile delinquency, such as the courts, police, corrections, law, schools, and family. About 350 persons from many parts of the country attended the three-day session and heard presentations by nationally known experts in the field. The program concluded with meetings of participants from each of the six Midwest states at which time affirmative action plans for each state were presented.

The results of the meeting were encouraging for two reasons. First, the meeting provided a current view of new experiences and forward thinking in the field of juvenile delinquency. Second, the meeting was the first joint undertaking of its kind between private foundations and government.

The meeting was sponsored by the Cleveland Foundation, Fordham University, and Region V, the Midwest Region of HEW. Representatives of about ten other private foundations attended and participated in the meetings. What emerged was a recognition of the mutuality of interest between private foundations and government in the examination and resolution of human-service problems.

Since the innovative aspect of the meeting was the fact that it was the first of its kind, it was designed to be national in scope by developing approaches that could be replicated in other parts of the country. A second joint undertaking between private foundations and government occurred in Columbus, Ohio, the week following the Cleveland meeting.

A number of leaders in Columbus recognized the need for co-ordinating existing human-service systems and approaches in their city. Under the leadership of the Borden Foundation, which is head-quartered in Columbus, the National Public Relations Council of Health and Welfare Services, which is supported by the Russell Sage Foundation, and Region V of HEW, a conference was held to identify resources and programs that relate to human-service prob-lems in Columbus. The objective of the meeting was modest and the result was encouraging. Community people in leadership roles were presented with specific information about programs, funding possibilities, and the availability of planning resources. This kind of meeting could be held in other communities with the active par-ticipation of a private foundation or a group of community private foundations and government.

The real test of the meeting will come when this broadened and strengthened group of individuals and institutions begins to attack some of the root social problems confronting the community. This kind of joint undertaking can serve to sensitize government to a com-munity problem when it is first identified, thus greatly accelerating the response of government through financial assistance, if it is needed.

PROGRAM EVALUATION

The issue of program evaluation opens up a new area that founda-tions should explore. It could become an area of primary interest to them. The threshold question is whether human-service pro-grams, funded and operated by either the public or the private sector, are achieving the goals and objectives for which they were established.

For many years we have assumed that the human-service programs of public and private agencies achieve a public and social good. But the relative merits of individual programs have not been tested in any structured way, and hence the costs of these programs to taxpayers and private donors cannot be compared with the good they achieve. Thus, recipients sometimes feel that weak or unproduc-tive programs are funded at the expense of promising new programs that are not funded. Seeing more and more of his money being spent on human-service programs, the taxpayer feels that problems in this area are proliferating faster than solutions.

Although human-service programs are not subject to precise mathematical measurements, techniques are available that can adequately quantify these kinds of programs. But more effort is needed to improve the techniques of human-service evaluation.

For private foundations, evaluation studies are expensive and professional expertise hard to find. The process of evaluation itself tends to be thought of as negative in nature and, of course, foundations feel that they do not really need another headache, particularly one which is self-induced. Cursory evaluation of a project could perhaps be done more quickly and cheaply by simply drafting a self-serving press release extolling the success of the project. In fact, much money is sometimes spent by private foundations in parochial and unproductive ways, free from the hassle of informed public debate about the wisdom or value of these expenditures. The result is that no critical evaluation is made.

Foundation self-evaluation is essential to the continued healthy operation of foundation activities. However, there is another area of evaluation that private foundations should seriously explore as they plan the allocation or reallocation of their resources. This area is the evaluation of publicly funded human-services programs by private foundations or by organizations funded by foundations.

EVALUATION OF GOVERNMENT HUMAN-SERVICES PROGRAMS

Private foundations do not adequately evaluate the programs they fund and operate. Perhaps more importantly, the human-services agencies of government—whose lead foundations frequently follow—sometimes experience difficulties in evaluating or monitoring the various programs they administer.

Some critics have suggested that what passes for evaluation may be after-the-fact justification of the expenditure of both public and private funds. A form is clearly lacking in which critical evaluative issues may be debated. Also lacking are objective data that can be used by program managers and public officials to talk to an informed public about these programs.

Government Evaluation—Sometimes, government program managers are not the best judges of the programs or projects they manage. There are two chief reasons for this. First, managers may be too far removed from the "street" where events occur and cannot measure their programs against reality; second, because of large workloads, they are often too occupied with administrative details to keep close tabs on their projects.

HEW Secretary Elliot L. Richardson made extraordinary efforts to try to achieve maximum efficiency in the use of federal funds during his years in office. His achievements were considerable, as were those of a number of other government-agency leaders. But problems still remain. Some programs, for example, may have lost their initial relevance after being operational for a relatively short time, because the circumstances which induced the programmatic response may have changed. Yet the programs may continue to be funded at the usual level. It is very difficult to cut back or terminate a program, because recipients tend to be vocal about losing their grants. Unless there is a sound objective evaluation of a program, it may appear to be neither fair nor feasible to discontinue it. Some programs appear to be weak because specific projects are not managed well. Sometimes a relatively simple evaluation can correct incipient deficiencies that jeopardize an entire program.

The amount of resources available to HEW is at the same time both vast and limited in terms of total need. Interestingly, however, the amount of money set aside each year for program evaluation is quite sufficient. These allocations are intended to encourage greater objectivity in government self-evaluation. However, one might easily conclude that even greater objectivity can be achieved as the result of evaluations of government programs by disinterested parties such as private foundations.

While there is a continuing responsibility for government agencies to monitor and evaluate themselves, it might well be an important new function for private foundations to support this work. Virtually every government program would benefit from some sort of objective evaluation undertaken by the private sector.

In HEW, the most commonly found forms of evaluation are process, structure, and outcome or output evaluation. Process evaluation refers to an examination of the procedures utilized in the direct delivery of services by grant recipients. Structure evaluation entails an examination of the applicant's tools or resources, such as staff, offices, and information systems. Outcome or output evaluation refers to a determination of whether or not the program in question is achieving the purpose for which it was designed. Is the Adult Basic Education Program, for example, in fact upgrading the skills of individuals and thereby permitting them to enter the work force and perform more complex work? Inquiries of this nature would constitute the activities which private foundations might pursue in assuring the accountability of government programs.

Foundation Involvement—The practical question raised is: how can foundations become involved in the evaluation of public human-service programs?

It is not feasible for private foundations themselves to develop an internal capacity that would enable them to make evaluation studies. However, larger private foundations could develop the capacity to identify programs to be evaluated and the ability to derive the wider significance from the results of the studies. It is within the capacity of foundations to develop the expertise to manage the work of evaluators engaged by them, and most importantly, to translate the results of the evaluation into change of individual programs and the recognition of circumstances that would lead to broad changes in the delivery of human services by private foundations and government.

The actual evaluation studies could appropriately be undertaken by the various "think tanks" and research institutes. Universities are another likely possibility. The important proviso is that foundations develop and maintain a management capability in this area.

Citizens rarely have private sector watchdog agencies operating on their behalf. There is, however, a new trend toward citizens monitoring government. One excellent example of this is Chicago's Better Government Association, a tax-exempt not-for-profit corporation. The objective of the BGA is to review instances of waste and inefficiency at all levels of government and report its findings to the public. The BGA operates in Illinois, primarily in the metropolitan Chicago area, with a small staff of about twelve and a budget of less than $200,000. During 1967–1972, it exposed about 40 major government scandals a year involving the annual waste of an average of $20 million. It has had a number of notable successes, such as the exposure of deplorable conditions in nursing homes, which contributed to a national movement for upgrading supervision and administration of these institutions. Yet the feeling of the BGA principals is that they are able only to scratch the surface because of their limited resources. The BGA concept could be replicated in many other areas of the country with great effect. However, a watchdog approach is only part of the solution. What is needed is the ability to follow up on disclosures or findings once they are made. Exposure of a scandal is dramatic, but the real payoff comes only with continuous and enlightened public debate which can compel real, fundamental change, not just amelioration of the worst symptoms of the problem.

Watchdog efforts must be augmented with highly objective and scientifically disciplined evaluations such as those that "think tanks" might produce. Harold Fleming, president of the Potomac Institute, has proposed that private foundations greatly expand their efforts in the evaluation and monitoring field, with special emphasis on continuous scrutiny of government agencies for cases of mismanagement, inefficiency, or corruption. Fleming points out that there is a crucial distinction to be made between lobbying by a private foundation, which is prohibited, and monitoring of executive programs and expenditures, which is not prohibited. Private foundations should not be reluctant either to expend or to accept funds for an intensive monitoring or evaluation effort, primarily directed toward government and, to a more limited extent, toward private foundations themselves.

In evaluating government programs, a private foundation has an initial problem of selecting appropriate ones. Many government programs are complex and appear to be inaccessible. However, the broadening of the interpretation of the Public Information Act will make it substantially easier for organizations in the private sector to gather relevant facts from government agencies. For example, the Act requires HEW to publish in the Federal Register complete statements describing the rules, procedures and structure of programs within the department. All final concurring and dissenting opinions in the adjudication of cases, all statement of policy and interpretation, and all other records not specifically exempted by the Act must be available for public inspection and copying, as must an index to the available information. Information centers are located in the headquarters of HEW and each of its operating agencies, as well as in each regional director's office. The policy of HEW is to liberalize access to information about its programs. But the experience is that inquiries from the private sector are infrequent.

As a start, individual private foundations or a consortium of private foundations ought to develop and identify issues and programs that for various reasons ought to be evaluated and monitored by the private sector. In such an enterprise, private foundations would be independent of government interference and the results would be widely disseminated and discussed. Both the public and private sectors would gain from each other, and opportunities for joint undertakings would certainly be presented as methodology is developed. The results of such a program may tend to be momentarily awkward for a government agency under scrutiny, but the purifying effects would far outweigh the initial apprehension.

Regulation, Information, and Small Foundations

IRS RELATIONSHIP TO PRIVATE FOUNDATIONS

There is a great deal of misinformation about the role of the Internal Revenue Service and its relationship to private foundations. This has at least two negative consequences. First, it impedes the ability of IRS to respond to private-foundation needs by fully utilizing the information resources it possesses; second, the suspicion with which foundation executives regard IRS is mistakenly directed at government human-service agencies as well, thus limiting the contacts that should be developed between private foundations and government agencies.

The threshold question is whether IRS, as it is at present constituted, is the appropriate agency to act as a matrix for all the disparate entities and objectives within government and the private foundation sector. The tentative answer is negative.

The relationship of IRS to government as a whole is important and often misunderstood. Congress develops imperatives, through legislative action, which are interpreted by the Department of the Treasury and set out in broad policy guidelines. IRS is a component of the Department of the Treasury and has the narrowly defined role of implementing Treasury policy. IRS is not a regulatory agency; its regulation of private foundations is only ancillary to its primary function.

IRS has the further responsibility of assuring that private foundations file returns. An audit procedure follows to determine whether there is liability for corporate tax. In this sense, IRS regards a private foundation the way it regards any profit-making corporation. If exemption from the corporate income tax is established, IRS must determine liability for the tax on unrelated business income and for any of the excise taxes that Congress has imposed on specific kinds of private-foundation activity. When these duties are performed, IRS has largely fulfilled its mandate.

What IRS has to do is to determine whether the program of a private foundation is charitable within the legal definition of that term. However, the definition of charity is very broad and extends far beyond the generally accepted definition of human services that is discussed in this paper. A private foundation may engage in a broad range of charitable undertakings, some quite esoteric, that have nothing to do with human services. IRS, therefore, as it is at present mandated, is not and has no need to be an agency which has expertise in the field of human services. Its role could be changed by Congress, and its traditional relationship to private foundations could be altered, but that would be grafting a system of constantly changing social judgments on to what is supposed to be an objective audit system. From the standpoint of the requirements of public administration or the more pressing needs of private foundations, there is no need to change the role of IRS.

EXPANDING IRS ROLE TO MEET INFORMATION NEEDS

But the role of IRS could be expanded to meet the information needs of the public, of private foundations, and of government. We lack an objective data base about what private foundations do, how and where they spend their money, which private foundations are terminated, and which private foundations come into being. The

Foundation Center has made important steps toward meeting these needs. However, more complete and detailed information is required for specific purposes which are not now being served.

Knowing what kinds of new foundations are being formed, and how many there are, would help us discern some of the directions which private groups are taking to deal with social problems. In addition, people who have previously had little contact with foundations would be aided by more immediately accessible information which could be useful in drafting grant proposals. This kind of information must be disseminated in an entirely new way so that it is on hand where it is needed. The reporting form filed by private foundations (990-AR) is available to the public at the Foundation Center Library and its eight branch libraries, as well as at each foundation office for 180 days. The real use for this information may occur in a community organization storefront in the inner city, light years away from the board rooms of charitable organizations and the development offices of universities, the traditional beneficiaries of private foundations.

Information developed by the IRS audit process carries with it statutory restrictions on disclosure and is not a promising source of data. A recent study conducted by F. Emerson Andrews disclosed that only 59 percent of a sample one thousand foundations filed acceptable tax returns in the previous year. Thirty-four percent made minor omissions such as failing to list possible payments to trustees; 2.9 percent of the foundations committed an apparent statistical error, while 4.2 percent were guilty of significant departures from the required return. Although the last group is relatively small, the fact remains that fewer than two-thirds of the sampled foundations provided tax returns in which all required schedules were filled out, statistics checked, and some analysis provided.

The IRS can require, within the bounds of reasonableness and fairness, any information about private foundation finances or programs. Where the needs of the federal socioeconomic agencies require, the information returns could be modified to develop specialized information. The mass of data available to IRS could be utilized by private foundations, the public, and government, and this should be explored further. Electronic retrieval (also being developed by the Foundation Center) could make the information readily available to anyone with an interest in the subject.

The principal and often sole point of contact between government and private foundations has been the IRS. This relationship is narrowly defined by statute and regulation. There has never been a stated government policy in the foundation field or a mechanism for developing such a policy. The Peterson Commission proposed the creation of a Philanthropic Policy Board—an idea that remains to be tested. Until very recently, there was no relationship between government and private foundations that could provide a basis for the careful formulation of policy. But now the human-service agencies of government and private foundations are beginning to work together. This relationship should be encouraged and accelerated. From this intensified encounter may come the kind of experience that will enable leaders of government and private foundations to evolve strategies and mechanisms which, in the long run, will result in enlightened policy.

DIFFUSION OF INFORMATION

We not only need to develop useful information about private foundations, we need to ensure that this information is adequately diffused to the general public, to social researchers, and to community organizations where the information can be translated into action.

Of the private foundations in the United States, only 193—about 3 percent of those listed in the 1971 *Foundation Directory*—published annual reports that year. It is not only small foundations which fail to publish. Twelve of the thirty-two foundations with assets over $100 million did not present reports in 1971. More than half of total foundation assets are not represented in the annual-report tally. The number of annual reports published by private foundations increased somewhat after 1969, the date of the Tax Reform Act, but the total number remains small. It would be useful if all private foundations published annual reports. This change will come about either through voluntary self-regulation by private foundations themselves or by a requirement imposed by legislation. The need for information is urgent and there are no apparent signs of a trend that will result in all private foundations' publishing annual reports in the next few years.

Although many of the annual reports are handsome documents indeed, profusely illustrated, with attractive covers, a sampling reveals glaring deficiencies in the presentation of information. Uniformity of presentation would be helpful in comparing and analyzing successes and failures in approaches to human service problems. However, present practice does not reflect any such uniformity. At a minimum, a private foundation's annual report should present the foundation's goals, an explanation of their grant-making process and the criteria employed in that process, an accurate financial statement, a description of projects, and a detailed evaluation of its projects. The broad purpose of an annual report is to inform. Too often, annual reports only advertise.

A standardized foundation annual report does not have to be dull or lock-stepped to the lowest common reporting denominator. It should meet uniform criteria for basic kinds of information but use great latitude in expressing the individual nature of a given foundation. It can be slick, artistic, or turned out on a mimeograph machine, as long as it contains adequate information.

A useful undertaking would be to develop a joint private foundations-IRS information project. A redesign of the present tax-form requirements and the development of the appropriate data-retrieval system by IRS would be very helpful. The best way to design and implement this information system would be through a planning committee of representatives from several related groups. The participants would include IRS and private-foundation representatives, lawyers, and accountants (through their professional associations), and, of course, members of the public, who are often forgotten when the configuration of such committees is being considered.

The grant-making process of a private foundation is the heart of its activity. Both government and the public have a right to know a great deal more about the process than is generally known. If grants are made on an elitist basis, for instance, the fact should be made public. If skill in grantsmanship is needed to provide the leverage for a grant, technical assistance should be provided to individuals or community groups to give them open access to grants. Lacking objectivity and access to the grant-making process, a new idea or new group is at a severe disadvantage, and the possibility of finding new approaches and solutions to human-service problems is diminished.

At present, when informative annual reports do become available, the benefits are limited. The reports are distributed to trustees, grant recipients, and a limited number of those with a peripheral interest in that foundation. Here the active dissemination process stops. Some annual reports are distributed to the branch libraries of the Foundation Center, such as the Newberry Library in Chicago and the Cleveland Foundation Library, but on the whole the general public is not provided with enlightenment about foundation activities.

Even the requirement that a private foundation Form 990-AR be available for inspection and that an announcement be made in a newspaper of general circulation does not move the information to the point where it can perform a public service. What is needed is access to the annual report, the 990-AR, and a narrative digest or summary of grant availability, classified by subject and geographic area and including the procedure for grant application, which is readily available to scholars, grantsmen, and community people alike. One possibility is to explore the use of either United States post offices or district offices of the Social Security Administration as repositories for information to be developed by IRS from the 990-AR forms.

THE SIGNIFICANCE OF SMALL FOUNDATIONS

Small private foundations, those with assets under $1 million, should be a vital component of any system of information-sharing or other types of cooperation aimed at strengthening the innovative capabilities of private foundations. About 30 percent of total private-foundation expenditures are made by these small foundations. The significance of the role played by small private foundations is so great that their decline would considerably reduce overall foundation flexibility.

John Davis, a former member of the Hartford Foundation for Public Giving, has pointed out that small foundations can provide fresh input into the study of problems such as drug addiction and alcoholism within a community. In turn, large foundations and government, which have specialists on their staffs, can direct small private foundations to specialized bodies of information and advise them concerning the types of projects they might fund. This could be done by commencing a series of recurring regional meetings on specific subjects, jointly sponsored by government and large private foundations, which would have as their purpose the introduction of small private foundations into the information stream.

It is not economically feasible for the vast numbers of small foundations to engage a full-time staff to review grant applications, evaluate grantee performance, or seek new opportunities for grants. Accordingly, these functions may be handled as an accommodation by lawyers and accountants who have had a professional relationship with the for-profit business of the donors of a private foundation. In these instances, those who undertake the administration of private foundations may not have the time or expertise in human-service matters to properly manage private foundation activities.

Since such a substantial percentage of private-foundation grants are made by these small private foundations, it is important that they be well administered. This entails the filing of adequate and complete annual reports and tax returns. If, because of lack of professional staff, these minimum standards become difficult to meet, small foundations should consider pooling their resources and coordinating their activities through a shared professional organization.

The cooperative ventures already noted in Chicago and Hartford, as well as in many other cities, whereby all types of foundations coordinate their activities, should be expanded and encouraged. There are three basic types of cooperative associations: informal, in which foundations share information and seek to increase the cumulative effectiveness of their grants; formal nongrant-making associations with a central research staff which make recommendations for program priorities; and, finally, formal grant-making associations which reflect the full extension of this concept.

These coordinated efforts can avoid duplication of funding and provide a broader perspective for planning a response to community human-service problems. Associations of this type can identify those local projects which are not receiving the needed funds from local foundations. They can serve as springboards, making sure that such worthwhile ventures reach the attention of larger foundations or government, whichever presents the better opportunity for funding.

The preservation and proliferation of small private foundations could have a refreshing impact on the way the nation spends the resources available for meeting human needs. The mere presence of such private foundations may well stimulate larger private foundations and government to reexamine their funding priorities and increase their investment in innovative high-risk projects.

Conclusion

As a unique American social institution, private foundations have a distinguished background. History has changed markedly over the past 60 years, and private foundations are now neither the big spenders nor the pioneers in the resolution of human service problems. The future direction of private-foundation activities is clear: foundations should use a much higher proportion of their funds in innovative and high-risk programs which will place them, once again, in the role of leading the way for government. There is a range of innovative projects that should appeal to the timid as well as the bold foundation executives.

To motivate a private foundation to accelerate and expand its innovative processes, it is necessary to provide both a spur to action and a source of comfort and support which can insulate them from repercussion if their innovative efforts go wrong. Joint undertakings with government are part of the answer. The other part of the solution is to have private foundations develop a constituency relationship with the people they serve in the delivery of human services.

The matrix of this new approach for private foundations is openness and candor about their affirmative responsibilities and activities. This will serve to correct misinformation and dispel latent hostility about the invisible nature of their operations.

Change need not be regarded as negative or potentially shattering to private foundations. The talent and resources to be used for redirection of effort are readily available to private foundations.

What is needed is an objective data base for bold decision-making. Even without such information, we can analyze the present condition of private foundations from a review of existing available data. Once the shibboleths are challenged, the direction for change becomes clear.

H. Thomas James

7

Perspectives on Internal Functioning of Foundations

For this discussion of the internal functioning of foundations I must of necessity draw heavily on personal experience, first as a mendicant professor and dean coming frequently with my tin cup to the chilly side of foundation desks (with, I might add, occasional success), and in more recent years, back to the wall but usually more relaxed, on the comfortable side of the desk. Since the Spencer Foundation had been virtually dormant for the two years prior to my arrival September 1, 1970, while the board searched for a president, we faced all the critical tasks of foundation management— selecting the staff, establishing a base of operations, expanding the board, money management decisions, program and grant decisions, coping with the 1969 Tax Reform Act—in quick succession. The Tax Reform Act was perhaps less traumatic to us than to established foundations, for we had no traditions to be disrupted; we formulated our policies and went about our business, with a law firm retained to see that we conformed with the rules as given.

H. THOMAS JAMES, *president of the Spencer Foundation, was dean of the School of Education, Stanford University, 1966–70. He has been assistant state superintendent for finance and research in Wisconsin and associate director of the Midwest Administration Center. Dr. James was assisted in this paper by Charles B. Strozier.*

Since my first contact with the Spencer Foundation occurred when two members of the board of trustees came to see me at Stanford in 1969 to explore ideas about what the foundation might do and who might administer it, I will begin with some comments about trustees.

Trustees

The trustees of endowed wealth are legally and morally responsible for the honest, prudent management of the monies under their control. The most basic principle guiding their duties is loyalty, both to the preservation and to the purposes of the trust. For some trusts and endowments the beneficiaries are clearly defined and the trustee's role is largely ministerial. But most foundations confer extensive discretionary powers on the trustees, allowing them to function as a governing board and to spend the money "for the benefit of mankind," "for the improvement of education," "to improve health," or for any number of broadly defined philanthropic goals. Definition of the terms by which the grant of power is made to the trustees is crucial in determining the uses to which the money will in fact be put. It is clear therefore that the individual and collective character of trustees has an important impact on the functioning of the foundation.

The board I came to know as our discussions began was, understandably, closely linked with the founder—two of his attorneys, a close business associate and friend, two long-time scholar-consultants, and his widow. To this nucleus were added a senior vice president of a large stock brokerage firm, the head of a banking system, a scholar in social psychology, and one of the founder's sons.

Earlier studies have revealed that the prototypical foundation trustee is in his sixties, a graduate of a private college, white, Anglo-Saxon, Protestant, and, most likely, a moderate Republican. Two-thirds of the trustees of the 25 largest foundations have backgrounds in business, banking, or the legal profession. Rarely are trustees drawn from organized labor, and there are few Catholics, Jews, Negroes, women, or young people among them. Although we have a broader representation on our board than the prototype referred to, it still cannot be said to reflect a cross-section of the educated, responsible public presumably fitted to serve as foundation trustees.

Foundation boards are and always have been co-optive and there-fore self-perpetuating. This operating principle has kept the boards restricted in composition. But despite the heavy hand of tradition, one must ask whether foundation boards of trustees should more adequately reflect the diversity of our society: First, Will the be-havior of trustees differ significantly if they are drawn from broader segments of the population? Second, Is society hurt by the present narrow social, economic, and political base of trustees? Answers are needed for both questions, and even though facts are scanty and evidence hard to come by, the necessary study is overdue.

In considering the possible alternatives suggested by these ques-tions, several major foundations are testing or considering a number of changes. Having a board of some kind is assumed to be worth-while, just as the sincerity, honesty, and diligence of most trustees of the large, independent foundations are not questioned. Neverthe-less there are logically persuasive arguments for a number of re-forms even though the essential role of trustees, as it has developed over the years, would be preserved, and there is little evidence that these reforms would make foundations significantly more responsive to the needs of a rapidly changing society.

One characteristic of trustees has always been advanced age. The national mean age of trustees in the United States in the late 1960s was approximately 60 years; one foundation had one-third of its trustees over 70, and tenure continuing into the nineties was not uncommon. Traditionally it has been left to the individual to decide when he should step down. Recent trends, however, indicate that this aspect of foundation boards will change substantially in the future. For one thing, many foundations have established retirement ages, usually 70. In addition, many have set up maximum lengths of consecutive years of service. Thus Carnegie permits a trustee to serve two four-year terms, while Ford allows two six-year terms. After that a trustee must retire. He can conceivably be brought back onto the board later, though this is explicitly discouraged. Terms of service for the chairman and the vice-chairman of the board of Carnegie each are for five years, but only the chairman's total length of service may be extended past the maximum eight years. For any foundation a retirement age and a fixed length of service should give it greater freedom to select younger trustees and trustees of more diverse backgrounds. The Spencer Foundation board in 1970 set a retirement age of 70 for board members then serving, and of 65 for new members; and the retirement age of the president, at the express request of the president-elect, was set at 65.

Few other concrete proposals have been made by the foundations themselves to make their boards more diverse and responsive. Some foundation boards have tried adding members from groups not formerly recruited, but these efforts have been neither systematic nor widely copied. Furthermore, it may turn out that a fixed retirement age and a fixed maximum length of service—reforms that have indeed found favor with some foundations—do little more than increase the mobility of the foundation trustee elite, without altering its narrow social, economic, educational, and religious basis. There is no compelling reason to believe that a 30-year-old white Protestant banker, lawyer, or businessman has a more empathetic understanding of the raw surge of American life than his 60-year-old colleague. Foundation boards are being encouraged by many critics to move voluntarily toward reform as a means of salvaging a worthy tradition in our civilization. Also urging them in that direction are proposals for a legislated end of self-perpetuation, the opening of previously private debates on internal policies, quotas for the newly elected trustees, and possibly direct government regulation.

Staff

The only paid staff member with the Spencer Foundation before my arrival was the secretary of the foundation. Hence I draw upon our experience from that date for these comments on staffing. The history of foundations before World War II reveals that only a handful had paid staffs. Even today, of some twenty-six thousand foundations, the majority operate essentially out of the back pocket of the donor or his lawyer. Unless annual grants total well over $100,000 it simply does not pay for a foundation to hire a full-time executive officer. Only the large independent foundations can justify the support of staffs, and many of these are operated by one man. Almost all foundations with assets exceeding $100 million have paid staffs, whereas very few with assets under $1 million have any staff at all.

I have used the term *paid staff* because I am sensitive to some ambiguities in the more widely used term *professional staff*. I was always comfortable with being described as a *professional educator,* for—though some may quarrel with the term—I accepted it as appropriate to my life's work, and I still think of myself as one. On the other hand, I have not been comfortable with the notion that I am, or might become, one of those who might be called professionals in the fine art of giving money away (is *philanthropoid* emerging as the right word?). Rather I prefer to think (as I am sure doctors, lawyers, ministers, physicists, and many other professionals before me have thought) that it is training and experience in my own professional field that equip me with some useful expertise in investing funds to stimulate inquiry in that field, and that funds so invested may promise larger returns to society than random distributions might offer. It was toward improving the breadth, depth, and quality of research on education that I directed my efforts while serving as dean of the School of Education at Stanford University. And it is precisely toward these same ends that my efforts are directed now as president of the Spencer Foundation, chartered as it is to support research in the behavioral sciences aimed at the improvement of education.

So while I will now feel free to use the term professional staff, I trust that I have made clear that I do so in the special sense of a professionalism based on training and experience related to a field of study and practice. This usage obviously does not rule out the development (or deny the existence) of a professionalism related to foundation practice. Such a professionalism must, however, be only one of a larger set of bases for professionalism of the staff of a foundation.

BUILDING A STAFF

The need for in-house portfolio management staff was quickly ruled out by our board's decision to employ investment management firms. With the help of competent consultants in the field and a survey of performance the board appointed three firms, divided the portfolio among them, and selected custodian banks. The investment policy outlined for the managers was simple and straightforward. We assume that the money market is efficient, and that it pays off in proportion to risks taken. The guidelines for risk are determined by our objectives, to bring the combination of capital growth and income to a level that will keep pace with inflation over the long run, permit payout at or slightly above the levels required by government, and conserve capital. Thus the staffing needs on the fiscal side were reduced to pre-audit, accounting, and budget control personnel, and an accounting firm was retained to perform the post-audit function and to prepare tax reports.

The range of staff skills we needed on the grant-making side of our operation was restricted by the specificity of our charter, requiring us to support research in the behavioral sciences aimed at the improvement of education. I accepted the role of generalist in research and practice in education, and developed with board and outside consultants, and for approval by the board, a set of guidelines intended to circumscribe broadly our areas of interest. Each proposal coming into the office was screened first at the clerical level to remove those clearly outside our purposes, such as capital grants, general institutional maintenance, and those clearly having nothing to do with either research or education. All remaining proposals were referred to professional staff, which meant me initially, then slowly expanding to three additional persons occupying roles which I will describe shortly. I might add that every turndown letter, even for requests screened out at the clerical level, is reviewed, along with the proposal, by both the president and the secretary of the foundation. Complete lists of turndowns are furnished to each board member every quarter. We agonized, of course, as others have before us, about phrasing the turndown letter. But we came to depend, as most foundations seem to do, upon defining the procedural grounds for rejection ("outside our area" or "we have attached higher priorities to other proposals now before us") rather than upon discussion of the merit of a proposal. The reason for this course seems obvious. Although one may not quarrel with the comment now going the rounds of foundation offices that "to fund one program out of ten gives a foundation nine enemies and one ingrate," there are still degrees of enmity, and we find it easier to live with someone who sees us as wrong-headed about our priorities rather than with one who persists in bickering with us about the merit of his proposal.

The blessing of obscurity made our work load light during the final months of 1970, but the publication of a guidelines brochure marked the beginning of the end of that blessing. As the work load mounted, I put into effect a plan that I had proposed earlier in my discussions with the board, namely, a staffing plan that would maintain a flat administrative hierarchy and maximum flexibility for future organization. We created three positions in the professional staff to be occupied half-time for short periods (as little as three months, and not longer than a year) by mature advanced graduate students. These young people were about to complete their dissertations (or had recently done so and had a book to write or some other useful activity to pursue in the remainder of their time) in fields related to education and the social and behavioral sciences. The strategy behind my plan was simple. First, purely personally, I knew I would miss the bright young minds that contribute so much to the education of a professor willing to listen; and second, I needed the viewpoints and perspectives to be expected from people with training and experience quite different from my own. The experiment was highly successful. To these roles we were able to attract an educator interested in economic analysis of school efficiency, a young lawyer pursuing the impact of the Serrano line of decisions on schools, a post-Master of Business Administration at work on the economics of education, and a young historian working on the psychological analysis of historical figures. Their common characteristics were unusually high intelligence, strength and independence enough to take a point of view and defend it with vigor, a disciplined way of knowing and testing reality, and broad knowledge of the literature and leadership in their field of study.

A comment on the interpersonal relationships involved in the staffing plan may be of interest. The flat hierarchy was, of course, advocated by James C. Worthy, then vice-president of Sears, Roebuck, in the literature on administration two decades ago. About the same time, research by Andrew W. Halpin and others showed that the three-man administrative unit was essentially and inevitably unstable because changing coalitions of two tended to gang up on the third. Accordingly, for my purposes in keeping our organization flexible, a combination of a flat hierarchy and a three-man team with short tenure seemed ideal. (I was also attentive to Parkinson's Law, which requires two or more appointments at a given level, so that they compete with each other and not with the boss.) But the best-laid plans of mice and men gang oft agley. Our permanent quarters included a good deal of unassigned space, because the staff is building gradually as needs dictate. The research assistants as they came in were given windowless offices along the back side of the suite; the two offices with windows next to mine were reserved for visiting scholars. However, the first visiting scholar chose the most remote cubicle office nearest the back door. Shortly thereafter, by processes still somewhat mysterious to me, the senior (by six months) research assistant appeared in the office with windows next to mine and by equally mysterious processes his correspondence thereafter was signed "research associate." The second research assistant stayed put, but the third (possessing special merit in the eyes of all three by being the first to hold the doctorate when appointed) showed up in the second windowed office (which, I learned only later, had precisely twelve square feet less glass than the first). Thus in that brief span of time, without any action on my part, and with salaries remaining the same, my flat hierarchy became three-tiered: a research associate (office next to me); an assistant who, to my knowledge, never appended any title to his correspondence (second office from me, twelve square feet less glass than the first) but demonstrated by his confident behavior that only six months difference in seniority justified any difference at all in his status vis-à-vis the research associate; and a research assistant, who clearly accepted his low-man-on-the-totem-pole status by signing himself "staff associate," going coatless, and leaving after three months. His successor, the post-MBA, sidestepped the whole issue by taking the office next to the foundation secretary and the accountant. He apparently established a new hierarchy on the business side which was flat but would, I assumed, begin to have steps downward as rapidly as he could acquire assistants. My great confidence in his judgment suggested that he would require two, and I waited with keen anticipation for his astonishment upon finding that he could not keep them equal in status.

The lessons for administrative scholars and practitioners which I draw from this experience are as follows: (1) The flat hierarchy is sound in principle but may be impossible to maintain. (2) An organization designed for instability will quickly rigidify. (3) Parkinson's Law doesn't work.

I concluded early in the assessment of our staffing needs that it would not be possible for us to assemble the expertise required to make sophisticated judgments upon all proposals across the entire range of scholarly interests we could expect to encounter. William James was too harsh when he said that any expert who could not explain what he was doing to an eight-year-old child was probably a charlatan. We are always inclined to give an applicant the benefit of the doubt when we do not understand the technicalities of his proposal, and consequently we seek an evaluation from the most competent specialists we can find in his field of work. We close acceptances of proposals one month before each quarterly board meeting for all proposals to be considered at that meeting, prepare in-house reviews, assemble them with our consultants' reports, estimate the funds available for grants at that meeting (using as a rough guide one-fourth of the annual payout to be made in the fiscal year), and set about the hard task of selecting from the proposals remaining (invariably more than we can fund), those that will be presented to the board with a favorable staff recommendation. Although these recommendations are generally accepted by the board, they are always thoroughly explored and tested—and on occasion, rejected. Two illustrations will suffice to indicate the flavor of the testing process. The first was a request to supply funds to one institution to bring a distinguished scholar from another institution in order to broaden the range of inquiry going forward in the first. The question put to me by a board member was: What return to society is to be expected from moving a productive body from one institution to another, thereby weakening one in some measure, and strengthening another, while the scholar presumably does what he is going to do in either setting? It was an illuminating question, one I am not likely to forget, and how I wished I had thought of it first! In the second instance, a sound proposal for a technically excellent study recommended for support by the staff was passed over by the board when an eminent scholar on the board pointed out some new horizons appearing in that field of study, and asked what the proposal under consideration, though technically excellent, would add by working over known ground? Again, I recognized the question as a right one, and regretted it had not come up in staff meetings.

ROLE OF PROFESSIONAL STAFF

I conclude this discussion of staffing with the following generalization, which I believe is supported in the still quite meager literature on foundations. Of all the factors that distinguish the modern American independent foundation from the endowments and charitable trusts of previous centuries, the most significant is the fact that they generally have staff with professional qualifications relevant to their fields of operation—staff whose primary function is to recommend ways to distribute the available funds for worthwhile projects, monitor their performance, and report back to the board and the public on their achievements. It is only with a staff that foundation activities become more than a casual, idiosyncratic—essentially personal—matter. Through the interaction of staff and the governing board the terms of the charter are spelled out and defined in a body of policy that is built up over time. When the governing board includes public-spirited citizens, broadly educated and attuned to the needs of society, and when they can interact with staff chosen for special expertise in the foundation's field of activities, the body of accumulated policy can shape contributions to the general welfare in very significant ways.

There are, of course, exceptions to any generalization about trends; among the larger foundations, the Fleischmann Foundation offers perhaps the most notable exception to the move toward professionalization of staff, for without staff the board of this foundation has launched remarkably effective programs. Yet the generalization remains that the quality of a foundation program usually can best be estimated by the quality of its professional staff. Furthermore, a staff is essential if the foundation is going to develop expertise and competence in a given field to seek out and develop valuable projects systematically, evaluate their results methodically, and report them in ways that contribute advancement in the field.

Under ideal operating conditions a foundation staff, upon receiving a proposal, finds either in-house or in the field the proper expertise to assess its quality and its potential for contributing to social gains. Suggestions for modifications may on occasion be discussed with the applicant. Site visits may be made to determine the appropriateness of facilities or to explore other questions. Staff will be available for follow-up visits as necessary. In short, staff permits the grantor to be more actively involved with the grant than any rich individual could ever hope to be (assuming philanthropy is not his full-time occupation). Since the end of World War II, there has been a greater tendency to recruit officials with special competence in the foundation's area of interest, and this in turn has led to frequent exchanges of personnel between foundations, colleges and universities, and government, a trend encouraged by John Gardner in his writings and by his actions. Donald Young comments that "in recent years the foundations best known for their philanthropic achievements increasingly have been staffed by men distinguished by relevant professional competence."

Critics of foundations have recently tended to judge them on scales of creativity, innovation, and activism, and to praise those ranking high on these scales. Few receive such praise. I asked Robert Maynard Hutchins what foundation grants had paid off best during the past twenty years. He said he could not give me a list, but he would give me a generalization: he suspected that payoff would run roughly in inverse proportion to the size of the grant! Yet I think history will show that much of the best work has been selected and sometimes shaped by professionally relevant and competent staff, and some of these grants have been large. In some cases this implies technical competence, as, for example, when a foundation wishes to concentrate its efforts in the natural sciences, or, as we are doing, in the social and behavioral sciences. In other cases, competence is more loosely defined and involves broad experience in public affairs, community action, or other nonspecific areas. The very large foundation is able to operate effectively in many fields. For example, the Ford Foundation has eight major divisions, Rockefeller five, and within each division there are a number of changing programs. For most middle-sized foundations ($10–100 million) such diversification is impossible, owing to their relatively small staffs. The middle-sized foundation can, however, profitably concentrate its efforts on one field, and find competence and expertise in occasional consultants.

If a foundation field of action or modus operandi creates a need for staff, then a problem is posed for smaller foundations which cannot afford one. Efforts are currently under way to create a staff to serve several foundations on a contractual basis, in much the way that investment counselors may now serve several foundation clients. Whether these efforts will establish a trend, however, remains to be seen.

Strong arguments can, of course, be made against staffing. For instance, each dollar spent on staff reduces the grant-making capabilities of the foundation by that amount, and the question, difficult to answer but necessary to consider, is: Does that staff dollar increase the efficiency and effectiveness of the grants made? Clearly, several alternatives to staffing exist. The trustees may have the time and the interest to donate relatively large amounts of time to work that would otherwise be done by staff, as in the case of the Fleischmann Foundation; or the foundation may choose to support either existing institutions working in the foundation's field of interest or the work of individuals, chosen either directly by the trustees or by an outside group. Doubtless there are other alternatives. The Spencer Foundation chose the professional staff alternative, but with the intention of keeping the staff small; my early estimate to the board was that all costs of administration, including staff costs, should come down to 8 percent of grants in four years, and stabilize around that percentage.

Program

DEVELOPING A PROGRAM

My own approach to program was a problem-solving one. The problem that faced me in the fall of 1970 was compound: the board wanted to get money flowing out early, and at the time I had neither time nor staff to generate a well-defined, comprehensive program. The solution I arrived at was simple. Since our prime purpose was support of research in the behavioral sciences aimed at the improvement of education, it seemed good strategy to begin attracting young behavioral scientists to the study of education as soon as possible. The method I recommended was to make annual grants of $30,000 each to ten universities with research-oriented schools of education and records of good communication across disciplines. The grants were to run for five years, but on a suggestion from the board this was modified to three years followed by a review before extension to five. Interdisciplinary committees at each university were to receive proposals from young faculty and make the individual awards, which were intended to fall in the range of funding between $500 and $5,000 that young faculty find hard to come by. In addition, we made two comparable grants to the National Academy of Education and a shorter-term, smaller one to Claremont Graduate School. This plan solved both parts of my problem. On the one hand, for the nonexistent staff it substituted senior university scholars who would do far better work than an inexperienced staff could have done in selecting good proposals to support: they were on the ground, knew the people— those who might write slick proposals but not deliver and those with good ideas who might not yet be adept at writing good proposals—and could, I knew from my experience, be counted upon to keep the dean's take for "administrative overhead" to a minimum. On the other hand, it started the flow of funds into the field in ways that contributed directly to our purposes. Furthermore, it promised a sort of radar network for us that should give us early information on some of the most promising young scholars in the social and behavioral sciences, many of whom we would doubtless work with for years to come.

With our brochure out and our income increasing rapidly, good opportunities for use of our funds increased also, more rapidly than income. As word of our purposes got around, the "out-of-program" requests declined sharply; so too did the number of what Orville Brim has called "long foul balls," excellent ideas close to, but not within the areas of interest of the foundation. From September 1970, when we began operating, until March 31, 1972, the board authorized about $3.7 million in grants.

These grants may be ordered in three sets. The first set, discussed earlier, comprising what we called "seed grants," was designed specifically to attract to the study of education young scholars from several disciplines. The second set of grants supported disciplined studies or projects by individual scholars or teams of scholars. The third major set of grants goes to support institutional development or change.

We became involved with these three categories in slightly different ways. In the first set, we took the initiative, in some instances inviting proposals from institutions noted for rich resources in the behavioral sciences and productive research in education. The effects of this effort over time should be to increase substantially the number of young behavioral scientists engaged in the study of education, especially as our offer fortuitously came at a time when funds supporting research were generally declining.

For the second set, the formal studies and projects of individuals and group of scholars, we selected, with the advice of consultants expert in the field of each applicant, from among the many applications made to us those few which seemed to hold the most promise for social gains and the improvement of education. Ralph Tyler has characterized operations in this category as not unlike playing the stock market in the business world—one gets the best advice one can, decides what level of risk one is willing to accept, and uses one's best judgment on the investments most likely to yield a high return.

The third category, funding institutional development and change, is extraordinarily important but also appallingly expensive. Our best hope in this category is to find the points of leverage where institutional development or change that can be initiated with our relatively small funds will show enough promise in its early stages to attract from other sources the additional resources needed for carrying through. Since other foundations, and government agencies as well, are also seeking these points of high leverage, we probably can anticipate relatively few attractive opportunities and even fewer successes.

There are, of course, other sets of objectives, or categories for funding, that we need to explore. One is the thematic approach to grant making, which requires that a foundation select some fairly specific theme, build in-house expertise around it, and become the acknowledged leader in that field, keeping in touch with all related work and focusing its resources steadily and sharply over a long period of time to achieve orderly and planned progress. The Markle

Foundation supported medical education for many years; then, under Lloyd Morrisett's leadership, it turned to improving communication in the processes of education, notably through the
Children's Television Workshop. The Kellogg Foundation supported the development of educational leadership broadly in the
early 1950s, then subsequently concentrated its interest on the development of leadership for the junior college movement. There
are many other illustrations. Clearly we must be alert in the years
ahead to opportunities for such thematic approaches. My own interest and practical experience in state and local school administration, school finance, and school law are in-house resources for a
development of efforts along these lines, and it may be that we will
pursue them in the future.

Another set of possibilities about which we have talked but to
date have taken no direct action involves young would-be scholars
and scientists. There is a need first to identify promising individuals
possessing talents with which they might make important contributions in education and then to help the individuals develop those
talents and channel them into productive use. One way to do this
is to select a promising point of intervention in the career lines of
individuals and make fellowship funds available at that point, assuming that these will help channel career lines in a specified direction. Another is to search out individuals with extraordinary
promise for development in selected directions and provide them
with the resources they need to maximize their talent. Some of
these individuals can be expected to emerge from our seed grants,
which have already drawn them into productive work in education.

DEFINING THE PROBLEM

In creative research it is usually impossible to know exactly how
long it will take to investigate a problem or what kind of data, or
products, if any, will emerge. A researcher often demands a good
deal of money and complete freedom to produce results according
to his own schedule. This distinctive feature of research has ex-
asperated more than one multimillionaire donor whose frame of
reference is the precisely defined problem, precise expectations for a
product, and equally precise expectations for returns on invested
capital.

The growing skill in building models of the engineering or economics type for problem solving has driven foundations in two directions: one is to spend more and more on the insoluble problems, and the other is to seek out individuals who ask the right questions, the kind that make old, insoluble problems come apart and suggest new models for attacking their components. Since we have no shortage of old, insoluble problems, or of those who like to restate them and carry forward the endless work of devising models for their solution, it is clear to me that to pursue the first course is to invite bankruptcy, both in money and ideas. Conversely, there seems to be good logic in seeking out and supporting those rare individuals who have the knack of asking the right questions, a course some of the more sophisticated foundations seem now to be pursuing. In my own field we have for the past twenty years been attempting to apply modern concepts drawn from decision theory to the administration of educational institutions. Recently, I thought I heard the ring of a right question when James G. March, upon turning his interests from analysis of the business firm to analysis of educational institutions, asked: "How does one make decisions in an institution whose aims are not clear?"

MONITORING GRANTS

Clearly, some kind of monitoring of grants is essential. A foundation must satisfy itself that its resources are being wisely and productively utilized, or withhold them. It must know from time to time whether the original plans are being followed, and if they are not, expect good reasons, clearly explained, for the changes. Since the reputation of the institution housing the scholar, whether it be university or independent research group, is also involved, foundations are not alone in this concern. Usually then, and quite satisfactorily, they can rely on the internal controls of the recipient institution.

In monitoring any grant, however, a foundation must accept the uncertainties inherent in inquiry. Investment in research is high-risk investment. Close supervision often characterizes the operating foundation, where the work is done in-house, but it is inconsistent with the purposes of a grant-making foundation, which seeks the best talent in a given field of inquiry and calculates its risks in terms of the value of the potential knowledge to be gained. Once the commitment is made, it is clear in principle that a grantee has the right to pursue his project independently of the foundation's inclinations and prejudices. The researcher, after all, is the expert, and only in rare situations should the foundation official presume to meddle with a research project. Close monitoring also takes the time and energy of the scholar and thus directly interferes with the progress of the research. The apt and often-cited analogy is the gardener who keeps pulling up his plants to see if the roots are growing properly. Finally, close monitoring can be politically dangerous, implicitly tying the foundation to the results of controversial projects.

The "proper" amount of monitoring must therefore be adjusted to circumstances and individual talent, as well as to the type of grant. For example, an award to build a new gymnasium requires little effort on the part of a foundation official. A more thorny question is whether a foundation should monitor closely an unseasoned agency but let a professor proceed totally unhampered, with no site visits and only a final report when he finishes after ten or twelve years. To stand back from the professor and let the reputation of his institution serve as adequate collateral on the worthiness of his research may be to abdicate responsibility, but to monitor closely may be presumptuous. To treat an unseasoned agency in a special way may open the foundation to charges of discrimination, but to pay no attention is equally likely to bring charges of irresponsibility. The proper balance can be struck if the foundation in both instances assumes fiscal responsibility, to see that the funds provided are spent for the purposes intended; then in both cases the institution is accountable, not to the foundation but to its various constituencies, for the quality of the results and the uses to which they are directed.

THE UNIVERSITY-CLIENT

Foundations have made grants to an infinite variety of recipients, but in recent times the most important relationship has come to be that between foundations and the universities. This peculiarly close relationship arose inevitably because the modern foundation, with its bias for getting at the root of a social problem, rather than alleviating the attendant sufferings of individuals, usually finds the best people for this task at the great research centers—the universities. The distribution of foundation funds to colleges and universities in the United States has never been uniform, for the simple reason that the best scholars congregate at the best universities.

The 1969 Tax Reform Act specified fiscal responsibilities, and differentiated the relationships between foundations and public charities (a class that includes universities), other private foundations, operating foundations, and individuals. Beyond fiscal responsibilities lies the whole question of evaluation of foundation efforts, which is dealt with in Orville Brim's chapter.

Reporting and Accountability: Problems for the Future

One of the important facts about foundations which is repeatedly and justifiably pointed out is the relatively small amount of money represented by their total assets of something more than $25 billion and of their annual expenditures of $1.7 or $1.8 billion. The annual expenditures of the Department of Health, Education and Welfare alone are substantially greater than the total assets of all foundations. In light of these magnitudes, the public's concern about the influence of foundations may appear to be misguided. But the explanation for this concern lies in the unique role foundation money plays in society, its virtually complete freedom from public control, and the charge that it is secretly managed by a social elite.

HISTORICAL PERSPECTIVES

Historically, much of the fear, both rational and irrational, of foundations has centered in the simple fact that they represent large concentrations of wealth in the hands of a few. To this tradition Representative Wright Patman and the "new populism" have introduced nothing new. In ancient Greece endowments and "foundations" were highly suspect for both political and economic reasons. In Roman times, Cicero believed that the foundations had participated in the Catiline conspiracy; yet in the attitude of the emperors, who coveted, rather than feared, the wealth concentrated in the various types of Roman endowments, one senses also opportunism. Throughout the Middle Ages, there were evidences of fear and resentment of the Church's wealth derived from bequests. Henry VIII attacked the institution that controlled something approaching half the landed wealth in his kingdom. The subsequent emergence in England of "foundations" that proved themselves consistently worthy in their alleviation of social distress helped reduce public and private fears of endowed wealth. In the eighteenth and nineteenth centuries, this favorable attitude was reversed by a substantial body of critics in England and on the Continent who decried mortmain, or the dead hand of the past, which through endowments inequitably controlled a significant portion of the country's wealth. Interestingly enough, this critical view of foundations has had a greater impact on European attitudes than those in America, with the result that foundations play a relatively unimportant role in contemporary Europe.

In America, on the whole, the colonial experience tended to establish public confidence in the uses of bequests, whether for religious or social purposes. This trust profoundly influenced the legal framework for foundations, which was clearly articulated before the nineteenth century began. It also helped mitigate, though by no means eliminate, criticism of the "robber barons" at the end of the nineteenth and beginning of the twentieth centuries. Nevertheless, the rapid industrialization which created the monstrous fortunes that in turn became the assets of the modern foundations —sweat from the brows of underpaid workers, many would say— has complicated modern attitudes toward foundations. In the public mind it was, and to some extent still is, difficult to dissociate the ruggedly individualistic, elitist characters of John D. Rockefeller, Andrew Carnegie, and Henry Ford from the philanthropic foundations which bear their name.

There is thus in contemporary America a complex set of feelings and attitudes toward foundations, as there is toward corporate structures in general. Great concentration of power and wealth is respected on the one hand, feared on the other. The popular rhetoric concerning the individual and his right to get rich tends to rub off on the rich man's foundation; but this rhetoric clashes with the equally popular rhetoric about supporting the underdog and seeing the mighty put down from their seats. The man in the street is therefore likely to be profoundly ambivalent about foundations and their contributions to society. Currently, no single attitude prevails, though it takes no stretch of the imagination to believe that the events of the 1960s indicate an increasing suspicion of foundations and their activities, and to sense that foundations will be caught up in broader concerns about large corporations in general.

FOUNDATION REPORTING

For the average citizen, the most offensive characteristic of foundations is the secrecy with which they are seen to operate. In 1964, when the Foundation Center was gathering basic information about foundations in America for the first *Foundation Directory,* it encountered stiff opposition from a great many foundations, opposition that is difficult to describe as anything but reprehensible. Similarly, the Peterson Commission felt that foundations had virtually invited public suspicion with their obtuse secrecy:

> By remaining a kind of closed society in an era when openness is a byword, the foundations excited public suspicion that they were engaged, not in a great range of activities that promoted the general welfare, but in secret things done in a dark corner. By their reluctance to discuss publicly their failures as well as their successes, the foundations foreclosed the right to their own fragile humanity. They became instead symbols of secret wealth which mysteriously used the levers of power to promote obscure, devious, or even sinister purposes.

Yet it is hard to understand how the public could inform themselves about such diversity, or to believe that they would take the trouble to do so if they could. The best hope for better understanding probably rests with the capabilities for informed reporting of the foundation field by the expanding activities of the Council on Foundations.

Apologists are fond of illustrating the irrationality of the public's attitude toward foundations by referring to the four congressional investigations of foundations, the first of which (1915) was initiated by the Progressives but the next three of which (1952, 1954, 1960s) derived their support from rightist fears of "radical" innovation. The implication clearly is that foundations can never hope to satisfy the public, so why attempt to explain anything? The problem with this line of argument is that the foundations themselves have fostered suspicion by the determination many of them have shown to remain secretive. It is not strange that the public is often irrational in its attack on foundations. It has traditionally lacked the essential information on which to base a clear, rational criticism. Foundations are, after all, in the final analysis quite readily held accountable to the public through the media, the Congress, and the courts, and the ability of foundations to foresee the conditions under which they may be called to account will in large measure determine their future.

The Tax Reform Act of 1969 of course changed the extent to which foundations can remain legally secret. But even under the new law the degree to which foundations must make available to the public information about their functioning remains largely a voluntary matter, except that they must put considerably more information on the public record in their Internal Revenue Service 990-Information Return. Yet clearly this is viewed as minimal, for another provision of the new law requires foundations, when they file their IRS forms, to place simultaneously "in a newspaper having general circulation" a notice that their IRS form is easily available for inspection for 180 days. Richard Magat of the Ford Foundation has pointed out that before May 17, 1971, which was the first due day for most foundations to file their IRS form under the Tax Reform Act of 1969, a total of 981 foundations had placed their required advertisements in the *New York Law Journal*. Magat commented: "However estimable the *New York Law Journal* may be in other respects, its circulation of 8,969 is somewhat less even than the 33,000 lawyers who practice in New York City." It is apparent that some foundations will surrender their "right" to absolute secrecy with the greatest reluctance. What probably is needed beyond these minimal efforts is a careful analysis by each foundation of the particular audiences presumed to be especially interested in various features of its work, and the preparation of special reports to be disseminated to these special audiences.

Even if all foundations had willingly reported their activities through the many means at their disposal, there is still a question whether they would have satisfied the popular criteria for accountability. Secrecy after all is a relatively superficial problem, an obvious abuse that is already well on the way to being ended. Accountability to popular criteria, on the other hand, is a more complicated issue.

OTHER POPULAR CRITERIA FOR ACCOUNTABILITY

The 1969 law provides some estimates, beyond the matter of secrecy, of what the popular criteria are, and the kinds of questions popular concern will prompt government regulatory agencies to raise. In general these questions will focus on relationships and linkages among the donor's family, the company that generated the foundation's assets, and the foundation's management. Thus the important general indexes to be evaluated will be the proportion of the board from the family, the proportion of foundation assets invested in the company, and the freedom of foundation management from ties either to the family or the company. Where foundation holdings in the company are large in proportion to total foundation assets, and especially when they are large in proportion to total company assets, then rate of divestiture will be an important index. Where board members are largely company-related or family-related, then the rate of decline in their proportional representation will be of interest. Similarly the selection of staff on the basis solely of professional and managerial criteria is likely to be of interest to regulatory agencies, although current political concerns about religious, racial, and ethnic balance may be of interim interest. Over the long run the larger concerns about the quality and direction of grant making, the financial relations with family and company, and the "arm's length" performance of foundation management are likely to persist as major concerns of the regulatory agencies. Clearly there is already abundant evidence that, while most of the prestigious foundations already had their houses in order, many improvements have occurred in all of these indexes since the passage of the 1969 Tax Reform Act.

RISK TAKING

Foundation work would be severely hampered without a significant margin for risk taking. Foundations have no external constituency, no voters, customers, or advertisers. This gives the foundations, in theory at least, the flexibility to adapt quickly to changes in society and to operate on the cutting edge of innovation. There are few social institutions with this built-in flexibility, and to eliminate them would be as serious a loss. Yet critics of foundations point out that few foundations seize their opportunities. Because of this flexibility, foundations, though operating with government in many fields, should be able to find areas of action that do not over-lap government services, and with the relatively small funds at their disposal support the experimental, play with the contro-versial, "comfort the afflicted and afflict the comfortable," provided of course, that they are willing to take the political heat that such a course often generates. Finding such a course is difficult, for the programs of the federal government are so diverse in research, health, and welfare activities, and in education, that a casual defi-nition of foundation programs in these areas is no longer sufficiently discriminating to be pioneering. At the same time, although it is expected that foundations will use their wealth as a lever to redress some of the inequities of American society, it is unrealistic to ex-pect them to do so by funding socially and politically controversial projects. At their best they appear now to be making contributions to improvement of the human condition by supporting efforts to generate new knowledge. Beyond that, one can hope only for moderately specific variations on the established and traditional foundation concerns that will contribute creatively to a wide range of human needs.

Like investors, foundations can be arrayed according to their grant-making policies on a continuum from conservative to rash. As the conservative banker contrasts with the stock market "gun-slinger," so foundations can calculate the risks involved in grant making and decide whether they will play the conservative game or face the possibilities of enormous losses in playing for enormous social gains. Foundations generally have stayed pretty much at the conservative-banker end of the grant-making continuum and are found playing the solid, low-risk, socially and politically acceptable conservative game. Donald Young comments:

> In so expending their funds foundations are serving the main function for which they have been granted privileged status by society. It is an

important function—if only because the resulting diversity of support and direction of scientific, educational, and charitable efforts is needed to help avoid stultifying homogeneity in management and operation.

Little more than this can be realistically anticipated from foundations as they exist today. The gnawing question for the future is whether that will be enough.

In closing I emphasize again the limitations imposed by my heavy reliance on very limited personal experience, experience that no doubt has been singularly blessed, for it has not equipped me to answer any of these questions, so important to many a foundation official. What do you do with the founder who has whims of iron? Or the tunnel-visioned staff member whose schooling in a particular mode of thought makes him view fresh ideas as naive or heretical? Or the one so emotionally involved with pet projects that he loses objectivity? Or the aggressive one who competes with others for larger sums and more prestigeful projects? Or the trustee who relies more heavily on cocktail party chit-chat than on reviews by the staff? Or the powerful politico, adept at arm-twisting? It would be presumptuous for me to attempt to diagnose problems like these, or to prescribe remedies, having never experienced them. Perhaps, if my good fortune holds, I never will. But if it does not, then my responses may be the stuff of a future paper, possibly entitled "After the First Seven Years."

Orville G. Brim, Jr.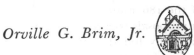

8

Do We Know What We Are Doing?

Knowledge and Decision Making

At Russell Sage Foundation in 1972 we were in the middle of a review of our work of the past ten years. In this period we appropriated about $13 million in support of 186 major studies or programs in the social sciences, mainly sociology. In this decade we turned down requests that were outside of the foundation's program—that is, out of the fields of current interest—at the rate of twenty proposals per week, or some ten thousand rejections. Among these were a number of excellent ideas close to, but not within, the areas of interest of the foundation. Note what this means: we already had made a decision about certain general problems of concern—broadly defined as "program areas."

In addition to these ten thousand "out of program" rejections, we turned down, at the rate of about five per week, proposals in the social sciences in our areas of interest, but in our judgment, without outstanding merit. Over the decade, this sums to twenty-five hundred more rejections. And, we gave serious staff review, leading to eventual rejection, to at least two proposals a week for the ten-year

Author and consultant, ORVILLE G. BRIM, JR., *was president of Russell Sage Foundation, 1964–72. He has been a member of numerous public commissions in the social sciences and serves on the boards of several eleemosynary organizations. Dr. Brim has written, or joined in writing, seven books in social science and more than two-score articles and reports.*

period, totaling another one thousand turndowns. Note again what this means: we were deciding which specific questions, within our general choice of problem areas, were best.

Of the 186 studies we supported, about 60 percent were selected from proposals coming from the outside. The other 40 percent were initiated by foundation staff. For the proposals started internally, the ratio of eventual support to rejection is substantially greater for the clear reason that we started within the areas of foundation interest. When staff-initiated ideas are rejected, it is because on further examination the question cannot be formulated or turns out not to be significant, or the time is not right, or it costs too much, or it is impossible to find someone competent and willing to do the work.

Russell Sage Foundation was started in 1907, when there were only a half-dozen other foundations in America, most smaller. During its half-century of history prior to the last decade, many decisions on appropriations were made. Moreover, Russell Sage Foundation is not one of the larger foundations: with its 45-million-dollar endowment, it ranks about seventy-fifth in size of assets, and about the same in amount of annual appropriations. There are, then, nearly 75 larger foundations where administrators are making decisions about where the money should go. At the same time, following after Russell Sage Foundation in size of assets or appropriations are another twenty-five thousand or so similar institutions. Let us say that out of this class of institutions there are perhaps one thousand where the donor and/or the administrators take their philanthropic work most seriously and aspire to a high level of performance as a foundation. Not all of these have "professional staff," for Zurcher and Dustan[1] report there are only about one thousand full-time foundation administrators in the United States (and over four hundred of these work for two foundations: Ford and Rockefeller). Nevertheless, professional staff or not, a substantial number of medium- or smaller-sized foundations attempt seriously to make wise and just decisions about the allocation of money.

With all of these decisions being made, and having been made

[1] Arnold J. Zurcher and Jane Dustan, *The Foundation Administrator: A Study of Those Who Manage America's Foundations* (New York: Russell Sage Foundation, 1972).

over decades, affecting the course of the lives of many persons, either directly or indirectly, one might suppose that each foundation, and foundations collectively, had accumulated a body of knowledge which led them directly to wise and effective administrative decisions about the most productive allocation of the money at their disposal. Indeed, we would expect foundation executives and administrators to be making decisions on the basis of knowledge about outcomes of their alternative actions, that is, foreseeable consequences of their decisions about who gets money. Instead, there is almost no codified information about "grants" and their outcomes which conceivably could be helpful to the foundation administrator. The fact is that these tens of thousands of decisions about what areas to go into, how the site should be selected, which person should receive money to do the work, when it is time to change, how a project should be administered, are based on such information and personal predilection as the administrator may have accumulated at that stage in life. There are a few maxims and some "traditional wisdom" that is shared among foundation executives and trustees, but it is very soft stuff, useful mainly in disposing of proposals for expeditions to capture an Abominable Snowman, or fervent but far-out requests, often hand-lettered in two colors— and occasionally full four-color jobs with arrows, mottos, flying objects, and exclamation points.

This ignorance exists whether a foundation tries to introduce change into society or seeks to maintain and strengthen existing institutions—libraries, hospitals, universities . . . Irving Kristol notes that planned social change usually has more unanticipated consequences that on the whole are less desirable than were expected, and this probably applies equally well to efforts to maintain existing American institutions.

At present these many decisions are made with inferior information. Most foundation trustees and executives clearly do not know what they are doing, in the sense that they do not know the consequences of the decisions they make for the society in which we live. Now, hardly anyone ever knows except occasionally in his life just "what he is doing" in terms of his influence on the world in which he lives, but life decisions must be guided by the information on hand, quite variable in its certainty from one person to the next and one situation to the next. The traditional wisdom drawn upon in foundation operations provides only partial information at best and compared with what most individuals use in personal decisions it is probably inferior.

However, the knowledge resources of the executive can be improved. The premise is that the best information is that tied to the organization's performance and directly related to known characteristics of the decision about appropriation of money and the characteristics of the project that receives these funds. Obviously lacking in the foundation field is the most valuable information from evaluations of foundation activities, i.e., knowledge derived from studies of performance, related to characteristics of decision and project. Informal as well as more formal scientific evaluative information is lacking. The executive is cut off from the usual flow of informal evaluation feedback, as well as the more systematic and more valuable formal evaluation of his work that might come from systematic analysis of empirical data.

Five Levels of Desired Evaluative Information

Diverse motives power the world's institutions: the universities, science, business corporations, and certainly foundations. Administrators pursue fame, power, love, prestige and money, not only good works or contributions to knowledge. But regardless of the diversity of motives, foundation administrators have a common interest: each wonders how he is doing. Did things work out the way he thought they would? Is he doing better than he expected? Is he doing better than someone else is doing, or might do in his place? Can his job, and indeed his institution, be justified, when there are other uses for the money he controls? As Zurcher and Dustan[2] point out in their survey of foundation administrators, respondents stated that the most frustrating aspect of their work comes from "the failure of a foundation to evaluate performance and measure what it does."

The administrator shares with the public this interest in how he is doing. The disgruntled rejected applicants, though not always vocal, still want to know "Why him, or her, and not me?" and often

[2] Zurcher and Dustan, op. cit.

look in silent interest at the course of success or failure of some foundation's project and smile inside and silently say, "I told them so," when a competitor fails. And the public, through its institutions, has a stake in the success or failure of foundations. The Tax Reform Act of 1969 challenged foundations to defend their position as contributors to pluralism, socially and politically, in a way distinguished from those activities of government and business. And, of course, in the two decades prior to the 1969 Act there were, through congressional activity, substantial expressions of public interest as to whether the public was getting its money's worth from the tax exemption granted to private foundations.

Knowledge gained from evaluation should have more than just personal interest to foundation administrators, for it may help them to sustain the institution in American life. Foundations have a fragile position in American life. Perhaps their case was proved during one period in history and their position was secure during the first four or five decades of this century, or better yet, prior to 1940. Still, like other institutions, their position is not won for all time, but must continually be maintained in a changing society, and now especially as the public sector assumes many of their former functions in society. In the absence of evidence one can argue that the waste is very high, and this belief, over time, erodes society's confidence in our efforts. Paraphrasing Oliver Wendell Holmes' "four generations of idiots are enough," American society may soon say that four generations of foundations are enough and discard the tax-exempt foundation as an experiment that has not paid off.

What is it that the administrator, and other persons, would like to know? *First,* there are questions about specific projects. What actually happened during the course of this project or study or grant? Ordinarily this interest is sparked when it seems that one particular project turned out to be unusually good, or unusually bad and troublesome, in the eyes of the executive, or the trustees, or the grant recipients, or the constituency involved, as might be true with schoolteachers, legal aid clients, or users of public libraries. The question is what actually happened—the who, what, when, where, and how, or the "who did what to whom?" type of inquiry.

Comparing two or more projects is the *second* level of information. Is a given project more successful than another of a similar kind? If so, and after the criteria of success presumably have been sorted out, is it because of the person, or the place, or the advice and guidance of the foundation, or for other reasons—or do none of these matter so far as one can tell so that the differential success is beyond our understanding? To the sophisticated administrator, and to the rejected grant applicant, the desirable comparison is whether a funded project is more successful than the competing project that was turned down. Can this question ever be answered?

Whether our program in law and social science is better, more worthwhile, than our program in social indicators and social change, is a question one might ask at Russell Sage Foundation, and it is this interprogram comparison that constitutes the *third* level of information. It is argued, and I certainly agree, that program areas are necessary in a foundation to set rational limits for planning and staffing and accumulating knowledge and sustaining effort so that a difference can be made. In the larger foundations, of course, there are many program areas; in smaller foundations concentration in a given area is often the practice. How can information be obtained to answer these questions: Should Russell Sage Foundation be in radioastronomy or oceanography rather than applied social science? Should the Markle Foundation have given up its medical scholar program and moved into the mass media? Should the Ford Foundation have phased out its program in the behavioral sciences? We see, now, that the interprogram level of inquiry involves not just comparisons of existing programs, within a foundation, but paralleling the interproject analysis, one must ask whether the program it supports is superior to that program area the foundation has passed by.

Fourth, how do foundations compare with each other? Can it be said that one foundation is better than another? The criterion problem, that is, the judgment of relative success or achievement, seems even more difficult at this level than when one compares projects or programs. Certainly different fields of interest are involved, and different sizes of appropriations. Nevertheless, it is a matter that is much thought about, at least among foundation executives and trustees. Not that this gets into the open very much, but it crops up enough in conversations and especially in annual reports and other institutional documents to make it clear that foundation administrators compare themselves and their institutions with others in the field.

Sometimes the distinction is made between business on the one hand and the nonprofit sector on the other, and the assumption is that the former is competitive and the latter cooperative. This seems to be more of an ideological statement than the actual truth. Cooperation in business organizations is such a natural tendency that antitrust laws barring collusion are a major effort of our times. And on the other hand, the competition between foundations for prestige, publicity, and association with famous grant recipients is impressive to those familiar with the inside picture. A word more should be said here, because foundations do vary substantially in more than their program interests. They vary in their operating style. I have noted distinct variability among foundations in such administrative matters as the contractual relationship with the grant recipient, the formality of the proposal and budget, the information presented by the staff to the trustees for the latter's decision, the way in which a proposal is suggested at staff meetings (i.e., does an individual staff member serve as protagonist, or are they all funneled through the executive officer?), the day-to-day or week-to-week control over the progress of a given activity, and so on. There is, then, enough variation in foundations, and enough competition for excellence among foundations so that if it were ever possible to sensibly compare their relative achievements, the information yielded might prove revolutionary.

Finally, the *fifth* and most elevated level of information would demand a comparison between the foundation's goals and activities and those of other institutions, public and private, pursuing public good. Would funds now going into foundations, or currently administered by foundations, be better employed by operating philanthropies such as libraries, hospitals, or universities, or by public agencies such as social rehabilitation services, or the Office of Economic Opportunity, or the National Endowment for the Humanities? Are foundation goals better than or different from those of other institutions concerned with income redistribution, public education, provision of health services, maintenance of historical landmarks, or preservation of wilderness? Can foundations justify their survival as an institution in American society on the basis of comparisons with alternative uses of the foundations' assets? Can we know whether society really is getting its money's worth?

The Usual Lack of Evaluative Information

INSTITUTIONAL ISOLATION

If, as I assume, foundation staffs and trustees are seriously interested in getting information, why does this group of American men and women so often fail to have the knowledge about their work and its effects that they want and need in order to make sensible decisions? I see a failure of the institution, rather than the administrators—a structural, not a personal problem. Foundations put their executives in a unique position in our society. The fact is that they operate with few, if any, reality checks. They are cut off from the natural flow of evaluative information that other institutions receive in American life. They do not know whether they are doing what they think they are doing—or whether what they are doing makes any difference to anyone or not. Institutional isolation breeds narcissism and illusory feelings of power, and separates administrators from the frontiers of thought.

The isolation is manifest in social process in five ways. First, foundation executives and trustees operate in a high state of autonomy. There are no voters to elect them, and no stockholders to judge their actions. Only rarely can the popular will be expressed in any effective mode of influence over foundations. This happened just recently in the Tax Reform Act of 1969. New constraints on foundations were widely supported, and the foundation administrators were shocked to realize that they were not held in high repute, and indeed had few supporters among the public. Characteristically enough, the response was not to reexamine the kinds of questions to which foundation funds were being directed, but to conclude that foundations were not getting their story told well enough and that the public did not appreciate the value of their work.

Secondly, there is no readily accessible hard-headed impersonal way to evaluate the performance of foundation administrators. There are no performance statistics; no batting average; no earned-run average. There is no bottom line showing profit or loss for the year's activity. There is no way to use dollar value as a measure of performance to check one's work. If a corporation wanted to buy a foundation, as they might a profit-making company, there is no way to make the usual appraisal. Dollar for dollar, would one pay more for Commonwealth or Carnegie? Would the Grant Foundation be more profitable than the Twentieth Century Fund?

Third, foundation executives and trustees are socially encapsulated. Surveys show that over 90 percent are eastern, male Wasps, and they live surrounded by friends and colleagues from the same background. They are effectively prevented by the social system from challenging contact with, and external criticism from, people of different viewpoints. The restricted sociometric network closes off penetration from the outside or escape from the inside. Dealing with applicants outside of their little circle generates credentialism of the highest degree because the executives have no other kind of experience to draw on. Moreover, there is little turnover in foundation administrators or trustees. There is almost no exchange of personnel between foundations, and while tenure is not the rule for foundation administrators, they do stay on and on and on. Boards of trustees tend to be self-perpetuating bodies, with no term limit or age limit on reelection.

Fourth, foundation executives rarely deal in truth in exchanges with their primary constituency—their grant applicants. When one is appointed to a foundation post, the usual line is "Congratulations, you'll never have another bad lunch, or hear another honest word." Few people will bite the hand that eventually might support them; when grant applicants speak critically, they speak with low voices.

Fifth and finally, foundations lack natural enemies in our society. This has two consequences. While there are some occasional critics, some muckraking, some intelligent challenges, there is a virtual absence of a body of criticism compared with what is received by other American institutions, such as universities, hospitals, government, and corporations.

There is no systematic continuous monitoring by journalists; no features, no foundation beat, no section on philanthropy, no continuing coverage. Nor is there any deadly competition from other institutions in American life; deadly, that is, in the sense that other institutions seek to put foundations out of business. In a sense, one might say that foundations have enemies, in that the projects that they support may be intrusive and disrupt other people's values. But it is really the project that has enemies, and the project directors take the punishment. The foundation is protected by its phalanxes of external grant recipients. The public, through the federal government, makes occasional intrusions into foundation autonomy, which may become more serious, but are not yet a mortal challenge. Foundations have no competing corporations, no competing technologies, no situation of scarce goods or resources, no competition for membership, no dependence on fund raising drives—none of the rough and tumble of dangerous competition that produces the sharpest information about where one stands vis-à-vis friends and enemies in the day-to-day course of work.

BASIC CONCEPTS OF EVALUATION RESEARCH

For the more formal systematic methods of getting the facts about how one is doing, the same lack exists and again for structural and contextual reasons. There is no easy, or perhaps even feasible, way to bring to bear on foundation activities the social science arsenal of evaluation procedures. Experimental designs, for instance, demand that what would be rejected proposals be funded on a random basis, and approved projects turned down in their place; target populations should be selected on a random basis in many cases, rather than for special need; objectives should have measurable criteria of success or failure, and so on. Nevertheless, since we will return to consideration of certain quasi-experimental fact-gathering efforts, we should have the basic concepts before us so we know what we are missing. Selected theoretical works on evaluation research elaborate these very well.[3]

[3] Donald T. Campbell, "Reforms as Experiments," *American Psychologist*, 24 (April 1969).

Francis G. Caro (ed.), *Readings in Evaluative Research* (New York: Russell Sage Foundation, 1971).

Jack Elinson, "Effectiveness of Social Action Programs in Health and Welfare" (1967).

Gerald Gordon, Odin W. Anderson, Henry P. Brehm and Sue Marquis, *Dis-*

Evaluation research is the application of social research to provide the administrator with accurate information on the consequences of his action. The main aim is to measure the benefits received from the program, particularly with respect to objectives that have been set by the program, and to relate these to costs incurred. More specifically, evaluative research must determine the extent to which a program achieves its goals, the relative impact of key program variables, and the role of the program itself versus external variables or influences. Even more hardheaded and more specific, the issues of methodological approach to the examination of goals and underlying assumptions of an activity have been succinctly delineated by Suchman.[4] (See Rieker.[5]) His contention is that the social scientist's approach must be different from the impressionistic evaluative procedures assumed by administrators, politicians, and journalists. Such an approach can be substantiated by (1) extensive examination of objectives of a program (including underlying assumptions); (2) development of measurable criteria specifically related to these objectives; (3) establishment of controlled situations

ease, the Individual, and Society: Social-Psychological Aspects of Disease: A Summary and Analysis of a Decade of Research (New Haven: College and University Press, 1968).

Caroline Hodges Persell, *The Quality of Research on Education: An Empirical Study of Researchers and Their Work* (Columbia University [BASR], May 1971).

Patricia P. Rieker, "Reflections on Evaluative Research: A Comprehensive Paper" (University of Pittsburgh, unpublished paper).

Alice M. Rivlin, *Systematic Thinking for Social Action* (Washington, D.C.: Brookings Institution, 1971).

Peter H. Rossi, "Practice, Method and Theory in Evaluating Social Action Programs," in Daniel P. Moynihan, ed., *In Understanding Poverty* (New York: Basic Books, 1969).

Peter H. Rossi and Walter Williams (eds.), *Evaluating Social Programs: Theory, Practice, and Politics* (New York, Seminar Press, 1972).

Eleanor B. Sheldon and Howard Freeman, "Notes on Social Indicators: Promises and Potential," *Policy Sciences*, 1 (1970), pp. 97–111.

Edward A. Suchman, *Evaluative Research* (New York: Russell Sage Foundation, 1967).

Carol Weiss (ed.), *Evaluating Action Programs: Readings in Social Action Education* (Boston: Allyn and Bacon, 1972).

Carol Weiss, *Evaluative Research* (Englewood Cliffs, N.J.: Prentice Hall, 1972).

Walter Williams, *Social Policy Research and Analysis* (New York: American Elsevier Publishing, 1971).

[4] Suchman, op. cit.

[5] Rieker, op. cit.

to determine the extent to which these objectives and negative side effects are achieved.

In order to determine and to measure the conditions influencing success or failure beyond the stated goals, Suchman has provided six aspects of a program around which variables could be determined for comparison:

1. Content—What is to be changed in terms of dimension of knowledge, beliefs, attitudes, and motivation

2. Target of program—What individuals, groups, organizations, communities, or social systems are to be affected

3. Time within which change is to occur—Immediate, intermediate, and/or long-range objectives

4. Number of objectives—Unitary or multiple

5. Is extent of expected effect aimed at widespread or concentrated results, impact or just coverage

6. Four subsidiary categories of effect
    a. Effort—amount of action
    b. Performance—degree of adequacy
    c. Process—how effect was achieved
    d. Efficiency—effect with respect to cost

I doubt that we will see any true program experiments along these lines in the next few years. Still, approximations to these specifications are possible; and the experimental attitude of mind is an important side product.

The State of Foundation Evaluations

I have said that most foundation administrators have a serious interest in finding out how they are doing. Also there is continuing exhortation both from within their ranks and from the outside to carry out more studies of how they are doing. The case is made almost routinely in the more recent general texts on foundation management and in statements of foundation philosophy.[6]

---

[6] Conference on Foundations, *The Future of Foundations: Their Institutional Role in Society*—A Condensed Transcript—(The Charles F. Kettering Foundation, 1971).

Merrimon Cuninggim, *Private Money and Public Service: The Role of Foundations in American Society* (New York: McGraw Hill, 1972).

Foundations, Private Giving, and Public Policy: Report and Recommendations

In spite of this interest, and the wide agreement in the administrative field and in the public mind that evaluation is much to be desired, we still have virtually no information relating foundation program consequences to administrative purpose and management. Here is a major class of American institutions numbering in the tens of thousands, a more-than-billion-dollar-a-year enterprise, and yet there are hardly a half-dozen published reports on any substantial efforts at evaluation of foundation activities.

INFORMAL

The administrators of foundations seem trapped in foundation lore about how decisions should be made. Many of the general works on foundation management attempt to codify this lore of the "profession" of foundation administration, dealing with such matters as the timing of an appropriation, that is, whether circumstances are right, the degree to which one should be active versus passive in developing grants, whether flexibility or sharp concentration in a field should be the rule, whether the venture capital investment model is appropriate, and so on.

But, wise as some of these observations may seem to be, much of the traditional wisdom consists of unexamined maxims which have come to be rather comfortable substitutes for hard-headed evaluative information. Many of these guidelines lead one to think

of the Commission on Foundations and Private Philanthropy (Chicago: University of Chicago Press, 1971). The Peterson Commission Report.

Fritz F. Heimann, "Developing a Contemporary Rationale for Foundations," *Foundation News,* Vol. 13, No. 1 (Jan/Feb 1972).

Irving L. Horowitz and Ruth L. Horowitz, "Tax Exempt Foundations: Their Effects on National Policy," *Science,* 168 (April 1970), pp. 220–228.

Waldemar Nielsen, *The Big Foundations* (New York: Columbia University Press, 1972).

Eugene C. Struckoff, "Should 'The Trusts' Publish a Report, 1955–1972?" (The Spaulding-Potter Charitable Trusts, 1971).

Stephen White, "Steps Toward Evaluation of Foundation Activities," *The MBA,* Vol. 5, No. 2 (Nov. 1970), pp. 8–18.

Alan Barnes, Evaluation of Activities of the Biomedical Sciences Division at (January 1968), pp. 1–4.

Donald R. Young and Wilbert E. Moore, *Trusteeship and the Management of Foundations* (New York: Russell Sage Foundation, 1969).

Arnold J. Zurcher, *The Management of Foundations* (New York: New York University Press, 1972).

Zurcher and Dustan, op. cit.

mistakenly that he is evaluating his work. One is that, "If you don't fail one out of four times in your projects, then you are not taking enough risk." This kind of thinking permits foundation administrators to shift their losses into the credit column, by saying the failures demonstrate their willingness to take chances. To my knowledge no one has ever examined whether those that failed were in fact viewed at initiation as high-risk projects. Examination might show instead that most or all the failures fall into the low-risk category.

The various informal attempts at evaluation range from case study reports on specific projects to the higher levels of generality —interfoundation comparisons and foundations contrasted with other institutions. Some are valuable; most are dangerous. What should concern us is the production of false and misleading information by untrained and incompetent reporters under the banner of solid "evaluation research." For instance, in a book written by a foundation administrative officer surveying the contributions of American philanthropic organizations, the author stated that much to his surprise, upon completing the book, he found that his own foundation was listed more than any other in the index, and thus concluded that it had had the most pervasive influence.

FORMAL

What we do have, on the positive side, are a few published studies of merit, and a few internal evaluation studies that I have had the opportunity to look at but which have not been publicly distributed.[7] The Suchman and Rieker study of the Maurice Falk Medical

---

[7] Winston O. Franklin, "The Delphi Technique as a Program Planning Tool for Foundations," *Foundation News*, XII (May/June 1971), pp. 106–109.

Lawrence Podell, "Evaluation Research Project of the Catalyst Demonstration Project to Employ Mature College-Graduated Women as Caseworkers in Public Welfare in Boston" (Spaulding-Potter Charitable Trusts, 1970).

Eugene C. Struckoff, *A Review of the Program of The New Haven Foundation* (New Haven Foundation, 1970).

Edward A. Suchman and Patricia P. Rieker, *Review and Evaluation of Maurice Falk Medical Fund* (Maurice Falk Medical Fund, 1969).

Alan Barnes, Evaluation of Activities of the Biomedical Sciences Division at Rockefeller Foundation (not distributed).

Robert Goldman, Project Evaluations at the Ford Foundation, Division of National Affairs (not distributed).

Fund and the Struckoff study of The New Haven Foundation are serious scholarly efforts dealing with the program and project levels, in which outcomes are related to objectives, project characteristics, and managerial activities. The information yield is sparse, but valuable. Franklin's report on the use of the Delphi technique at the Charles F. Kettering Foundation deals with evaluation, prospectively, of the merits of alternative programs. Podell's evaluation of a specific project of the Spaulding-Potter Charitable Trusts is well done, a model for a project case study, although it does not make interproject comparisons. Unpublished reports of good quality include evaluations of funded versus rejected projects in the Biomedical Sciences division of The Rockefeller Foundation, Alfred P. Sloan Foundation's evaluation of its Cooperative College Development Program, many project and program assessments at The Ford Foundation, and the appraisal of the Scholars in Medical Science program of the John and Mary R. Markle Foundation. No doubt I have missed some published studies, though I do not think many. I surely have missed some material in the annual reports of foundations, although the bulk of this is innocuously descriptive rather than analytical. And, I am sure, that there are a large number of internal evaluation documents, or at least I hope so, about which the public has no knowledge. Still, in connection with our own Russell Sage Foundation look at the past decade, we discussed the problem with quite a large number of foundation administrators and did not turn up a pool of so-called hidden documents. It appears to me, therefore, that this is more or less the state of affairs.

Two Evaluation Efforts at Russell Sage Foundation

During 1970–1972 we pursued two methods of evaluation at Russell Sage Foundation. One of these, noted previously, looked at the studies of projects supported during the 1960s decade; the other was a year-long analysis and critique of the foundation by

---

Donald B. Strauss, Evaluation of *Scholars in Medical Science* Program of the John and Mary R. Markle Foundation, 1962 (not distributed).

Stephen White, Evaluation Report: Cooperative College Development Program, Sloan Foundation, 1970 (not distributed).

John Wholey, Evaluation of Redevelopment Projects in Urban Locations, Division of National Affairs, Ford Foundation (not distributed).

several radical sociologists. Thinking in terms of the levels of inquiry mentioned above, the first study focused primarily on interproject comparisons, within specific foundation program areas, although there is some interprogram comparison. The radical critique, in contrast, looked primarily at program activities in comparison not with each other but with alternative program possibilities not then being supported by the foundation.

A RADICAL VIEW

Let me take up the radical evaluation first. In the summer of 1970 I employed three radical sociologists in the East to review the program of Russell Sage Foundation from their perspective, and to write a report giving their criticisms and recommendations for changes. We had met in connection with some administrative matters of the Eastern Sociological Society, and it seemed to me in our brief discussions that most of the activities of the foundation, which I and others had initiated in the past half dozen years, were viewed by them as harmful, or at best irrelevant, to the general good of American society. It seemed wise to find out why they believed this. They accepted the invitation to serve as consultants to the foundation on a per diem basis, for as many days and as long a period as would be necessary to complete their evaluation. Our understanding was that the information they obtained, and the report they prepared, were to belong equally to them and to the foundation, with both parties having the right to publish or otherwise distribute the resulting materials.

They were much concerned at the outset, and to some extent throughout, about being co-opted by an "establishment institution" —or perhaps more accurately not about actual co-optation but about the way in which their radical colleagues would view our relationship. It is important to note that their first decision, prior to accepting the appointment, was whether or not Russell Sage Foundation should be terminated, with its endowment put to some other use, or whether it should be maintained and changed. Their conclusion was that it might be possible to work through this institution and help to transform it to something that would better serve their own moral concerns, rather than seek its destruction. I had my own concerns, to be sure. One had to do with possible public embarrassment of my staff colleagues, the foundation trustees, and perhaps the concept of foundations itself. Another had to do with a general uneasiness about the rules of the game. One of our working conditions was that the consultants had direct access to all organization records—and I do mean all. The fact that they would work in the office on weekends and during evenings, when usually no one else was there, took a while to get used to. Nevertheless, over a period of months, a fragile relationship of mutual trust was maintained, and the work went along.

Their procedure was to work only with documents, only with written records. My contribution was to provide as complete an inventory as possible of all organization documents, archival or current. It was not until the draft of their report was prepared and I had read it, that we sat down to discussions of the data they had used and their interpretations. At that time the operating rules were that they would accept changes of fact, where the records might be misleading, or had omitted something. Also, they eliminated from the report a number of statements imputing motives, so-called "mind-reading" statements, that went beyond the data and in fact, as they recognized, were in contradiction to their research principles. Finally, we discussed a number of interpretations of the analysis. I learned a lot in these post-report discussions. I believe that they did too. A number of their conclusions and recommendations were acceptable almost at once; on others there was discussion and some reworking. On other recommendations there was simply honest disagreement.

Specifically, their report was a narrative account of findings and some statistical data concerning the functions and activities of the Russell Sage Foundation as they delineated the inability of philanthropic organizations in general to contend with the hard-core problems confronting society. The researchers considered the foundation's activities from 1948 through 1970. They based their findings upon examination of (1) trustee agendas and minutes; (2) staff memoranda; (3) annual reports; (4) résumés and proposals; (5) other documents pertaining to the foundation and its role in the social sciences; and (6) later on, interviews with major foundation personnel and associates. However, the team did not interview grant recipients; did not directly observe the staff's decision-making processes nor its interaction; and did not make inquiries into policy circles concerning the effects of foundation programs.

Four major substantive discussions constituted this document: the structure of the foundation; its operations; its external linkages; and how the effects of its structure, activities, and linkages were manifest in the kind of appropriations made during the twenty-year period.

In examining the structure of the foundation, the researchers attested to the professional excellence of the staff and its devotion to social science. However, they felt that it had succeeded in further institutionalizing social science and in becoming more out of touch with society. That the foundation seemed to have failed to produce imaginative ideas that could suggest new, more relevant programs, was due to its upper-middle-class constituency, whose affiliations and perspectives have been too closely aligned with the knowledge industry and the bureaucratic nature of corporate business and government agencies. The radical consultants believed that the trustees and the staff represented the establishment and had accepted the theory of social change in which social scientists function as a knowledge transmission belt for the rational policy-makers who are supposed to be the agents of social change.

Summarizing operational strategies, the researchers found that Russell Sage Foundation sought to: (1) promote social science and its utilization within practicing professions, e.g., law, education, medicine; (2) promote efficiency and effectiveness of existing organizations; and (3) mitigate some of the human and social costs of technology, specialization, bureaucratization, and racism. Selection of a project seemed to be based on its potential to fulfill at least one of five developmental rules: (1) to enhance the foundation's scholarly reputation; (2) to increase its influence in sociology; (3) to last beyond the life of initial funding by creating new professional positions or by producing publications; (4) to achieve outside funding beyond the foundation's initial support; and (5) to make possible the determining new target opportunities.

Several guidelines seemed inherent in the foundation's activities in order to seek new ideas and to implement programs: (1) the selection of highly qualified professional personnel (many of whom had had prior contact with the foundation); (2) the establishment of a power base within target organizations it was trying to change; and (3) the sponsoring of conferences, symposia, commissions, and organizations in order to reach the outside environment.

Nonetheless, the team drew the following conclusions about the foundation's spectrum of influence: (1) it had restricted its organizational linkages to the knowledge industry, i.e., social science and its elite personnel, in order to control the organizational structures of the social sciences; (2) its dissemination practices had been restricted to the knowledge industry with little attention to influencing policy-makers; and (3) it had remained totally isolated from insurgent and oppressed groups and has thus decreased the amount of knowledge available to the members of society who need it in order to solve their problems.

The concluding section of the report consisted of specific recommendations to Russell Sage Foundation as a key institution in the organization of the social science enterprise. In general, it was recommended that the foundation should "consider as its constituency the powerless majority of American people and support through its research and actions political movements and social movements which seek to establish democracy and equality."

After receiving the report, we had a number of staff and trustee discussions of the specific recommendations. For instance, we had never really solved the problem of what to do with grant applicants with important ideas who lack the evident credentials to carry out the work. Since lack of credentials and critical insurgency tend to be correlated, we found ourselves pressed into working with academics or less exciting challenges. Now we deal with each of these as special cases, and make provision for substantially more staff inquiry into the uncredentialized competence of the grant applicant. We instituted a fund from which grants for planning research projects can be made, with this money being marked for a class of applicants who have unusually creative research ideas, but who for various reasons have been unable to obtain support. These funds provide for expert consultation in setting up the study and in plans to monitor its progress.

With respect to dissemination of the results of some of our studies, the consultants noted that the very fine report by Scott on services for the blind [8] was given free distribution, with accompanying publicity, to administrators of agencies for the blind, but not to leaders of critical groups, nor was any provision made for a Braille edition and its distribution so that the blind clients of the agencies might have in their possession the powerful critique that Scott made of agency operations. The important book by Moskos on enlisted men[9] was made directly available, with promotional material, to military officers, administrators, and agencies, but not to organized groups of veterans. And the influential guidelines for elementary and secondary school record keeping, developed by David H. Goslin and his colleagues[10] and specifically directed to the protection of privacy by parents of their children's school records, was widely distributed to professionals and administrators in education, but not to organized groups of parents. I hardly need to say that we now give much more attention to the audience of a particular study, to how the work might be used by counter-establishment groups in our society, and to the wider dissemination of results.

We disagreed, as noted, on several points. For instance, the sentiments of the foundation administration were against providing on the board of trustees for specific, designated representation of the many diverse views in American society of what the foundation might do. Instead, further effort would be made to expose the organization to challenges. Productive tension would be sought, but not paralyzing conflict.

INTERPROJECT COMPARISONS

As stated above, about $13 million was appropriated in support of 186 projects or studies at Russell Sage Foundation during the decade of the 1960s. We had a natural interest in what happened to these projects, and whether we could rank them according to different degrees of "success" so that we might gain some insight into why some went better than others. Unlike the radical consultant report,

[8] Robert A. Scott, *The Making of Blind Men* (New York: Russell Sage Foundation, 1969).
[9] Charles C. Moskos, Jr., *The American Enlisted Man* (New York: Russell Sage Foundation, 1970).
[10] *Guidelines for the Collection, Maintenance and Dissemination of Pupil Records* (New York: Russell Sage Foundation, 1970).

this one had not yet yielded results in 1972, but there were some instructive aspects of the research which are worth discussing.[11]

Our first step was to classify the appropriations by type, according to the general objective of the project. Most of Russell Sage Foundation activity had been in the area of applied social science, and 110 of the 186 projects were classified as "research projects." These were research studies, oriented to publication of results; an example is Kurt Back's study of sensitivity training, and his book, *Beyond Words*. The second class consisted of research and training programs (N = 11); an example here is the support of the Center of the Study of Law and Society at the University of California, Berkeley. These tended to be large, long-term, expensive projects, and they constituted an important part of the foundation's activity during the decade. Institutional support and development activities (N = 9) made up the third class; included here are appropriations to the Institute for Advanced Study, Princeton, New Jersey, to help in the first steps in establishing a School of Social Science.

Fourth were training programs (N = 10), including fellowship programs for postdoctoral training in law schools and fellowships in social science and journalism. A fifth category, "planning projects," was needed to take care of some fifteen appropriations; an example here is an appropriation to the law school at Stanford University to plan a program on law and social science. The sixth category included projects in "dissemination" (N = 16). Examples here are the support of a half dozen conferences to exchange information, support of the *Law and Society Review*, appropriations to the Foundation Center in support of the *Foundation Directory*. Seventh, and last, were the fifteen visiting scholars who had spent up to a year in residence at the foundation planning new work or completing work in progress, and participating in foundation staff activities during the year.

Data about each project were available from the records; these included age, sex, and organization of principal investigators, type

[11] This research study was under the direction of Dr. Lindsey Churchill, associate professor, Department of Sociology, Graduate Division of the City University of New York, and former staff member at Russell Sage Foundation, in collaboration with the author. Michele Kucker and Arlene Amidon assisted with the study.

of fiscal agent, size of appropriation, whether or not additional contingency or supplemental appropriations were made, the duration of the project, whether it was internally or externally initiated, the area of foundation program interest, and others.

A questionnaire with some three dozen new questions was distributed to all the project directors. The primary purpose was to find out certain outcomes of the project activities. Both objective (publications, public appearances, university courses taught, etc.) and subjective (attitudes, etc.) items were used. More data about the project characteristics and characteristics of the director also were obtained from the questionnaire: e.g., changes in his occupational life that interfered with or facilitated work on the project; other changes in his life, such as illness or personal matters.

Even from the simple frequency distributions of projects by selected characteristics we find some provocation to thought. The distribution of the projects by age shows few project directors to have been 50 or over, and even fewer under 29: why, in particular, was the mature social scientist underrepresented? Only 9 of the 186 projects were given to nonuniversity-based research institutes: this had never set a policy, so what was the reason for this uneven distribution? An examination of the duration of funded projects shows a bimodal distribution, with high frequency in the 6- to 18-month category, and another high frequency at the three-year-or-more period. Should we be making more use of projects with a short life, that is, to be completed in six months?

Moving on from the frequency tables, developing the criteria of success or failure is of course the most important and most difficult task and one that we are not at all confident that we can solve in an acceptable way. We expect that we will have to work with imperfect criteria—just how imperfect is yet to be seen. Objective measures are preferable in that they are explicitly based on selected criteria, such as a book production measure that is largely independent of the people doing the evaluation. The major problem is that frequently these are not applicable to all of the projects, or classes of projects, being compared. (Certain of them may be oriented not to scholarly or written production, but rather to training or planning.) Moreover, the consequences of foundation-supported projects are numerous and multidimensional, and using only objective measures means that one usually can appraise only a few of the many possible effects. On the subjective side, general ratings of quality and influence of projects can be made by reviewers familiar with the activity and the field of interest. These global ratings usually can be applied to almost all projects and presumably present a summation of multifold consequences. What we do not know is the "reason" for the overall rating; nor its reliability between raters, or over time with a given rater, nor its validity in the sense of its correlation with what actually took place.

When all this work is done, and the data are at hand, the ratings can be averaged for each project, and for program areas, and then correlated with the various types of project characteristics and administrative processes listed earlier. If we find no strong positive or negative correlations between the various measures of success and the characteristics of projects and methods of operation, then we must consider at least three instructive reasons for the lack of findings. First, the cause may lie in unreliable or invalid ratings of success. Second, we may not have in our battery of potential predictors the truly significant factors that influence differential success of outcomes—we may not have the information in our records, and we did not think to ask it. Or, third, perhaps both the ratings of success and the predictive factors are satisfactory and the reason there is no significant relationship between project outcome and our antecedent predictive characteristics of the project or administration is that success and failure are much too dependent on chance factors, that is, a number of unsystematically distributed effects on the course of a given program that cannot be anticipated. We can speculate about what this would imply for guidelines for "rational" foundation management.

A Look at Federal Evaluation Research

Sharply contrasting with the state of affairs for private foundations, the federal government has developed a strong interest in and commitment to evaluation research of both traditional and innovative social action programs. While, strictly speaking, these federal programs are not grants in the sense used by private foundations, and although there are very few evaluations of true "grants programs," [12] the similarities in the required decision-making process in the allocation of limited funds are close enough so that foundations can learn from these federal evaluation efforts.

There are many specific reasons for employing social research techniques to determine the nature of human resources programs and the allocation of economic and personnel resources to them. As noted, social action programs in health, education, and welfare have been expanding, yet little evidence has accumulated concerning their effectiveness. Moreover, competition is ever increasing for resources, both human and material, and often there is little basis for deciding intelligently where to allocate these resources. Further, policy makers, public administrators, and social researchers now work together more closely; all three groups have come to recognize the potential utility of the evaluation of their efforts. Finally, increased methodological knowledge, the availability of computers, and a better understanding of statistical methods now permit more effective treatment of evaluation data, and thus more sophisticated investigations.

MAGNITUDE

It would not be an exaggeration to say that evaluative research is now a very popular concept. The Office of Management and Budget and the General Accounting Office are active, and Congress itself is insisting that agencies produce real evidence of the effectiveness of their programs. Illustrative of the extent of interest is the fact that certain major legislation (the Economic Opportunity Act of 1964; the Elementary and Secondary Education Act of 1965) included both the requirement for evaluation and the funding for carrying it out. Federal expenditures for evaluation research in fiscal 1970 provided approximately $45 to 50 million in the general areas of social welfare and social services, housing, education, etc., with the largest portion being expended by the Department of Health, Education and Welfare (HEW), and the remainder by the

[12] E.g., Review of Program of National Institute of Mental Health, an internal review under direction of Julius Segal, chief of program planning and analysis, National Institute of Mental Health.

Dorwin Cartwright, "A Study in Research Evaluation: The Case of Research on Group Decision-Making," *American Psychologist* (in press).

Departments of Labor, Justice, Agriculture, and Housing and Urban Development (HUD), and the Office of Economic Opportunity (OEO) and the National Science Foundation. In HEW alone, for instance, in 1969 approximately $5 million went for evaluation; in fiscal year 1970, $18 million, and then $30 million in 1971.[12a]

There is good information on who does the evaluation work, on some of the problems faced in carrying it out, and on the differential quality of evaluation research on social programs. For example, in fiscal year 1970 the $18 million programmed for evaluation research in health, education, and welfare went primarily to profit-making research firms. The distribution was the following:

Type of Organization	Total Evaluation Dollars	Percent
Profit	7,761,413	45
Not-for-profit	4,959,467	29
Universities	3,658,196	21
State and federal gov't agencies	642,273	4
Independent consultants	184,138	1

FREEMAN STUDY

More precise information on who is carrying out the evaluation research of the federal government, and how variable its quality may be, is now becoming available from studies of the field of evaluation research.[13] The Freeman, Bernstein, and Rieker study deals with federally funded evaluation studies initiated in 1970. A list was compiled of all federally funded evaluation studies of social action programs in the areas of health, education, welfare, public safety,

---

[12a] James G. Abert, "Case Studies on Evaluation" (Research in Progress), Russell Sage Foundation.

[13] Abert, op. cit.

Albert D. Biderman and Laure M. Sharp, *The Competitive Evaluation Research Industry* (Washington, D.C.: Bureau of Social Science Research, Inc., 1972).

Committee on Federal Evaluation Research, Division of Behavioral Sciences, National Academy of Sciences–National Research Council.

Howard E. Freeman, Ilene H. Bernstein, and Patricia P. Rieker, "Survey on Evaluation Studies of Social Action Programs," Russell Sage Foundation.

Peter H. Sossi, "Booby Traps and Pitfalls in Evaluation of Social Action Programs," Proceedings of Social Statistics Section of the American Statistical Association, 1966.

income security, manpower, and housing. Additionally, only contracts and grants which were allotted $10,000 or more and whose initiation date was in fiscal 1970 were included. For purposes of drawing as wide a net as possible, studies were included if: (1) they were identified by the federal funding agency to be evaluative studies, (2) the abstract submitted for approval stated that they focused on either the description or the assessment of service, treatment, intervention, or social change programs, and/or (3) they were categorized by the funding agency as either field-experiment, demonstration-research projects, or action-research programs in any of the above stated areas. Approximately 420 studies met the criteria identified above.

Questionnaires were sent to the project directors of each study to obtain a descriptive picture of the type of organization doing evaluation, personnel, etc., and to address the question of how the social context, e.g., organizational characteristics, personnel, nature of target population, and funding arrangements, influence the kind of evaluation done, e.g., measurement of input, measurement of output, and plans for utilization and dissemination of findings.

This study utilizes the five-fold classification of federal grant recipients given just above. Questions often are raised about the quality of the evaluation research done under these different auspices. For instance, a large number of grants and contracts are provided by the federal government to university-affiliated persons and university research centers. The problem is that such funds may be accepted by academicians who in many cases proceed to do research consistent with their theoretical and scholarly interests but not remotely evaluative in terms of program goals. Also, the time budgets of academicians limit their ability to carry out extended field operations. Another important group is composed of profit-making and nonprofit-making corporations which frequently engage in competitive bidding for evaluative research contracts. However, many of these corporations, it is fair to say, do not have the necessary talent and are far more interested in the size and number of grants they solicit than in being able to carry out the research well. Their relation to the sponsoring agency is often that of a customer to supplier, with more concern to satisfy the customer than to do objective evaluation studies.

Freeman's study suggests in its preliminary analyses some conclusions of considerable importance. If these preliminary results hold up, our views of federal evaluation research must be changed. A distinction is made, as it is in most analyses of evaluation research, between a description of how social programs operate, and on assessment of impact. The first measures process, usually according to whether it went in accord with the time plan and the budgetary plan, and the second studies what changes occurred. Rossi[14] in his review of certain federal evaluation programs finds that most of these were primarily loose narrative accounts of the program activities. Although these reports contained so-called systematic social bookkeeping data, they usually lack systematic observations on the effects of the program. The Freeman review finds, perhaps surprisingly, that it is public service agencies, such as the Tennessee welfare department, which most often include measurement of effects or impact in their evaluation studies.

It is also indicated in preliminary results that on the whole, profit-making corporations, while they receive a substantial amount of evaluation money, do less adequate research in terms of sampling techniques, overall design, etc., than the other types of organizations. Related to this is the report that research produced by principal investigators receiving grants is more often of a higher quality than that produced by persons working on contracts; and, as expected, those with higher educational degrees do better quality research than those with lesser degrees. Since profit-making corporations tend to receive contracts, not grants, and have less highly qualified personnel, these facts are correlated.

Another engaging preliminary finding is that when the evaluation of an action program is made by the same organization as that carrying on the program (either with same or different staff), the evaluation is of a higher research quality than when an evaluation is conducted by persons totally independent of the action program, that is, the evaluation and action being done by different organizations. This last finding, of course, goes contrary to the belief in the value of "independence of judgment" and seems to show that knowledge about the program is more valuable to high quality

[14] Rossi, op. cit.

evaluation research than is completely "independent judgment" purchased at the price of substantive ignorance.

POLICY INFLUENCE

The importance of this large and rapidly growing body of evaluation research at the federal level must not be underestimated. The course of American society may be substantially changed by the outcome of these evaluation studies, because of their influence on federal policy. For examples, the results of evaluation of the negative income tax experiment in New Jersey may change the national welfare policy; the results of evaluation of performance contracting by school systems may alter policies in thousands of school districts.

Lessons for the foundations as, and if, they begin to move into evaluation of their activities are still to be dug out from the experience and made explicit, but we will return to some of these emerging guidelines in the discussion that follows.

Innovation in Foundation Evaluation

The positive sentiment of many in our society is that pluralism among our institutions should be maintained, and particularly that there should be organizations relatively free from governmental pressure and not directly subject to the influence of mass public opinion. Foundations have the luxury of this position in our society. It is dangerous, though. The lack of external influence that gives the foundations autonomy also deprives them of any systematic feedback on their performance and influence in American life. Foundations thus are in a position of ignorance which over time is dangerous to society and to their own survival. The primary task of foundations today is to get the information they need about their effects on the world, without losing their freedom.

Earlier five levels of desirable information were delineated: project case studies; comparisons between projects; between programs of a foundation; comparisons between foundations; and comparisons between foundations and alternate forms of grants or philanthropic activity. Evaluations of projects and programs, that is, information dealing with intramural aspects of a given foundation,

seem to me to be quite different from comparisons between foundations themselves, and between them and other institutions. Certain
methods seem appropriate to getting facts about a given foundation's work, whereas the comparisons between institutions demand
different research techniques and may force us to exchange freedom
for information of questionable value.

ELICITING CRITICISM FROM OUTSIDERS

Taking up first the evaluation of projects and programs, we have
noted that foundation administrators are isolated from most of the
usual sources of external feedback about their procedures and consequences, and it certainly appears that some of the weaknesses of
the administrators' position can be partly eliminated by deliberate
efforts to introduce reality checks in the day-to-day operation. The
solution is simple in concept: foundations must find their critics and
provide a means for them to speak!

POLLS

As for the public voice being heard, periodic systematic taking of
opinion would seem straightforward. An informed public is a
requisite for getting useful data, so the samples to be polled should
stress the potential constituency of a given foundation. For example,
with reference to the programs of social-science oriented foundations, samples of judgments from the membership of several social
science professional associations are appropriate. How many know
what is being done? If not many, why not? What are viewed as
frontiers for important work? What might be done by a foundation
that cannot be done by universities, or institutes, or the public
sector?

INVITED CRITIQUES

An approach to evaluation can be made through invited critiques
of foundation programs by outside teams of knowledgeable critics.
Journalists, other foundation executives, experts in the field, are
suggested as good members of "outside review panels." While some
foundation executives make use of consultants and panels and conferences to comment on the effectiveness of their work, most are

friends of the executives, and little effort is made to search for diverse panels to give testimony.

Occupational stagnation can be solved by deliberate policies of staff and trustee turnover, with deliberate intent to bring in enough diversity of viewpoint so that beneficial criticism is produced and new and important ideas hammered out through mutual challenge.

The isolation of the foundation administrator within his own sociometric network is more difficult to solve, because most of our social processes operate to constrain one from breaking out of one's own group. Still, visiting staff members or consultants deliberately selected to challenge the administrator's values in a tough but constructive way would help to open up new horizons.

Systematic questioning of grant recipients during the progress of a given project or program, as well as a terminal questionnaire-based report, would provide the administrator with knowledge about the attitudes and beliefs of recipients and their suggestions for how things might have been done otherwise. This is certainly more than the administrator has at present.

All of these straightforward, not very novel methods may still yield only innocuous feedback. The problem remains that foundations have money; foundation administrators usually are persons of power in our society. Several years ago a number of us in the foundation administrative field were trying to get some impartial research done on foundation activities in the United States and were canvassing likely sites for a well-supported, long-term research center for this purpose. The leading institutional candidate, whose chief executive officer I approached informally on the matter, immediately said *no,* on the clear grounds that since the organization was dependent on grants from foundations, it would be very difficult for him to maintain a critical stance toward the foundation in research reviews, and fatal if he did so.

GRANT APPLICANTS

In casting about for another way to find critics from whom one might learn it seems to me that the rejected grant applicant is a possible source of useful candor that has not been used. To set the stage for the desired interchange, the first move belongs to the administrator. When administrators deal with applicants that they are turning down, or about to cool out, they are less than truthful and substantially less than candid. Someone once said that a foundation executive is a friend who stabs you in the front. Would that it were true. The usual commentary on a rejected proposal is evasive, philanthropic doubletalk that avoids the real reasons for the rejection: "We have nothing but praise for your proposal . . ." or "We shall waste no time in reading it . . ." The bemused rejectees do not understand why the decision was made, and have no true recourse to debate or to challenge constructively the project or program decision. This paragraph, entitled "Japanese Rejection Slip," helps make the point:

> We have read your work with inexpressible pleasure. We swear on the sacred memory of our ancestors that we have never before encountered such a masterpiece. If we publish your admirable work His Majesty the Emperor will undoubtedly insist on its being a model for all future writing and will forbid our publishing any work inferior to yours. Since talents like yours emerge only once in every thousand years, this would put us out of business, and we must therefore refuse your divine work and deposit at your feet, trembling at the thought of the severe judgement we shall receive from future generations for failing to include in our pages, work of such sheer genius.[15]

Where it is clear that the applicant is out of his depth, is clearly proposing work that he or she is incompetent to do, then the administrator owes the applicant a direct answer and comment on that fact. A friend of mine who is a saxophone player says that when he used to judge music competition he wished he had a big rubber stamp that said "Give up!" This may be too rough, but it moves in the right direction. Where the proposal is clearly competent, a quality idea, but outside the foundation's area of interest, this should be accurately stated, and information provided on other more likely funding agencies, as well as how to compete in the foundation's favored areas. This is usually done by most administrators, but the failure is that this "out of program" reply is used in place of candid answers on competence or deep disagreement. In the

[15] *Authors Guild Bulletin,* Reprint from *Survival,* a Civil Defense publication in Alberta, Canada, in 1963 as the contribution of Paul Juhl, news editor of the *Record-Gazette* of Peace River, Alberta.

latter instances we should hope that the reasons will be thought through and clearly set forth, to set the stage for the discussion. To illustrate from a recent letter:

> Your letter of March 28th was a refreshing contrast, in our experience at least, to the murky norm in communications between foundations and applicants. You were open and candid and we appreciate this most sincerely. It gives us an opportunity to speak to your mind directly.
>
> Responding in the same spirit, we disagree strongly with the critique of our proposal which you quoted at length. We think it reflects a limited and defeatist reading of reality within the world of white institutional power and that it is, therefore, inadequate as a basis for judging the effectiveness of . . . as a strategy for promoting change within the world.

One long and candid discussion per week with a legitimate antagonist—one viewed as incompetent, one viewed as irrelevant, or wrong, and one viewed as close to the foundation's work but with a low priority—in which the administrator is required to defend his position would be an instructive novelty. If these sessions were recorded and made available for comment by various critics of different ideological persuasions, then each would constitute a case study of how decisions can be made and worked through, the analysis of which would give much both to the executive and to the rejected applicant.

The foregoing has dealt with eliciting criticism from outsiders. Moving on now to consider what might be done on the inside—by the administrator—I want to mention three matters: record-keeping, case analyses of successes and failures, and quasi-experimentation in evaluation.

RECORD-KEEPING

First, project or program record-keeping for most foundations, even among the top 200 or so in size, is not geared to providing good information about the course and outcome of a program or project, so that evaluative judgments can be made later. Full record-keeping should have data about characteristics of the project's personnel, the project itself, and the site, as well as data about the foundation side of the matter, that is, minutes on the decision, informal records concerning the estimated degree of hazard or confidence, some clear statement of objectives and the time schedule of work to meet them, and so on. The administration should provide for systematic periodic monitoring of the project during its life, with standard rating data on budget control, personnel management, adherence to time schedule, and the like, as well as field notes, being made part of the project or program file. This minimal information provides a basis for subsequent quasi-evaluative models to be employed if one wishes, and certainly should help to stimulate the foundation administration to think about what each effort is trying to do, and what is going right or wrong during the course of its life. All of this reaching out for information, even though simple, descriptive and factual in nature, causes one to think about data in relation to outcomes and decisions and sets the stage for more sophisticated inquiries.

CASE ANALYSES

Second, foundation administrators usually have a sense of what are their specific successes and failures both among projects and program areas. My own inquiries at Russell Sage Foundation and elsewhere demonstrate that administrators can rank completed studies or projects according to degree of success. Without considering right now what criteria are being used, this fact provides a basis for two or three interesting and potentially valuable studies.

One could profitably spend some time analyzing those instances ranked as most successful. Professional journalists, viewed as informal investigators, might be employed to "get the facts" and tell the story, a technique used by a number of foundations. Beyond this, in instances where ratings of studies by knowledgeable administrators are in disagreement, recorded discussions of the resolution of their disagreements about the success of the projects would help make evident the criteria involved in their judgments of success and lead on to making these defined and communicable, and therefore available for healthy debate within the foundation.

We might establish a national award contest. The Council on Foundations, the membership organization of foundations, could take the lead. Each member foundation could submit annually three candidates as their best completed programs or projects for that year. A distinguished review committee would then have the responsibility, under Council auspices, to provide annual awards, by categories (according to size, action or research, deliberate seeking of change versus supporting existing organizations, and so on), for the most successful foundation achievement for that year.

If the various annual awards for achievements in literature can survive, with as great diversity as exists in literary production, and with as inexplicit, subjective, and strongly felt criteria for merit as there are in the literary community, then we should be able to do it in the foundation field. These awards would have the merit of focusing national attention on what are alleged to be, by the distinguished review committee and the foundation nominators, the best work of the foundations of that year. Debate about the character of excellence, the criteria used, and all the rest would inevitably follow, as would serious self-examination of project and program by administrators and particularly by foundation trustees concerned with why no nominee from their institution won a prize. If this is too much for the Council on Foundations to assume, as indeed it might be, considering that action on this matter would have to go through a membership screening and approval and could fall by the wayside because of the threat that it promises to be, then why not another institution—a major newspaper or other institution in journalism, or a smaller foundation looking for an important role to play, endowed and therefore not dependent on foundation largess.

Now, if we are to study our successes, we might also study our failures. The professional journalist or other external analyst should be engaged to tell the story of the failure as well as the success. The same revealed difference technique on administrative ratings must be used here, so that the discussion between the disagreeing judges on what constitutes failure elicits the submerged criteria and gets them into a form where the matters can be debated.

We cannot tell what we might turn up here. Foundations, like humans, tend to hide or forget their failures. In annual reports, failing projects are not scandalized, they simply disappear. I know of no data on the number of instances where a foundation has terminated a project rather than let it run its course because it began to look like a failure. Conversely, how many of the projects that failed could one say in retrospect should have been terminated but were not for one reason or another, usually to avoid embarrassment? Of course, foundations would be less interested in portraying their failures to their constituents, to their colleagues and competitors, and to the public, but there seems to be no reason to hold back because of problems of libel, since these are factually straight stories. Rather it is simple embarrassment to the recipient, and some discomfort to the foundation, that seem to keep these skeletons in the closet, even though the insiders know they are there.

QUASI-EXPERIMENTATION

Third on the list of innovative actions by foundation administrators is to engage in quasi-experimental evaluations of projects and programs—to adapt creatively the experimental model to our institutional uniqueness. To begin with, one needs to get into an experimental frame of thought. Foundation projects or programs always are experimental in the sense that there is some uncertainty as to what will happen. This is true not only of the innovative school but also those foundations that believe in standing pat, and supporting ongoing organizations of society. Does the grant to the museum do what everyone believes it does? Should it be used for something else? Should it go to a hospital? Should it go to another museum?

Part of the experimental frame of mind is the belief that the costs of research or action, and the disruption of the smooth administrative procedures of the foundation, and the surliness of the grant recipient, are negligible prices to pay for the time and money that might be saved by the foundation in the years ahead because of what was learned. But this belief should be balanced by caution governing the quasi-experimental procedures. We have learned some things from the federal government about the problem of excess and haste in evaluation. As a forthcoming report from a Social Science Research Council committee[16] states, experimentation is a superior means of getting dependable knowledge about social action, but one cannot advocate an indiscriminate and total adoption of the

---

[16] Forthcoming book-length report of SSRC Committee on Experimentation as a Method for Planning and Evaluating Social Intervention.

procedure. There are many cases in which the program, institutional auspices, the stage of the art and the rest, weigh heavily on the attempt at experimentation and may cause the conclusion that it is not worthwhile in this instance.

From the proposed quasi-experimental activity of foundation administrators we should expect increased sensitivity to questions about their work, their effectiveness, and what is going on, as well as a gain in sharpness about objectives of appropriations and characteristics of their own administrative styles. All of this lays the basis for a further information gain in the times ahead, regardless of the outcome of any given experimental effort. As the Social Science Research Council committee has stated,[17]

> Experimentation usually has some serendipitous advantages too. Designing an experiment forces one to confront certain problems that might otherwise be ignored or left in ambiguity. It forces one to define clearly (and in operational terms) what the objectives of the treatment (the intervention program) are; what effects are expected; and what measures are to be made of effects. Further, one is forced to design requirements to spell out rather explicitly what the treatment will consist of, i.e., what particular actions and operations will be carried out. Furthermore, when the treatment is actually carried out for experimental purposes, program operators will learn much about how to implement their purposes and what some of the obstacles and problems are.

Frequently, the objectives are very fuzzy. Many times during the past decade, social scientists have talked with me about their interests, identifying an area of potential inquiry, and asking "Now, don't I have a problem?" And I have to answer, "Yes, you do, it is a very important problem, but no one is going to finance a problem." A problem is not a critical question; "problems" are the beginning, critical questions are where the action is. Questions are phrased in ways that permit you to establish criteria of whether they are answered or not. At all times, the pressures must be on making the creativity used in identifying significant problem areas yield sharply phrased operational questions, where one can tell if the answer is yes or no or neither.

[17] SSRC committee report, op. cit.

DIFFERENCES OF STYLE

One general area of quasi-experimental evaluation would deal with differences in administrative decision-making and managerial style with reference to a given project or program. There is substantial interfoundation variability in administrative procedures, but there may not be enough natural variation within a given foundation to be worth major examination. In any case, it is better to delineate self-consciously the administrative options and variability for quasi-experimental purposes, than to deal with embedded variations that may be confounded or confused with specific personalities, or program areas, or other historical accidents. Specifically, then, one could introduce into one group of projects, but not another, certain variations to be evaluated. The experimental and control groups of projects could be produced either by matched pairs, or by random assignment of subsets of projects to the experimental or control groups. Each foundation will have its own particular interests to explore. Certain illustrative examples come to mind that I believe have not yet been examined. What if bonuses were awarded, as the Twentieth Century Fund does, for a satisfactory and on-time completion of work, but only to some projects and not to others, to see if the bonus matters? In like manner, what about having the second half of an appropriation contingent on a mid-project review and a satisfactory completion check, the alternative being the termination of the project and retention of remaining funds? Would universities and non-university research institutes accept an appropriation for one of their staff members in which the usual overhead fee to the institution was made contingent, payable at the end, on the successful completion of the staff member's project? Would this be a way of engaging the university or research institute administrative personnel as watchdogs? Would it really make any difference anyway? Could a given foundation administration make the decision and stick to it, whereby one out of ten proposals that fall within its program areas but did not qualify on other grounds (e.g., low competence) was randomly selected and funded in place of one that was recommended and about to be funded, the latter also randomly selected for replacement? Would the yield on the experimentally supported proposals be any different from those initially selected for support? If not, what conclusions must we draw? What if they turn out to be better?

Similarly, would any foundation administration commit itself to a trial program in which in 10 percent of the approved programs or projects, a nearly identical project was also supported, but of course with different personnel and at a different site, with the full knowledge of both projects' personnel? Assuming that there would be variable success during the course of the work and at the termination date between such pairs of funded projects, would the post hoc analyses of the differences turn up any insights into how projects should be set up and administered? Somewhat more experimentally, a foundation could systematically introduce differences between two similar projects at the outset. For instance, we recently had before us at Russell Sage Foundation a proposal from some lawyers for a research study. Administrative discussion seemed seriously concerned with the deficiency of the social science input to the research, but recognized that it was equally a problem requiring the professional knowledge of lawyers. Rather than try to bring together both sets of skills in a forced marriage to a single project, why not support the research twice, with the same objective, the same questions to be answered, but with one study carried out by lawyers, and the matching study by social scientists? Would it really make any difference? Once one gets into it and begins to think about experimentation many more leads come fairly readily to mind.

The Evaluation Expert—If and when the foundation administrator moves ahead in experimentation, the search should be on for the evaluation expert. There are many pitfalls, and much erroneous information, as dangers to the unsophisticated. The layman methodologist, however gifted as an administrator, cannot suddenly become an expert in sampling, questionnaire construction, experimental design, and statistical analysis. I am not trying to make jobs for social scientists, but they do many things of importance in our society, and evaluation research is one of them. Some of the things we have learned from the review of government evaluation are pertinent here in flashing caution signals. The university-affiliated persons have certain timing problems that limit their capability for getting involved in field operations, while the more independent profit-making corporations may not possess the necessary talent and in their relationship to the foundation may be more concerned to satisfy the extraneous interests of the foundation administrator rather than to do good evaluation research. We also saw that the quality of the evaluation research improved when the program administration and evaluation came out of the same organization, that is, from the same staff group. If the foundation administration is to look outside, as it will have to in most instances for expert social science knowledge in evaluation, the best bet would seem to be university-affiliated persons, clearly free enough of other commitments to give the time needed and be made familiar as soon as possible with the content and style of the day-to-day operation. The latter may take some time but may be a necessary prelude to designing an evaluation study.

At the same time, considering what has been said earlier about the inability to speak critically—the lack of candor on the part of a potential foundation constituent which is likely to be the case for a social scientist employed from the outside—some device must be invented to facilitate the consultant's criticism. One might be to engage a second team of evaluation consultants to monitor the activities of the first. Again, Russell Sage Foundation has been sponsoring special reviews of major evaluation efforts, such as the income-maintenance experiment in New Jersey, in an effort to provide a balanced review of this very important kind of work. These reviews express our concern with the time gap between the reporting of findings of evaluation studies and the careful review by peers of the research investigations. Typically, a policy decision has been made by the sponsoring agency of the evaluation study long before the merit and validity of the study itself can be reviewed by competent independent critics. This may apply to foundation administrators in their programs as it does to the federal government, and it would seem wise to have a coterminous review by a second group of peers of the evaluation work of the primary consultants.

The Limits of Evaluation Research

I stated earlier that there were fourth and fifth levels of desired information, about how foundations compare to each other, and how foundations compare to other institutions. Can it be said that one foundation is better than another? Can it be said that funds now going into foundations, or currently administered by foundations, are better employed than they would be by public agencies, or by operating philanthropies such as libraries or universities? These are sharply different questions from those faced by a foundation concerned about just its own activities, and, frankly, I see no way to produce useful comparative information from evaluation studies that bear on them.

In the first place, the goals of the various institutions are most often different, e.g., The Rockefeller Foundation and the Division of Social Sciences of the National Science Foundation, and are sometimes in sharp competition, e.g., the Stern Fund and the Pew Memorial Trust. One does not evaluate these goals, but debates them. Where the goals are roughly the same, e.g., the Grant Foundation and certain divisions of the National Institute of Mental Health, Carnegie Corporation and certain Office of Education programs, several Russell Sage Foundation and Twentieth Century Fund projects, there are practical difficulties of such magnitude as to make me conclude that it is impossible to carry out any worthwhile comparative studies. The cooperation of the institutions in providing data concerning operations and programs seems unlikely, and the data probably are not comparable anyway. I see no prospect of establishing collaboration along quasi-experimental lines in which the institutions agree to alter their procedures according to specifications, so that these differences could be linked to possibly different outcomes.

POPULARITY

This seems to leave us dependent on some other kind of knowledge of the consequences of foundation activity, if we are to say that one foundation is superior to another, or that foundations are doing something better with their money than would be done if the money were distributed in other ways, such as directly by the donor, or by federal and state and local government. In the last analysis this knowledge comes to us through the expression of the public will in a democratic society. We know the effects of the public will, working through our governing system, often take a long period of time to appear, and I assert that there is a grave danger in trying to speed up this process, or to get approximations to true public reaction, because this leads to the search for popularity indicators and seriously endangers the autonomy of foundations.

Several methods come to mind of appraising popularity short of the working of the democratic process. One is a recourse to public opinion polls. There are, and have been, several foundations taking polls of public knowledge about them, and public reactions to their activities. However, information about the characteristics of the polls, e.g., items used, sample base, as well as results, are confidential. The Council on Foundations has under way a national survey of public understanding of foundations and of what the public thinks of foundations; at present the results are not in. The value of sample survey data on the public's view of foundations cannot be appraised at this time, but most certainly an evaluation should be made of their usefulness. It may turn out, of course, that the populace simply has little knowledge of and no real attitudes toward foundations—which would be important information to have.

It is often suggested that we move from opinion research to behavioral measures of interest; for instance, a fund-raising drive by a foundation would provide a more hard-headed criterion of public acclaim. Recently I received this little note:

> Though I know your foundation has quite a lot of money, here is a small amount as a gift in support of one of the most incredible foundation programs going, from what I've read.
>
> Have a good day.

This letter certainly was heartening to me, as I suppose it would be to most foundation administrators, but then I reminded myself that testimonials, longer than this and with substantially more money changing hands, came in every day to astrologers and tea leaf readers.

Perhaps media coverage is the answer, on the premise that the profession of journalism is sensitive to the public interest, and through its selection of what is newsworthy provides indicators of what is judged to be in the public good. However, I think that in the absence of any demonstrable and measurable achievement by foundations, as compared with each other or with other institutions, too often popularity is accorded for promise, or position, or power—

and, I would add, persiflage. I would not want the journalism profession to be the arbiter of the value of a given foundation, or of foundations generally.

Do we really want, after all, such indices of popularity to be our measure of good work? Once this criterion is established, the foundations are led inevitably into a competition for establishing themselves as popular cultural institutions among the public, with appropriations likely to go to those activities most widely used, most highly favored. I doubt if this means that they are therefore contributing more to mankind.

RESPONSE TO PROBLEM

There appears to be a fundamental and perhaps unique problem for foundations in American life, but I think the response must be along the following lines. American culture believes in and provides for individualism, pursuit of distinction, freedom of speech on diverse views and, for institutions, diversity and pluralism. Foundations as one class of American institutions derive their legitimacy in part from this principle. Nevertheless, pluralism in institutions is always worrisome to society, more so, it seems to me, than is the concept of individual freedom. Even though the principles of freedom and pluralism are strong in American society, there is always pressure to revalidate, and for institutions with no well-agreed-upon contribution to American life, the pressure to validate must be more intense. The arguments supporting foundations solely on the principle of pluralism, apart from evidence on their actual contributions, are numerous and varied in source. Both supporters and critics testify to our need for diversity. The Treasury Department itself says:

> Private philanthropy plays a special and vital role in our society. Beyond providing for areas into which government cannot and should not advance (such as religion) . . . they enable individuals or small groups to establish new charitable endeavors and to express their own bents, concerns and experience. In doing so, they enrich the pluralism of our social order.[18]

[18] Cited in William H. Rudy, *The Foundations: Their Use and Abuse* (Washington, D.C.: Public Affairs Press, 1970), p. 6.

Now, I want to stress very strongly that arguments for pluralism are dramatically different from unsubstantiated foundation claims to grandeur. Foundation rhetoric is choked with phrases like "cutting edge of progress," "frontier thinking," "limitless horizons," and "leverage," and "courage to take risks," and I say that this kind of unctuous, self-serving foundation belly-scratching gets us nowhere except deeper and deeper into ignorance.

What, then, are the foundation administrators to do? The course on the one hand seems clear; with respect to improving the quality of information they have about various aspects of their own projects and programs, various straightforward fact-gathering and evaluative actions can be taken. Whatever else may happen, or how the debate may go, one can be more confident that at least internally there is some rational management of means to ends. But on the other hand, when administrators are challenged (or challenge themselves) to show a foundation is better than another, or that foundations do something better with their money than other institutions, I see the reasoned response to be that the challenge is not immediately answerable, and never completely answerable; that one must live with this ignorance and consequent uncertainty; that the attempt to answer the challenge leads toward a dangerous loss of autonomy and the use of shabby little deceits to one's self and the public. The case for foundations today must rest on the premise that pluralism is desirable and that over time, in the long run, the public through our political process will make the final evaluation as to whether foundations are a desirable component of our society.

Fritz F. Heimann

9

Foundations and Government:
Perspectives for the Future

Any effort to consider the future of foundations must deal with the ultimate question: is there a continuing rationale for foundations? Foundations are in a difficult period in their history. The legislative battles of 1969 demonstrated that they have very limited political support and no effective popular constituency. The pervasive role of government programs means that the traditional rationale for foundations has largely disappeared. That rationale, though never very explicitly formulated, rested on the premise that there were spheres of activities in which the federal government had little or no active role, but which were of sufficient public interest to justify the use of tax incentives to stimulate private initiative.

In the face of political hostility, foundations could resign themselves to a low visibility role as disbursing agencies for noncontroversial projects whose priority is too low to secure government support. The financial pressures on all private sector institutions—museums, universities, hospitals, symphony orchestras—are so great that there would be no difficulty disbursing the $1.5 to 2 billion per year which the foundations have to spend.

However, as tax-favored institutions, foundations are certain to be under renewed scrutiny, and will be required to justify their existence. Not having made anybody mad may not be an adequate defense. If foundations support only what is popular with politicians, their role will be insignificant because such projects will have access to much larger government funds. If they limit their grants to the institutions supported by individual giving, they are vulnerable to the attack that they are unnecessary middlemen.

In the long run, the only real justification for an institution is that it does things which others cannot do as well. Foundations have made many distinctive contributions in the past, but that was much easier before government agencies became active with vastly greater resources. Foundations must prove that they can continue to make distinctive contributions in an environment of massive governmental involvement if they are to develop sufficient public support to maintain their existence.

A Rationale for Foundations

I believe that their ability to make distinctive contributions is considerable. Of all of our institutions, foundations are potentially the most flexible, because they are least encumbered by internal or external constraints. This is of enormous value in a time of rapid change when most public and private institutions cannot cope with the need for change because of the constraints under which they operate.

Foundations are less constrained than any other type of organization by the pressures of their ongoing activities. Because they are essentially grant-making rather than operating institutions, their internal needs are quite modest and the bulk of their available funds are uncommitted. Thus, they have the potential to respond to change by launching new programs. Even though existing programs generate pressure for continued funding, it is far more difficult to eliminate or reduce a program carried on by an in-house staff than it is to cut support going to another organization. This phenomenon operates also with government programs and in the corporate world. The unique characteristic of foundations is the ratio of in-house expenditures to external grants. Only a very small percentage of the available funds are needed to keep the internal show running. Thus, the inertial force of ongoing activities is much smaller, and the ability to reallocate resources is correspondingly greater.

The fact that foundations are not required to raise money frees them from many external pressures. An endowed foundation does not have to satisfy the demands of an external constituency, such as voters, customers, or advertisers, to assure its continued existence. It may be argued that, in view of political and other public criticism, foundations are hardly free from external pressure. There is, however, a basic difference between having to earn the active and continuing support of outside constituencies to remain in existence, and having to avoid activities which could trigger widespread opposition. The latter is at most a negative discipline. Our basic premise is still true: external constituencies do not impose any affirmative demands which foundations must meet.

The freedom from internal and external constraints gives foundations great flexibility to respond to the changing needs of American society. This flexibility provides the best basis for defining a useful role for foundations, because it suggests that there are activities which foundations can perform better than other institutions.

It is clearly easier for a foundation to engage in experimental activity than it is for a government agency. The system of checks and balances under which government programs are conceived and executed makes it extremely difficult to tolerate the failures that are an inevitable concomitant of experimentation. The same constraints also make it very difficult for government agencies to operate either on a small scale or on a long-time cycle. This introduces a twofold bias. An experimental program which looks as though it may produce negative results is likely to be killed too early. A program which appears promising may well be given broad application prematurely. For example, one of the major problems of such antipoverty programs as community action was that experimental approaches were proliferated too early.

The very fact that foundations do not respond to a political constituency means that it is possible for them to sponsor a project in one community without being exposed to irresistible pressure to duplicate the experiment in other communities. Similarly, the freedom from political checks and balances, Budget Bureau reviews, appropriation committees, and partisan criticism means that a foundation can accept the consequences of an unsuccessful experiment without the risks inherent in a governmental program.

The absence of political checks and balances also means that foundations can be much more selective in their allocation of resources. A foundation can decide to support only the best law school or hospital, or other institution, without being subjected to pressure for even-handed distribution to all similar institutions. It appears that some foundations have in recent years become concerned about charges of "elitism." This has led to the distribution of grants to broader groups of recipients. Without debating the wisdom of any particular program, I believe that foundations lose their ability to be distinctive if they adopt grant-making criteria which closely resemble those of government agencies.

Foundations can also enter sensitive or controversial areas more readily than government agencies. Strong opposition by a vocal minority can often stop a government program. Foundations can be considerably more venturesome. For example, foundations began working in the birth control field at least two decades before the government entered it. Most observers credit the initial work financed by foundations with laying the basis for the government's ultimate entry.

The development of higher-yield food grains is probably the greatest success of the foundation field since World War II. The crucial importance of increasing agricultural productivity in countries like India with rapidly growing populations and limited available land, was widely recognized. However, for several decades the dominant political interest in Washington was the disposal of United States agricultural surpluses. Increasing the productivity of foreign countries had no political support. Thus here, too, political inhibitions on governmental action created an opportunity for foundation initiatives.

The greater flexibility with which foundation programs can be administered provides opportunities in such fields as support for artists, where subjective judgments are inevitably more useful than objective criteria. Government-financed programs must necessarily be operated with relatively formal procedures. Thus, it is questionable whether government programs in the humanities and in the arts could, even with increased funding, be as successful as, for example, the fellowship program of the Guggenheim Foundation.

Another obvious opportunity is the field of religion, from which the government is excluded by the Constitution. Here foundations can operate free from the competition of government programs. Surprisingly, relatively little foundation spending has gone for religious purposes.

It appears to be fashionable to be critical of large foundations which operate on a local, rather than a broader geographical scale. To me such a local emphasis would seem to be at least one justified response to the unequal competition with large-scale government programs. By concentrating on a limited area, a foundation is more likely to bring to bear meaningful expertise, and its available resources are more likely to have a perceptible impact.

To my mind, there are ample opportunities for foundations to play a role which is both unique and important. To play this role successfully requires first of all a realistic recognition of the role of government. This requires a much more sophisticated model than the simplistic "private sector-public sector" dichotomy with which the foundation literature abounds. Foundations must understand both the enormous scope and resources of government programs and their inherent limitations. Against this backdrop the role of foundations can be defined.

There is room for collaboration between foundations and government programs, as Richard Friedman suggests in his chapter. However, collaboration with government programs has its dangers. The role of being a junior partner in government-dominated programs does not provide an adequate solution to the future role of foundations. The traditional reluctance of many foundations to become closely involved with government-operated programs reflects a fear which, while perhaps exaggerated, is not unfounded in view of the much greater resources of the government, not merely in money but in other important factors, such as experienced manpower. The concern that foundations might lose any individualty or impact if their programs were closely coordinated with government programs cannot be dismissed. The reality, however, is that the government is active in most fields of foundation activity and unless foundations learn to operate in that environment there is very little scope left for them.

The Management of Foundations

Our discussion of the future role of foundations makes clear that there are no simple answers. Careful and sophisticated determinations must be made within each field of activity to find areas where foundations can make a distinctive contribution. The development of such programs is no job for dilettantes. A foundation which decides how to spend its money after the trustees have finished their drinks at an annual dinner is unlikely to be very effective. It does not follow from this that there is need for "professionalization in giving." What is required is detailed knowledge and convictions with respect to the particular field of activity, not expertise in the methodology and procedures of philanthropy. Effective philanthropy is serious work. However, if the donor or the trustees are willing to do the work, that's fine. If not, they should obtain the necessary help to make sure the job is done right.

The argument that "independent" professionals will necessarily do more useful work than the donor or his family is far from clear. Any judgment is bound to be impressionistic at best. However, even Waldemar Nielsen, whose book on *The Big Foundations* is strongly critical of donor control, describes various instances where highly productive programs were originated by donor-controlled foundations. In fact if the emphasis in foundation work should be on innovation, donors and trustees may at times be more venturesome than the foundation professionals. As one case in point, it is worth noting that John D. Rockefeller 3rd was unable to get the Rockefeller Foundation, of which he was then chairman, to become interested in the population problem. Because of his strong convictions regarding the importance of the subject, he finally established a separate organization, the Population Council, to work in this area. Only many years later, after the subject had become more widely recognized and much less controversial, did the Rockefeller Foundation itself begin to participate.

In a review of foundation activity in the field of economics, George Stigler made the following perceptive observations about foundation professionals:

The large foundations in general are staffed by men whose personal convictions on the proper type of research are fairly representative of the consensus of respectable professional opinion. It would be considered irresponsible or dangerous for a larger foundation to plunge on a large scale into an eccentric program, and men who seek to do this do not get on or stay on foundation staffs. This trait is probably due to the professionalization of the administration of large foundations and possibly also to their vulnerability to criticism.

People working for foundations, like beauticians and undertakers, want their work to be granted "professional" status. However, it is a gross oversimplification to associate good foundation work with professionals and bad foundation work with donor- and family-run foundations. The need for staff depends primarily on the complexity of the programs which are undertaken. Even a very large foundation can get along with little or no staff if it limits itself, for example, to making unrestricted grants to universities. A foundation which wishes to become involved in a substantial volume of complex activities will certainly require a staff.

Amending the Tax Law

One of the key issues for the future is whether and how the foundation provisions of the 1969 Tax Reform Act should be amended. The Act was the result of a complex process of political pulling and hauling and the results show it. There were some useful reforms, notably the payout requirement. While its formulation could be improved, the principle that there be a minimum level of payout to charity seems unassailable. It cured a serious flaw in the prior law. No one should get a current tax deduction when he creates a foundation, unless the foundation promptly commences its charitable activities and continues to maintain a minimum level of payout.

At the other end of the spectrum is the 4 percent tax on the investment income of foundations. It is an indefensible absurdity which should be repealed at the earliest opportunity. In fiscal year 1972 the Treasury collected over $50 million from foundations. This amount was lost to charity. It was more than double the Treasury's estimated cost for auditing all tax-exempt organizations. If the tax is not promptly repealed, there is a danger that, in accordance with Professor Parkinson's first law, the amount of work performed by the Internal Revenue Service will rise to the level necessary to eat up all the dollars available.

The restriction on transactions between foundations on the one hand and donors, trustees, and other "related persons" represents an exercise in overkill. A more sensible balance between the cure and the disease should be developed.

The requirement that foundations exercise "expenditure responsibility" when grants are made to organizations other than tax-exempt charitable organizations is sound. That it appears to be having the effect of discouraging grants to minority and poverty groups is a commentary on the administrative weakness or timidity of many foundations, not on the desirability of the requirement. Foundations should learn to live with the expenditure responsibility requirement and not use it as an excuse for failing to make grants which should receive adequate supervision.

Conversely, the fact that the Treasury has drafted fairly reasonable regulations interpreting the statutory restrictions on legislative activities, and that most foundations find they can live with these restrictions, should not divert attention from the inherent unsoundness of the restrictions. Congress does not need to be shielded from foundation-financed lobbying. Every other interest group is busy lobbying, including unions and corporations, churches and veterans' groups, and most powerfully of all, the executive branch of the government. The process is and should be wide open. There is no very persuasive reason for excluding foundation-financed inputs. They will add only a trickle to the torrent and their product will be no worse, and might occasionally be a little better and a little more disinterested, than most lobbying.

Professor Bittker's chapter demonstrates there is little or no logical or factual justification for most of the distinctions in treatment between foundations and other types of charitable organizations. Over a period of time the less favored status of foundations is likely to have a serious effect on the birth rate of new foundations. In particular, the restriction on the percentage of stock holdings in a corporation which may be owned by a corporation will almost certainly have an adverse effect on the creation of large foundations. Here too we seem to have a case where Congress made the remedy more severe than the disease warrants. In all likelihood, the minimum payout requirement will cure the most serious dangers presented by foundation ownership of controlling blocks of stock; namely, failure to provide an adequate financial return to charity. I would be inclined to drop the excess business holding requirement until after the effects of the minimum payout requirement can be determined. If there still is a problem at that time, the more drastic remedy can be reimposed.

While hard proof is not available, the Tax Reform Act is probably having a sharp impact on the creation of very small foundations. These have constituted an overwhelming percentage of the total number of foundations. (In 1969 more than 80 percent of all foundations had less than $500,000 in assets.) The legal and accounting requirements established by the 1969 law appear sufficiently burdensome to discourage the creation of small foundations. Tax and estate planners no longer bother with foundations when only a modest amount of money is involved. To my mind, this is a welcome development, which illustrates the serendipitous delights of our legislative process. Students of foundations have long questioned whether the same tax incentives which encourage the establishment of multimillion-dollar foundations should be available to individuals who create a foundation which, because of its small size, is bound to be nothing more than another checkbook for the donor's personal giving. Unfortunately, it has never been possible to draw a practical line of demarcation between the "incorporated checkbook" and the "real" foundation. Any size test—whether it be $100,000 or $1 million—has the political defect of looking like discrimination in favor of the very rich. Conceptual distinctions are even harder to define. The burden of paperwork created by the 1969 law seems to be accomplishing by indirect means what was impossible to do directly. It will probably take several years before we will know how high the entry barrier really is.

Congress should make a thorough review of the foundation provisions of the tax law. Such a review should preferably be undertaken as a separate matter and not, as in 1969, as part of a broad tax reform effort. The foundation provisions are very complex and will require detailed attention by the Treasury Department and by the congressional committees responsible for tax legislation. If the foundation provisions are taken up as part of an omnibus package together with issues of greater fiscal impact or political sensitivity, the foundation provisions will not receive the attention they require. While something different from the 1969 amendments might emerge, the results would probably be another ill-considered response to then current charges and countercharges.

The Government as Regulator and the Role of the IRS

Because federal encouragement for foundations has come through tax incentives, the regulation of foundations has inevitably become the province of the Internal Revenue Service. However, the principal interest of the IRS is to bring dollars into the Treasury. As a result, its interest in foundations has been directed primarily to questions of fiscal abuse. Moreover, because the auditing of tax-exempt organizations is not a very productive way of bringing dollars into the Treasury, the IRS has, during much of its history, paid only scant attention even to the fiscal regulation of foundations. With continuing public concern about tax equity, the need for adequate policing of foundations is beyond argument. However, the need for additional tax audits hardly justifies the tax on foundation income.

Much more difficult than determining the proper level of policing of fiscal abuses are the issues raised by government regulation of foundation program activities. The 1969 law enacted more detailed restrictions on foundation programs. The mere existence of the statutory provisions means that some regulation to achieve compliance is necessary. Furthermore, because many of the provisions raise problems of interpretation, it is necessary to develop regulations which will enable foundations to find their way through the complex statutory maze. In the area of foundation programs, however, the role of the Internal Revenue Service is more questionable than in the field of fiscal abuses. Very few people would ordinarily consult a tax lawyer or tax accountant in order to define, for example, a meaningful line between proper educational activities and improper participation in politics.

If we question the competence of the IRS in such areas, the issue is presented, if not the IRS, what other agency should do the job? Here we have a dilemma. It is true that some other agencies may have more sophistication than IRS with respect to questions raised by foundation program regulation. However, such sophistication is likely to have been obtained by engaging in government programs which in a real sense are competitive with those of foundations. Asking some branch of HEW to pass on the propriety of foundation programs is probably even less desirable than letting IRS do so. The alternative of setting up a new agency has its own problems. For one thing, do the problems really justify the creation of even a small new agency? Should we run the risk that an agency with a limited mandate will inevitably work to create a bigger job for itself?

As indicated earlier, I would cut back on the scope of program regulation. (By eliminating the restriction on legislative activities, some of the more insoluble definitional problems disappear.) On balance I would be inclined to leave the remaining program regulation to the Treasury, as the lesser evil. Benign or even uncomprehending neglect is probably better than overzealous attention.

While the lack of external constraints gives foundations flexibility to launch new and useful programs, it also leaves them free to continue old programs which have outlived their usefulness. That some percentage of foundation grants will be dull and unimaginative is inevitable. However, I question whether government regulation can do more than deal with the quantitative aspect of foundation work by insisting on a minimum payout level. I do not see any practical basis for government action with respect to the qualitative aspect of foundation work.

This presents almost insurmountable definitional problems. No group of legislators or administrators are likely to agree on any workable standards for distinguishing between good and bad foundation work. Even if by some miracle of the politics of consensus the definitional problem could be solved, the result would inevitably undermine the rationale for foundations previously suggested. If foundations were to spend their funds on the basis of government-defined standards of what is good and bad philanthropy, foundation programs will wind up resembling government programs. Unless we are willing to let foundations spend their money differently from the way government agencies would spend it, there is no point having foundations. The IRS might as well collect the money and let the government spend it.

Perspective on Foundation Performance

Any study of the foundation field should conclude with some overall evaluation. Are foundations healthy or are they sick? Should the institution be encouraged, discouraged, or eliminated? Like all ultimate questions these are hard to answer in any meaningful way. Even to make an approach requires, first, a realization of the limitations of the evaluative process and, second, a fair perspective of the strengths and capabilities of foundations.

In the course of the work of the Peterson Commission, much time was spent wrestling with the question of how to make some overall evaluation of the work of foundations. In particular the possibility was considered of making a "cost-benefit analysis" comparing the cost of the tax subsidies with the benefits to society resulting from foundations. After consulting some of the foremost experts in the arcane techniques of cost-benefit analysis, it was concluded that the job was impossible. The number of indeterminable variables is just too large. Even the "cost" of foundations, in terms of lost taxes, is impossible to measure. If there would be no tax benefit for contributions to a foundation, would a donor give the same amount directly to his university or to some other tax-exempt organization? Would he buy a bigger yacht, or improve his wine cellar? Would he leave the money to his children and, if so, by taxable or nontaxable methods? Would he set up a foundation even without tax incentives? A number of the major foundations were created before there were any strong tax incentives for doing so.

The analysis becomes even more unfathomable when we go beyond the donor's options. Let us assume that there had been no tax incentive for foundations, and that foundation donors had not availed themselves of other opportunities to keep the money away from the tax collector—what would the government have done with the extra taxes? Would tax rates have been lower? Would the national debt be somewhat smaller? Would the government have been impelled to spend more money in the fields in which foundations have been operating? If the latter is the case, would the money have been spent more or less productively than the way the foundations have spent it? It is self-evident that there are no good answers to any of these questions and that the whole notion of a cost-benefit analysis of the role of foundations is unworkable.

Accepting the reality that the role of the institution as a whole cannot be evaluated in any meaningful way, there is left the possibility of appraising the work of individual foundations and then somehow building up to a cumulative judgment of the institution. This is the approach taken by Waldemar Nielsen in his book *The Big Foundations*. He reviews the work of the 33 largest foundations, those which in 1970 had assets exceeding $100 million. Based on that review Nielsen concludes that foundations are sick and malfunctioning institutions with little hope for recovery. He is willing to grant them a brief term of years in which to improve. Failing to achieve adequate improvement they should be allowed to expire.

Whether Nielsen's assessment of foundations is justified depends largely on one's judgment of American society as a whole. If one begins with a vision of a society overwhelmed by problems with which our existing institutions are incapable of coping, and then asks what the foundations are doing to prevent the apocalypse, the obvious answer is: not enough. However, is it reasonable to expect foundations to sponsor programs which will change the system? As Nielsen correctly points out, the foundations are very much a part of "the system" and are interconnected with many of our other private-sector institutions, including corporations, banks, and universities. They are also dependent on the continued favor of the government. To expect them to play the part of well-financed and well-mannered Nader's Raiders is hardly realistic.

In defense of Mr. Nielsen, it should be recognized that he does little more than take the foundations on their own terms. After a thorough immersion in the pretentious prose of foundation annual reports and other statements of purpose, he compares the accomplishments with the rhetoric. Not surprisingly he finds a large gap. I will grant that anyone who has suffered through as much foundation prose as Mr. Nielsen has deserves to get even. However, I question the perspectives underlying his analysis.

In order to achieve a realistic perspective on foundations, we ought to look at resources rather than rhetoric. The annual expenditures of foundations are in the range of $1.5 to 2 billion. In a nation with a gross national product exceeding $1 trillion, there are serious limits as to what can be accomplished by foundations. Furthermore, there are thousands of foundations—most of them very small—and their funds are spent over a wide range of activities. Even the Ford Foundation, whose size disturbs Mr. Nielsen sufficiently that he wants to break it up into three or four pieces, is hardly a big institution when we lift our view beyond the foundation field. When we use yardsticks other than financial resources, the size of foundations seems even less significant. The number of people employed by foundations is in the range of two to three thousand. Even Ford with a disproportionate total of the manpower has fewer than five hundred professional employees. I would suggest that the real starting point for the assessment of foundations is the recognition that we are dealing with institutions of modest resources which for a whole variety of reasons can exercise only limited influence.

How useful such organizations can be depends on one's perspective of the problems which need to be addressed. As already noted, if we start from the premise that our society is doomed without radical restructuring of all of our principal institutions, foundations are hardly relevant. It is true that the prophet Jonah was able to save Niniveh even without a foundation grant. However, he lived in another age and had connections which even the Ford Foundation is unable to draw upon.

If evolutionary change, rather than radical overhaul is required, then an institution which is a part of the system, but free from many of the constraints of other institutions, can make some useful contributions. Financing the development of improved food grains at a time when the Department of Agriculture would not do so, supporting the creation of children's TV programs better than those which are produced within the profit limitation of commercial TV, sponsoring research in birth control when government was immobilized, are all very useful. There are no reasons to believe that foundations cannot continue to make similar contributions.

To my mind foundations have a useful role because we have

an extraordinarily complex society whose problems must be addressed in a wide variety of ways. Even though many of our problems are interrelated, there are no large, simple solutions. Foundations are important because they are different from other institutions in that they are largely free from the internal and external constraints which tend to keep other organizations in their accustomed orbits. This gives them the potential to address a great variety of problems to which other institutions are not attending. One of the most difficult challenges for the leaders of the foundation field is to inspire foundations to come close to realizing their potential, without at the same time elevating the level of rhetoric to a point where totally unrealistic expectations and anxieties are aroused.

At this time of uncertainties, it seems appropriate to recall the wise words of William the Silent, at the beginning of the Eighty Years War:

> It is not necessary to hope in order to undertake.
> It is not necessary to succeed in order to persevere.

Index

274

The American Assembly

COLUMBIA UNIVERSITY

About The American Assembly

The American Assembly was established by Dwight D. Eisenhower at Columbia University in 1950. It holds nonpartisan meetings and publishes authoritative books to illuminate issues of United States policy.

An affiliate of Columbia, with offices in the Graduate School of Business, the Assembly is a national educational institution incorporated in the State of New York.

The Assembly seeks to provide information, stimulate discussion, and evoke independent conclusions in matters of vital public interest.

AMERICAN ASSEMBLY SESSIONS

At least two national programs are initiated each year. Authorities are retained to write background papers presenting essential data and defining the main issues in each subject.

About sixty men and women representing a broad range of experience, competence, and American leadership meet for several days to discuss the Assembly topic and consider alternatives for national policy.

All Assemblies follow the same procedure. The background papers are sent to participants in advance of the Assembly. The Assembly meets in small groups for four or five lengthy periods. All groups use the same agenda. At the close of these informal sessions, participants adopt in plenary session a final report of findings and recommendations.

Regional, state, and local Assemblies are held following the national session at Arden House. Assemblies have also been held in England, Switzerland, Malaysia, Canada, the Caribbean, South America, Central America, the Philippines, and Japan. Over one hundred institutions have co-sponsored one or more Assemblies.

ARDEN HOUSE

Home of The American Assembly and scene of the national sessions is Arden House, which was given to Columbia University in 1950 by W. Averell Harriman. E. Roland Harriman joined his brother in contributing toward adaptation of the property for conference purposes. The buildings and surrounding land, known as the Harriman Campus of Columbia University, are fifty miles north of New York City.

Arden House is a distinguished conference center. It is self-supporting and operates throughout the year for use by organizations with educational objectives.

AMERICAN ASSEMBLY BOOKS

The background papers for each Assembly program are published in cloth and paperbound editions for use by individuals, libraries, businesses, public agencies, nongovernmental organizations, educational institutions, discussion and service groups. In this way the deliberations of Assembly sessions are continued and extended.

The subjects of Assembly programs to date are:

1951——United States–Western Europe Relationships
1952——Inflation
1953——Economic Security for Americans
1954——The United States' Stake in the United Nations
——The Federal Government Service
1955——United States Agriculture
——The Forty-Eight States
1956——The Representation of the United States Abroad
——The United States and the Far East
1957——International Stability and Progress
——Atoms for Power
1958——The United States and Africa
——United States Monetary Policy
1959——Wages, Prices, Profits, and Productivity
——The United States and Latin America
1960——The Federal Government and Higher Education
——The Secretary of State
——Goals for Americans
1961——Arms Control: Issues for the Public
——Outer Space: Prospects for Man and Society
1962——Automation and Technological Change
——Cultural Affairs and Foreign Relations
1963——The Population Dilemma
——The United States and the Middle East
1964——The United States and Canada
——The Congress and America's Future
1965——The Courts, the Public, and the Law Explosion
——The United States and Japan
1966——State Legislatures in American Politics
——A World of Nuclear Powers?
——The United States and the Philippines
——Challenges to Collective Bargaining